PENGUIN BOOKS

THE PENGUIN WODEHOUSE COMPANION

Richard Usborne was born in India in 1910. After graduating from Oxford, he worked in advertising. In 1935 he became part-owner and unpaid editor of the infant (and soon ailing) *What's On?*, which had to be resuscitated by wiser men. He returned to advertising. In the Second World War he served with the S.O.E. in the Middle East. After demobilization he became Assistant Editor of the moribund *Strand* magazine, 'and he wrote the much-praised *Clubland Heroes* (1953), a critical evaluation of three authors who had been his boyhood favourites, John Buchan, 'Sapper' and Dornford Yates. P. G. Wodehouse had read it, and when his publishers wanted a book to be written on his works to mark his eightieth birthday, he advised them to get Richard Usborne to do it. Always an admirer of P. G. Wodehouse, Richard Usborne now became an addict and, after *Wodehouse at Work* (1961), an authority. He contributed, along with eleven other eminent devotees, to a Festschrift, *Homage to P. G. Wodehouse*, which was presented to the author in time for his knighthood at the age of ninety-two. Richard Usborne has edited *Sunset at Blandings* (1977), *Vintage Wodehouse* (1977) and *Wodehouse Nuggets* (1983). His *Wodehouse at Work* (1961) was published in a revised and updated edition as *Wodehouse at Work to the End* in 1976. He has adapted numerous Wodehouse novels and short stories for B.B.C. radio, and has written for *Punch*, *The Times*, *The Times Literary Supplement*, the *Sunday Times*, the *Guardian* and other papers. For a period after the war he was a regular book-reviewer for B.B.C. radio.

D0684355

RICHARD USBORNE

~

The Penguin

WODEHOUSE
COMPANION

~

PENGUIN BOOKS

PENGUIN BOOKS

Published by the Penguin Group
27 Wrights Lane, London W8 5TZ, England
Viking Penguin Inc., 40 West 23rd Street, New York, New York 10010, USA
Penguin Books Australia Ltd, Ringwood, Victoria, Australia
Penguin Books Canada Ltd, 2801 John Street, Markham, Ontario, Canada L3R 1B4
Penguin Books (NZ) Ltd, 182–190 Wairau Road, Auckland 10, New Zealand

Penguin Books Ltd, Registered Offices: Harmondsworth, Middlesex, England

First published 1988
3 5 7 9 10 8 6 4 2

Parts of this book first appeared in *Wodehouse at Work to the End*
(Barrie & Jenkins, 1976) and *A Wodehouse Companion* (Elm Tree
Books/Hamish Hamilton Ltd, 1981)

Printed and bound in Great Britain by
Cox & Wyman Ltd, Reading
Filmset in Goudy Old Style (Linotron 202) by
Rowland Phototypesetting Ltd, Bury St Edmunds, Suffolk

for Jimmy Heineman,
collector and bibliographer

ACKNOWLEDGEMENTS

———————— ~ ————————

The illustrations on pages 2 and 122 are from the *Captain* magazine, which published most of Wodehouse's school stories from the first years of the century. Those on pages 45 and 61 are from the *Strand*. The other ten, by Peter van Straaten of the Netherlands, are the copyright of Mr James Heineman of New York.

CONTENTS

_____ ~ _____

INTRODUCTION

———————————— ～ ————————————

You may remember that, towards the end of *Right Ho, Jeeves*, Jeeves sends his poor master off on an eighteen-mile ride through Worcestershire country lanes at night on a borrowed bone-shaker bicycle without a lamp.

'But I may come a fearful stinker without a lamp. Suppose I barge into something.'
I broke off and eyed him rigidly.
'You smile, Jeeves. The thought amuses you?'
'I beg your pardon, sir. I was thinking of a tale my Uncle Cyril used to tell me as a child. An absurd little story, sir, though I confess I have always found it droll. According to my Uncle Cyril, two men named Nicholls and Jackson set out to ride to Brighton on a tandem bicycle, and were so unfortunate as to come into collision with a brewer's van. And when the rescue party arrived on the scene of the accident, it was discovered that they had been hurled together with such force that it was impossible to sort them out at all adequately. The keenest eye could not discern which portion of the fragments was Nicholls and which Jackson. So they collected as much as they could, and called it Nixon. I remember laughing very much at that story when I was a child, sir.'
I had to pause a moment to master my feelings . . .

This book is a conflation and updating of two books that have my name on their spines, *Wodehouse at Work to the End* (Herbert Jenkins, 1961; revised edition, Barrie & Jenkins, 1976) and *A Wodehouse Companion* (Elm Tree Books/Hamish Hamilton Ltd, 1981). I hope I have chosen the right fragments of those two books for collection here.

Sir Pelham Grenville Wodehouse, K.B.E., D. Litt. (Oxon.), died of a heart attack in hospital in America on St Valentine's Day 1975. He was ninety-three. He had received his knighthood forty days earlier. He and his wife Ethel had lived in the village of Remsenburg, on Long Island, New York, for the last twenty years and more. At his death the Remsenburg post office lowered its flag to half-mast, just clear of the piled-up snow. A great writer, he had been better known to the locals as the giver of the P. G. Wodehouse Shelter for stray cats and dogs.

Wodehouse had, in fact, lived more years of his life in America than in England. In 1955 he had taken American, in addition to his British, citizenship. But his roots were in England and his absorbent youth had been spent there. To the end of his life he preferred to write about English people in English settings.

'From my earliest years I had always wanted to be a writer,' he wrote when in his eighties. 'I started turning out the stuff at the age of five. (What I was doing before that I don't remember. Just loafing, I suppose.)' In 1903, aged twenty-two, when his first novel was being serialized in the

> Oh ah that Sorryful day
> When on the batted field the pets did lay in sorryful disgrace.
> With red blud Streaming fast
> There life was pasing fast
> And in the camp there lay
> Thousands of dead Men.
>
> P G Wodehouse
>
> this is a bit of poertory I made up

The writer, aged five

Captain, they printed a photograph of him, serious, broad-shouldered, tall, upstanding, stiff-collared, pipe in hand . . . every inch a writer. In 1907, when he was all of twenty-five and with seven published books to his name, he allowed the same magazine to print facsimile a poem he had written twenty years earlier.

Latin and Greek, well taught in scholarship forms at Dulwich, disciplined the structure of his English sentences. He read voraciously: Dickens for his funny characters (he couldn't bear the way Dickens treated children in his books – beatings, starvation, humiliations); W. S. Gilbert's verse; Anstey, Hornung, Conan Doyle, Kipling; all the stories in all the magazines, especially the trashy ones. The trash he read paid handsome dividends later in giving him a treasury of clichés for the burble of Bertie Wooster and other Drones Club narrators. He chose clichés, of words, situations and attitudes, as material with which to make many of his verbal jokes, situation jokes and morality jokes. His popular novelist, Rosie M. Banks (a purposeful echo of Ruby M. Ayres, a top-class professional writer of 'molasses for the masses' in Wodehouse's day) is too sensible to believe that a sane young man in love with a girl would stand beneath her window at night, quietly adoring. But she is also too sensible to omit such a situation from her books.

The Latin tags that he remembered and the Sixth-Form English – Shakespeare, Tennyson, Longfellow – Wodehouse gave thriftily to Jeeves. The Bible that he had studied in 'Divinity' and heard Sunday after Sunday from lectern and pulpit in Chapel at school and Church in the holidays gave him parsonical rhythms and references for his frequent clergymen, from the pale young curate who had been bullied at Theological College to the Bishop of Stortford who had, in his day, won the Curates' Open Heavyweight Championship two years running.

When he died he had nearly a hundred books to his credit, ninety-two of them being novels and collections of short stories. None of them was wholly serious; most of them, and the best of them, were farce. He collaborated in more than thirty stage plays, mostly musical. He was in the front rank of writers of lyrics, words fitted to music, especially Jerome Kern's, for the stage. The great American song-writers, Larry Hart, Richard Rodgers, Oscar Hammerstein and Howard Dietz, acknowledged their debt to him. He was an expert composer of light verse and had contributed a great deal of it to newspapers, *Punch* and other magazines in England from 1902 onwards. For three stretches he was highly paid and, he thought, underworked as a writer in Hollywood. He was happily married for sixty-one years. He and Ethel had no children together, but she, a widow when he married her, had a daughter, Leonora, who was a great joy to her stepfather and everybody else. He adopted her and changed her name to Leonora Wodehouse.

He was a shy and very private man. He had few close friends. He worked hard. Trollope said that the most important equipment for a writer was a large piece of sealing-wax with which to affix his posterior to a chair. Wodehouse did not need the sealing-wax. He loved working. He made merry, but only at his desk and typewriter. He was a humorist, not a wit, not a satirist. He was a craftsman manufacturer of the ludicrous – words, phrases, characters and situations in intricate and tightly controlled plots. For farce fiction, at the rate of more than a book a year in a *floruit* period of fifty years, he had no rivals.

His books were always young and all his elders, even the stuffed shirts, had been foolishly young once. The awesome Roderick Spode, Lord Sidcup, had in his youth stolen a policeman's helmet on Boat Race Night – that night in Wodehouse's calendar when Leicester Square seethed with young *boulevardiers* stalking policemen – and was still proud of it. The awesome shipping magnate Lord Worplesdon had, in his youth, held the record for being thrown out of Covent Garden balls, with or without the girl Tottie. Wodehouse uses the age-transference hinge of plot in many novels and stories: Lord Emsworth shooting Baxter with his grandson's confiscated air-gun; the bishop visiting his old school and his gaitered legs wobbling when the current Captain of Football passes by; the bishop and the headmaster, late at night under the influence of that great rejuvenator Buck-U-Uppo, painting the statue in the school close; the new boy at school who proves to be the prefect's uncle; the atheist policeman coshed into sudden piety and wishing to join the Infants' Bible Class preparatory to singing in the choir. You can be sure, with Wodehouse, that David will defeat Goliath, the schoolboy will outwit the master, the page-boy will outrun the furious footman, the chorus girl will rise to be a star or, at very least, will marry an earl, the poor will inherit riches and the Pekinese will rout the Alsatian. Those are the sorts of novels, outside the Blandings and Wooster sagas, Wodehouse wanted to write, and he wrote them exuberantly. Only in his extreme old age did his plots become strained and his flow of verbal felicities, in narrative and dialogue, comparatively thin.

He wrote about himself very little, and then in jest. His publishers put together three of his autobiographical books in one volume, with the title *Wodehouse on Wodehouse*. Don't take it all as gospel. For instance, that story of his about being sacked by the bank for defacing a new ledger. He told that one a number of times in print, and I heard him, at the age of ninety, trying to get it past Robert Robinson's defences in a TV interview. He was never sacked from the bank. As a trainee he had not been any better, or much worse, than the other boys from the public schools who had got nominations to the Hong Kong and Shanghai Bank in the City. But Wodehouse had determined, and known, that he was going to be a writer, and when he was offered a job for five weeks at five guineas a week to write the By-The-Way column for the *Globe* newspaper, he said yes and the bank agreed to let him go. The ledger-defacement/angry-head-clerk/banishment-in-disgrace-of-young-Wodehouse made a good story, and young Wodehouse worked it up and sold it profitably. Old Wodehouse knew it by heart and thought Robert Robinson might not.

He was born in 1881, the third of four boys in a sisterless and, for long stretches in his childhood, parentless family. His father was a civil servant, eventually a judge, in Hong Kong, and the boys had to be educated at good English schools. Separation of parents and children, boarding schools, holidays spent farmed out to real or proxy aunts, these were prices paid by thousands of middle-class English families in the days of our far-flung Empire.

They were a talented lot, the Wodehouse boys. Armine, a brother two years senior to Pelham ('Plum' to his friends, 'Plummie' to his family), was a scholar at Dulwich and went on with a scholarship to Oxford. He got a Double First (Latin, Greek, Philosophy and Ancient History) in a four-year course. He won the Newdigate Poetry Prize, was a good cricketer, played the piano well and wrote good light verse. He went out to India to teach, became a theosophist and, for a period, was in charge of the young Krishnamurti, whom he believed, with other followers of Annie Besant, to be a new Messiah.

Except for piano-playing, Plum might have made a name like Armine's had he gone to Oxford. He had done well at Dulwich – Sixth Form, Editor of the magazine, a good cricketer, footballer and boxer – but his father could not afford university for a second boy. When he left Dulwich, Plum went, at a salary of £80 a year, into the bank. He soon doubled his salary by writing in the evenings. He was single-minded and very industrious. He was determined to get out of the bank before they sent him to the Far East. He had a light touch and was soon earning, freelance, enough to enable him to live by his typewriter: that By-The-Way column in the *Globe*, bits and pieces in *Punch*, short stories in magazines (there were dozens of magazines wanting stories and verse in those days), novels about school life and, very soon, lyrics for shows.

He found that editors in America paid much better prices for short stories. So he went to New York, lived as cheaply as possible (see 'In Alcala' in *The Man Upstairs*) and bombarded the magazines with offerings. He had made a bit of a name in England with his school stories, but he put those behind him when he set up shop in America. He wanted to go for the adult markets now. He became attached, over a number of by-lines, to a smart New York magazine, *Vanity Fair*, and was its theatre critic. He handed that job over to a certain Miss Dorothy Parker and teamed up with Guy Bolton and Jerome Kern to write musicals. Their names, Bolton, Kern and Wodehouse, and the names of their succession of shows were up in lights throughout the 1920s and 30s.

Wodehouse came to command top prices for short stories and serializations of novels in the prestigious *Saturday Evening Post* in America and the *Strand Magazine* in England. Bertie and Jeeves came on, in bit parts, during the First World War. So did Lord Emsworth, his son Frederick and his secretary Baxter (*Something Fresh*, 1915). Ukridge, the Oldest Member, Mr Mulliner, Eggs, Beans and Crumpets – they told their stories in their own styles and made books for the fast-filling Wodehouse shelf.

He earned a great deal of money between the wars, lost some in the Wall Street crash, and made a great deal more. He earned $104,000 (£10,000-plus in those days) in a single year from Hollywood and, with time on his hands there, continued the lucrative flow of his own work. Benny Green, a shrewd critic, says that Wodehouse's stories of Dottyville-on-the-Pacific, with its moronic magnificos, temperamental stars and staffs of serfs, are purposeful satire, that Wodehouse had been professionally insulted by being lavishly paid for doing practically nothing.

Guy Bolton told me that Plum as a boy had heard his mother and father quarrelling about money and had sworn that, whomever he married, she should have sole charge of the exchequer. So what he happily earned Ethel happily spent – on looking after him, renting and decorating houses and apartments in Mayfair, Norfolk, Sussex, Hollywood, New York and France, bringing Leonora out, giving parties, racing and gambling. She could always economize, if it came to the pinch, by not answering income tax demands.

They were devoted to their dogs, generally Pekinese. A combination of the English quarantine laws, pressing income taxes in America, Canada and England, and Ethel's enjoyment of gambling brought them to Le Touquet in 1935. Ethel bought a comfortable house there, Low Wood in 'The Forest', by the side of the fourteenth fairway of a good golf-course (with girl caddies). This became their official and only home. London was just across the Channel for them (one at a time; the other stayed at home with the dogs). They could take their dogs to America and back without hindrance. Wodehouse came to England in July 1939 to receive an Honorary Degree at Oxford. He came a second time in July on business and to watch a school cricket match at Dulwich. Never again.

The German armies overran Le Touquet in 1940. Wodehouse, aged fifty-eight, was taken off to civilian internment with hundreds of other British male citizens, now enemy aliens, including, from Le Touquet, a golf-pro, a caddie-master, a billiard-marker, two bar-keepers and a piano-tuner. After uncomfortable journeys between uncomfortable stop-overs, they ended up at Tost in Upper Silesia, on the border with Poland, in a converted lunatic asylum. Ethel, with Wonder the Pekinese, found rooms as a paying guest at Hesdin, inland from the fortifications that the Germans were building along the Channel coast for their *Festung Europa*. Low Wood was occupied by a general of the Luftwaffe.

With France collapsing and the British armies struggling to and from the Dunkirk beaches, the fate of the Wodehouses rated a sentence or two down-column in one or two English papers. A year later the name Wodehouse became headline news in a big way. Bad news.

If you know in detail the sad story of Wodehouse's broadcast talks to neutral America from Berlin in the summer of 1941, and how the English authorities allowed their innocence to be doubted for thirty-nine years – in fact till five years after Wodehouse's death – you should skip the next thirteen pages. I still find that some people, indeed sometimes people who love the Wodehouse books, are going to their graves thinking that Wodehouse did something worse than foolish, something disgraceful, when a captive of the Nazis during the war. Here again, in case any one of those is reading this, is the sad story, with a happy ending but thirty-nine years too late.

The Commandant of Tost, Lagerführer Buchelt, had been a prisoner of war in England in the First World War and was reckoned as moderate and lenient in his treatment of his internees in the Second. He allowed Wodehouse to hire a typewriter and found a desk for him. An American journalist, Angus Thuermer, visited Wodehouse in camp at Christmas-time 1940 and told him, in the presence of Buchelt, that *Time Magazine* wanted an article from him about his experiences in internment. Wodehouse wrote it and, doubtless with Buchelt's approval, it had gone to America. Wodehouse thought *Time* must have found it too light. It appeared in the *Saturday Evening Post*, under the title 'My War with Germany'. A photograph in it of Wodehouse looking thin and cold in the camp moved Guy Bolton, Senator Barbour of New Jersey and other big-name admirers and friends in America to petition the German Embassy in Washington for care to be taken of Wodehouse's parlous health, suggesting that he might, as a special case, be sent back to America, where he belonged. This appeal, passed back to Berlin, may have put an idea into someone's head in the appropriate department of the German Foreign Office. It is known that Wodehouse, after the war, was never effusive in his thanks to Bolton or Senator Barbour for their intervention at this stage.

In May 1941 Buchelt told Wodehouse that he had enjoyed the article and then said, 'Why don't you do some broadcasts on similar lines for your American readers?' And Wodehouse had said there was nothing he would like better. Buchelt's suggestion may have been impromptu. Or he may have been prompted by a propaganda office in Berlin to sound Wodehouse out. Conceivably Thuermer himself had been prompted, in Berlin, to start the ball rolling. At all events, within a month, on the evening of 21 June, when Wodehouse was in a game of camp cricket, he got the order to go to his dormitory and pack his bag. It was nearly four months to his sixtieth birthday. At sixty an internee might officially be released to make his own arrangements to live as a private person under supervision.

With another British internee from Tost, Wodehouse was escorted by soldiers to Berlin and installed at the Adlon Hotel, a preserve of the German Foreign Office in the sense that the British Foreign Office has first call on Claridges for topmost foreign visitors to London. Paul Schmidt, Hitler's official interpreter and a fan of Wodehouse's books, was head of a department in Ribbentrop's Foreign Office which looked after the neutral press and enemy nationals. Werner Plack, one of

Schmidt's staff, had known the Wodehouses slightly in Hollywood, and Plack's friend Major 'Raven' Barnekow had known them well. Plack and Barnekow met Wodehouse at the Adlon shortly after his arrival from Tost and they repeated Buchelt's suggestion that Wodehouse might like to talk on the radio to his friends in neutral America. Wodehouse again said yes, enthusiastically. It did not take him long to script five talks. He had kept notes and a diary from the day he left Le Touquet, and each stage of his odyssey from Le Touquet to Tost made a professional 2,000-plus words for the radio. Plack arranged for Wodehouse to record them on wax in two visits some days apart at a studio.

Oddly enough, Wodehouse met Lagerführer Buchelt in civilian clothes in the Adlon and told him he was going to broadcast his internment experiences. Buchelt congratulated him on his release, but made no reference to their previous conversation in camp about the possibility of broadcasting.

Wodehouse's five talks were cheerful, often funny. They had no political or propaganda content whatsoever. But he had been an ass not to realize that the fact of his giving them, a British citizen on the Nazi radio from Berlin while England was at war with Germany, might make his name 'a hissing and a byword' in England and, to a lesser extent, in America. Duff Cooper, then our Minister of Information, had briefed a journalist, William Connor, 'Cassandra' of the *Daily Mirror*, to denounce Wodehouse on the B.B.C. radio, and he denounced him with a will. The B.B.C. had monitorings of the first two of Wodehouse's talks by then, and Connor might well have asked for them and read them while preparing his own talk. But it is clear from his script that he had not read them nor seen how harmless they were. His line was 'Traitor Wodehouse is broadcasting for the Nazis. In return for release from internment and the comfort of the Adlon Hotel he has joined Goebbels's team of propagandists.'

The B.B.C. protested against putting Connor's philippic on the air but Duff Cooper overruled them. Hardly anybody in England then heard Wodehouse's talks: they were beamed to America on shortwave and went out at 4 a.m. English time. But millions heard Connor at peak listening time, in the 'Postscript', after the 9 o'clock news. 'A rich man, trying to make his last and greatest sale . . . that of his own country . . . a hireling of Dr Goebbels . . . playboy, traitor to his country, his class and his old school, Dulwich . . . gambling at Le Touquet . . . throwing a cocktail party when the stormtroopers clumped into his shallow life . . .

a soft bed in a luxury suite . . . thirty pieces of silver.' Duff Cooper's purpose was reasonable: that America should not think England approved of Wodehouse speaking comfortable words to them across the Atlantic. England, expecting invasion, was hoping that America would come into the war and turn the tide. Americans must not think that Englishman Wodehouse was speaking for England.

Of course, the German propagandists would be happy if some Americans got the impression from Wodehouse's amusing talks that Germany was not really a land of whips, scorpions, Jew-baiting and atrocities. The Germans repeated the five talks, one a week, to England in the late evenings. But Connor had spoken. The damage had been done.

Ethel and Wonder the Peke had been allowed to come from France and join Plum at the Adlon in Berlin. They were all three allowed to go to Paris in 1943 when the Allies stepped up their bombings of Berlin. Wodehouse reported to the first Allied officer he could see, an American, when Paris was liberated in September 1944.

Major Cussen, a barrister before the war and a judge at the Old Bailey after, headed a department of M.I.5 in London that was to concern itself with British 'renegades', such as William Joyce/'Lord Haw-Haw' and others (mercifully not Wodehouse) so closely studied by Rebecca West in her book *The Meaning of Treason*. As the armies advanced across France into Germany, their intelligence officers had Cussen's list of renegades to look out for. The Americans had their own list of Wanteds. The British got the American list too, and the Americans the British. The French, from London and Algiers, had their own, much longer, lists.

Cussen had formulated rules of procedure for intelligence officers in the field: what to do with people on the British list when their capture was reported – safeguarding, isolation, preliminary interrogation, statements taken, written reports. The first 'renegade' reported as captured on Cussen's list was Wodehouse. Cussen decided to go over from London to Paris and test the guidelines he had laid down.

Until Cussen's arrival, Malcolm Muggeridge, an English M.I.6 liaison officer who had come up to Paris from Algiers with the French, was given the duty of keeping an eye on the Wodehouses. Muggeridge has written, in articles and books, about this, the start of his long friendship with the Wodehouses. Muggeridge had not been a great reader of Wodehouse's books and did not become one. But he very soon decided that, in Paris in 1944, the Wodehouses should be protected against 'the monstrous buffooneries of war'. Our Ambassador-elect to France was none other than Duff Cooper, the man who, as Minister of Information, had had Wodehouse put in the pillory three and a half years earlier. And to what hotel did Duff Cooper, his wife and some staff come, pending the reopening of the Embassy in the Rue du Faubourg St Honoré? The Bristol, where the German Foreign Office had installed the Wodehouses and Wonder. As the lift stopped working whenever, as was frequent, the electricity broke down or was switched off, the Wodehouses and Duff Coopers sometimes met on the stairs. It was Malcolm Muggeridge who, at Duff Cooper's request, found the Wodehouses other accommodation. Duff Cooper, in Paris in 1944, was not in the mood, nor did he have a duty, to continue the persecution of Wodehouse. He said that he had always been an admirer of Wodehouse's books. But when, in subsequent years, it became perfectly obvious that Wodehouse's broadcast talks had been utterly harmless except to himself, when even William Connor had sought, and immediately found, mercy in expiation and friendship with Wodehouse, Duff Cooper never publicly admitted that he had had very rough justice done to Wodehouse in 1941 by turning Connor on to denounce him as a traitor and forcing the B.B.C. to carry the denunciation in prime time.

Cussen completed his long interrogation of the Wodehouses, got Wodehouse to sign his statement and sent the papers to London. Cussen was sure that there was no case against him sufficient to warrant his being brought back to London. He too became a friend of Wodehouse. He advised him to write a detailed account of all that he had told him and have it published. He also tried to make it clear to Wodehouse that he should not demand to come back to London, that he should 'keep out of the jurisdiction'. Wodehouse, still mistakenly thinking that everybody in England knew by now that what he had spoken was harmless, couldn't see why it was dangerous for him to go back. He arranged to meet his London barrister friend, Raymond Needham, K.C., in Switzerland. Needham assured him that he should stay in France and keep a low profile. If he came back to England privately, the Beaverbrook press and some members of parliament might start a witch-hunt; he might find himself in the dock charged with treason, and a jury, tired by the war, hungry through rationing and shabby in old clothes, might turn savage against a wealthy humorist who seemed to have made light of it all in the Adlon Hotel. When the Labour Government came into power in the 1945 election, the Attorney-General was Old Alleynian Hartley

Shawcross. A written question was put to him in Parliament: what about Wodehouse? His answer was that so far there was not enough evidence to justify bringing him for trial, but he suggested that for his own sake he ought to keep 'out of the jurisdiction'. Discouraging. And still, to Wodehouse himself, baffling. It took him more than ten years to realize, and accept, that hardly anybody in England had heard his talks or had been able to read their texts. The first time they appeared in print anywhere was in *Encounter*, a magazine high of brow, low of circulation, in 1954. The second time was in 1961 – that was twenty years after their delivery into the microphone – at the end of the Penguin edition of *Performing Flea*.

The Wodehouses lived in France while the war rolled eastwards. When they could get visas they went to America. Ethel came back to England once or twice, for a wedding or a visit; Wodehouse never. They lived in New York, a rooftop flat, with something of a garden for airing Wonder, at 1000 Park Avenue. One day, when Wodehouse was in his brisk early seventies, he collapsed while out walking, alone, in New York. He managed to get himself to a doctor, who, thinking he was either very drunk or very ill, called an ambulance to have him taken to Bellevue Hospital, where the police often sent derelicts off the streets for attention. Then the doctor's secretary found a Savile Row label inside Wodehouse's dilapidated corduroy coat, and his fingernails were well tended. So the ambulance took him to a private hospital. The secretary, still brooding, remembered she had seen the patient before, with Oscar Hammerstein, no less. The doctor rang Hammerstein and described the Englishman who had stumbled into his office. Hammerstein said, 'Of course, it must be P.G. I'll call his wife.' Frances Donaldson tells this macabre story in her biography. It had been a minor stroke and Wodehouse recovered.

There was a house on offer in Remsenburg, Long Island, near where Virginia and Guy Bolton lived. Ethel bought it. It was their last home. As reshaped and furnished by Ethel, it might have been a house near the golf-course at Wentworth or Sunningdale. It stood in nine acres of woodland which went down to a bay that opened to the Atlantic. In the last ten years of his life, Wodehouse hardly ever ventured further from the house than to the post office with Guy to collect mail. He was perfectly happy doing his exercises, taking the dogs, and sometimes cats, for walks, getting his own breakfast, reading, writing, watching television and letting Ethel look after him. They were well-to-do and comfortable. Ethel, having been poor when young, thoroughly enjoyed being rich, but she never got used to it. She had periods of thinking they must economize drastically. In his last years Wodehouse had arthritis in his knees and asked Ethel if he could have a shower fitted over his bath so that he wouldn't have to sit down. But Ethel said they couldn't afford it and he never (Guy Bolton told me) did get his shower.

At the time of his ninetieth birthday he was much visited, and sometimes harassed, by television teams and interviewers, and he had another slight stroke. His knighthood was announced in the New Year's Honours list when he was ninety-three. Charlie Chaplin, in the same list, managed to get to London and, in a wheelchair, to the Palace to receive the accolade. Wodehouse had largely lost the use of his legs and couldn't get to New York, let alone London. The Queen Mother, a great fan of the Wodehouse books, suggested that she should go across and do the honours at his home. But it could not be fitted into her schedules. By the time the insignia had arrived in New York from London and the Consul had found an opportunity to take them out to Remsenburg, Wodehouse had died. Ethel, Lady Wodehouse, lived on in the house to the age of ninety-nine.

The knighthood indicated that Wodehouse's broadcasts from Berlin in 1941 had been officially forgiven, if not forgotten, by the millions who had heard Connor's denunciation on B.B.C. radio. In 1961, when Wodehouse was about to reach eighty, Evelyn Waugh, who revered Wodehouse as a writer, had suggested to his friend and eventual biographer Christopher Sykes that he, Waugh, should broadcast a birthday 'Tribute and Reparation to Dr Wodehouse' on the B.B.C. Sykes was the producer of many of the B.B.C.'s most important literary programmes. He wrote in the biography very interestingly about the opposition he met inside the B.B.C. twenty years later to any tribute to a man the B.B.C. had been forced, against the unanimous will of its hierarchy, to allow Connor to blackguard in 1941.

Wodehouse himself had heard, in America, that Waugh was preparing this broadcast and he wrote to him begging him not to attack Connor, with whom, he said, he had now become friends. Waugh complied, surely with regret. But, in relating how people had absurdly over-reacted in wartime, Waugh said that, in revenge for the broadcasts, some R.A.F. types had flown to Le Touquet to bomb the Wodehouse villa (Ethel Wodehouse had been moved out a year earlier) and had in fact pranged somebody else's villa. Wodehouse learnt about this

~ Nuggets ~

Evelyn Waugh, in explaining to Frances Donaldson why he called Wodehouse 'the Master', wrote that Wodehouse's books had 'on average three uniquely brilliant and entirely original similes to each page', and that that by itself would justify the title 'Master'. Similes, images, mixed metaphors, pulpit sentences deflated by slang, mad logic, clashing clichés, quotations blissfully botched, gags, nifties, one-liners, goodies or, to be pompous, verbal felicities. I have called them Nuggets. It is open-cast mining to dig them out of the texts.

The Oxford Dictionary of Quotations has a dozen good ones under Pelham Grenville Wodehouse. *The Penguin Dictionary of Modern Quotations* has another, bigger crop: sixty-nine. I gave ninety-eight in my *Wodehouse at Work to the End.* Here I have tried to add to, rather than repeat from, those selections. Frances Donaldson, in her biography *P. G. Wodehouse*, quotes from a letter Wodehouse wrote to Denis Mackail in 1946:

Lindsay is the man who was given the job of rewriting *Anything Goes* [Bolton and Wodehouse] for New York and after terms had been arranged he wrote to me, apropos of his share, that he was not disgruntled but, on the other hand, not gruntled. I have used this once in a book and I see that Guy has used it in the play he sent me the other day, but if you would care to have it, help yourself. It's good.

This refers to a nugget in *The Code of the Woosters* which tops *The Oxford Dictionary of Quotations* list:

He spoke with a certain what-is-it in his voice, and I could see that, if not actually disgruntled, he was far from being gruntled.

He worked at these things; they didn't just float out of his mind. He wrote and rewrote, cut, balanced and polished. The lord of language. The master craftsman.

~ *'After all, golf is only a game,'* said Millicent.

Women say these things without thinking. It does not mean that there is any kink in their character. They simply don't realize what they are saying.

~ The Duke of Wigan, who, as so many British Dukes do, was at this time passing slowly through Hollywood.

~ Maiden Eggesford, like so many of our rural hamlets, is not at its brightest and best on a Sunday. When you have walked down the main street and looked at the Jubilee Watering Trough, there is nothing much to do except go home and then come out again and walk down the main street once more and take another look at the Jubilee Watering Trough.

~ The two-forty-five express stood at the platform with that air of well-bred reserve which is characteristic of Paddington trains. Lord Ickenham was all that was jovial and debonair. Tilting his hat at a jaunty angle, he gazed about him with approval at the decorous station which has for so many years echoed to the tread of county families.

'To one like myself,' he said, 'who, living in Hampshire, gets out of the metropolis, when he is fortunate enough to get into it, via Waterloo, there is something very soothing in the note of refined calm which Paddington strikes. At Waterloo, all is hustle and bustle, and the society tends to be mixed. Here a leisured peace prevails, and you get only the best people – cultured men accustomed to mingle with basset hounds and women in tailored suits who look like horses.'

~ 'The last time I played in a village cricket match,' said Psmith, 'I was caught at point by a man in braces. It would have been madness to risk another such shock to my system.'

escapade when the B.B.C. sent him a tape of Waugh's broadcast. Guy Bolton told me that the thought of this raid, presumably authorized, had hung in Wodehouse's mind till his death fourteen years later.

There was no truth in Waugh's story. The raid could not have happened unauthorized. It did not happen authorized. The *mairie* of Le Touquet has assured me that after the German occupation in 1940 no bombs fell on Le Touquet till 1944, when (to suggest that the Allied invasion might land there) the R.A.F. had done some diversionary bombing. Wodehouse never knew that. Evelyn Waugh never knew that; nor, perhaps mercifully, did Waugh know that he had thus saddened, and for so long, the man he so much honoured. Wodehouse came to dislike talking about the whole sad business of his broadcasts from Berlin. He hoped that others would forget it, and he went on working. Work had always been his favourite pastime and he had a sheaf of typescript and notes for a new Blandings novel in hospital with him when he died. He was also roughing out new stanzas for an old song, 'Kissing Time'.

In the late 1950s I was preparing *Wodehouse at Work*, a book about his books, which his English publishers (on Wodehouse's recommendation, I have been flattered to learn) had commissioned me to write for his eightieth birthday in 1961. I had been in the Middle East at the time of the broadcasts in 1941 and had heard little, and thought less, about them. Now I researched the subject, read the 'as broadcast' script of Connor's ranting philippic at the B.B.C. (his producer had been Norman Collins) and read the newspapers, especially *The Times*, *Daily Telegraph* and *Mirror* (Connor's paper) of that period, June and July of 1941. I read the B.B.C.'s partial monitorings of his voice as it had come into their listening camp near Evesham. I met Wodehouse's old friend Bill Townend. I corresponded with Guy Bolton. I went to see another old friend, Denis Mackail. Both he and Bill Townend had heard Wodehouse's voice at 4 a.m., but they were the only two people I ever met who had. I had a long talk with William Connor, who had foul-mouthed Wodehouse on the B.B.C. radio. He was still standing pat on the theme of his 1941 'Postscript': that Wodehouse deserved everything that he had given him and that 85 per cent of the letters he had received on the subject at the *Daily Mirror* had congratulated him on his broadcast. I went to talk to the 'Mr Chips' of Dulwich, 'Slacker' Christison, who, as a boy there, had known both Armine and Plum Wodehouse. I read what had been written about the defamed Old Boy in the school magazine, *The Alleynian*. And I read Harry Flannery's 1942 book, *Assignment to Berlin*, and, via a Berlin telephone book, pursued Werner Plack, who, on Flannery's evidence, had been the man at the German Foreign Office who had brought Wodehouse to the microphone.

In 1956 Plack, who then ran a public relations business in Berlin, came to London and we became friends. The primary cause of his visit that summer was to persuade Princess Margaret to be seen, and photographed, smoking a pipe. One of Plack's German clients had produced elegant small pipes and specially scented tobacco for women to smoke and to be seen smoking in elegant places. Plack had written to Princess Margaret, then very much in the news, suggesting that she might like to receive samples of such pipes and tobaccos and have her photograph taken enjoying them. He had received an answer from a lady on the Princess's staff, and he showed it to me. It was clear to me that she was saying no on behalf of the Princess, though with great courtesy. Plack thought it showed a hint of willingness, at least for further correspondence, and he hoped to push the project along by a visit to London and by meeting the lady-in-waiting who had written the letter, if not the Princess herself. He showed me pictures from the German magazines of jet-set German ladies at nightclubs smoking these long-stalked pipes with bowls the size of acorn shells.

Plack's English was rusty but it had been fluent, learnt mostly in Hollywood in the 1930s. He spoke fondly of 'Ethel' and 'Plummie', of the American war correspondents who had been in his charge, of the British and American film stars he had known in pre-war Hollywood, of his friendships with David Niven and, during the war, with Douglas Bader and some of the prisoners in Colditz. Bader, in prison camp in Germany, had broken one of his artificial legs and an R.A.F. plane had been allowed to fly over and drop a new one for him. Plack told me that he had organized that bit of public relations. And he told me how, shortly after the war and the death of his lovely young wife, he had gone to New York and the Wodehouses had been kind to him; Ethel had agreed to be godmother to his son and had given him a toy horse. (Ethel later had no memory of this and had forgotten the name Plack.)

It was clear to me that Plack, in the manner of good public relations operators, had tried to be nice to everybody. He had regarded the Wodehouses in Berlin as his special wards. John Amery, who was also under Plack's supervision, had wanted to meet Wodehouse in Berlin, but Plack kept them apart. Plack had had the job of escorting the American diplomatic personnel from Berlin to Lisbon when America came into the war against Germany. Ethel, then in Berlin, had been worrying about a parrot, Coco, that she had left behind with the French lady at whose house she had been a paying guest in Hesdin after vacating Low Wood for the Luftwaffe general. Coco was off his feed. Ethel, knowing that Plack was going to Lisbon and thinking that there might be a supply in neutral Lisbon of a special parrot food that Coco liked, had asked Plack to look around for it. There was none available in France or Germany. Plack had, on his return from Lisbon, brought a supply of this food to Paris and thence, in a staff car borrowed from the army, raced up to Hesdin with it and presented it to the grateful lady and Coco. Plack told me that he had had to square this extra-curricular journey with Schmidt, Hitler's interpreter, who was his immediate boss at the Foreign Office. They had agreed to a mutually cooked-up story for the records. In return for this special food, and perhaps stimulated by it, Coco was to be taught to scream *Deutschland über Alles!* or something similar for the radio. One has to assume that, when the papers of the German Foreign Office were captured in Berlin and examined in 1945 and later, this particular item missed the eyes of historians.

Plack has died. Iain Sproat had been to see him in Berlin. My chief memories of him on his London visits were of taking him to the Imperial War Museum, of walking with him in Kensington Gardens and showing him the palace where I believed Princess Margaret lived, and, again in Kensington Gardens, being startled by loud explosions south of us. These proved to be the attack on the Iranian Embassy by S.A.S. troops.

The Home Office kept its file on the Wodehouses and the Berlin broadcasts closed until 1980, five years after Wodehouse's knighthood and death. Why? I myself studied the papers there when they were released. I have read the chapters in Frances Donaldson's biography and Iain Sproat's book, *Wodehouse at War*, with great care. But I am still not clear about the answer. It seems to have had something to do with that fellow-internee who came out of Tost with Wodehouse and, with him, to Berlin and the Adlon under guard. His name was in the Cussen papers. Sproat was told that that name was the reason why the papers were still under wraps. Sproat suggested to the Home Office that they black out the fellow-traveller's name if that was the cause of the hold-up. This had not, till then, occurred to the Home Office custodian (who was on the point of retirement). I remember asking him why that name (which I had not seen) had caused the papers to be kept under wraps. He implied that I was asking him a question to which I could guess the answer. I couldn't. Frances Donaldson told me that he had told her that 'the security people' had disallowed the publication of the papers because this man's name was in them. I can only think now that Mr A. N. Other had been an M.I.6 man who had been given his partial freedom from internment in 1941 because he had reached the age of sixty.

It was all very bad luck on Wodehouse. Because the papers that confirmed his innocence were not released even when he was knighted, even when he died, many of his greatest admirers and friends felt there *must* have been something in them that someone did not want us to know, something presumably discreditable to the Wodehouses. Sproat tells us that he, a Conservative Member of Parliament and later a Junior Minister, had applied to the Prime Minister, Edward Heath, in 1972, to press for a knighthood for Wodehouse. The answer was no, and 'I had a clear and strong impression – although it was never said officially – that the reason for the refusal was some deeply damaging revelation about Wodehouse in the Home Office file'. Heath must have been misinformed, as there was no such revelation in the file when it was opened.

Only the most sensitive textual geiger-counter could pick up any hint of a reference to the distressing wartime events in Wodehouse's post-war novels and short stories. In *Joy in the Morning* Nobby Hopwood wails, when her beloved Boko Fittleworth, trying, by a display of good humour, to win Lord Worplesdon's approval for their marriage, puts a surprise salt-shaker on the table and (as far as I remember) a dribbling glass for Lord W. to drink from, 'You can never trust a writer not to make an ass of himself', and this has always seemed to me to be Wodehouse speaking purposely for himself in the Berlin broadcasts context. In *The Mating Season* Gussie Fink-Nottle gets hauled into a London magistrate's court for 'wading in the Trafalgar Square fountain at five ack emma' in search of newts. But he has given his name as Alfred Duff Cooper and as such he gets fourteen days in the slammer. At a village concert one of the acts is a violin solo by a Miss Eustacia Pulbrook, of which Bertie reported, 'It was loud in spots and less loud in other spots, and it had that quality which I have noticed in all violin solos, of seeming to last much longer than it actually did . . .' I don't suppose Sir Eustace Pulbrook, Old Alleynian and twice Chairman of Lloyds, had ever had that drawn to his attention. But undoubtedly Wodehouse would have chosen the name for his violinist as a tiny raspberry to the good Sir Eustace (he was a charming man; I knew him, but he had died before I thought of asking him) for something derogatory he had said *ex cathedra* at their mutual Old School about Wodehouse and the broadcasts.

A. A. Milne, claiming to have been a friend of Wodehouse, wrote a sly and damaging letter to the *Daily Telegraph* at the time of the broadcasts. In *The Mating Season* Bertie Wooster, for his sins, is made to get up at that concert and, in the name of Gussie Fink-Nottle, whom he is at that time impersonating, recite Christopher Robin verses. To Bertie's great agony. And there is a fine golf story, 'Rodney Has a Relapse', in which Rodney Spelvin, apparently cured by golf of writing poetry, has a relapse and starts writing Milne-ish verses to his son, 'Timothy Bobbin'. Such as:

> Timothy Bobbin has ten little toes.
> He takes them out walking wherever he goes.
> And if Timothy gets a cold in the head,
> His ten little toes stay with him in bed.

Milne's letter to the *Daily Telegraph* had been one of the first of a number heaving bricks at Wodehouse after Connor had given the lead. I think Milne would have agreed with Confucius's statement, 'There is no spectacle more agreeable than to observe an old friend fall from a roof-top.' The letter, which you will find in full in Sproat's book, said, in précis, 'Poor, silly Plum, he's escaped again. He ought to have fought in the first War, but he stayed in America and didn't. He ought to have paid his income taxes between the wars, but he didn't. And now, for the sake of a comfortable suite in the Adlon Hotel in Berlin, he is giving weekly talks on the Nazi radio. He has escaped again . . .' Milne's letter continues:

I remember that he told me once that he wished he had a son, and he added characteristically (and quite sincerely): 'But he would have to be born at the age of fifteen, when he was just getting into his House eleven.' You see the advantage of that. Bringing up a son throws a considerable responsibility on a man; but by the time the boy is fifteen one has shifted the responsibility on to the house-master, without forfeiting any reflected glory that may be about. This, I felt, has always been Wodehouse's attitude to life . . . But . . . irresponsibility in what the papers call a 'licensed humorist' can be carried too far. Wodehouse has been given a good deal of licence in the past, but I fancy now that his licence will be withdrawn . . .

It wasn't till I found myself involved, in the late 1950s, in writing a book about Wodehouse's books that I set myself to catch up on them, reading and rereading and, in a number of Saturday visits to the British

Library newspaper archive at Colindale, to see what the 1941 papers had said about the broadcasts, and why all the fuss. I happened to be reading *Psmith in the City* (1910) when Milne's letter to the *Daily Telegraph* was fresh in my mind. In that early novel I found young Mike Jackson, Psmith's friend, voicing, or rather having the narrator voice for him, an opinion in print significantly similar to that imputed to Wodehouse himself in alleged conversation with Milne. Listen to this:

Mike got on with small girls reasonably well. He preferred them at a distance, but, if cornered by them, could put up a fairly good show. Small boys, however, filled him with a sort of frozen horror. It was his view that a boy should not be exhibited publicly until he reached an age when he might be in the running for some sort of colours at a public school.

I wrote to Wodehouse about this, thinking that he might just possibly not have spotted the echo. He hadn't. He told me Milne hadn't really been a friend of his and he certainly had never said that, or anything like it, to Milne. But the imputed remark, in Milne's letter to the *Daily Telegraph*, had rung a distant bell for him and now I had located its source.

I am glad to say that Compton Mackenzie had been infuriated by Milne's letter, and he wrote the Editor a snorter: 'a disgrace that the man who had made such a good thing out of his own son as Milne, should have attacked Wodehouse in this way . . .' Alas, the *Daily Telegraph* didn't print Mackenzie's letter. But it is in his many-volumed *Memoirs*.

Wodehouse's fiction – his world of drones, Drones, fortnight-long house-parties, butlers, chefs and valets – was never contemporary, nor had he been part of any such world. He had, on his typewriter, practised, polished and perfected an accent, a world and an outlook which was acceptable on both sides of the Atlantic and ignored wars, Depressions, strikes, ageing and death. Many people have tried, in print or conversation, to place the Wodehouse manner into some exact historical era: to fit Bertie Wooster and his friends, say, into a decade when they could be taken for real. It never works. The Wodehouse worlds and the three or four Wodehouse languages – Psmith, Jeeves, the burbler, the buzzer – are artefacts.

I had, in 1942 and far from England, what I thought at the time was a revelation on this subject. Syria and Lebanon, Arab countries, had been, as far as living memory went back, ruled by the Turks and the French, and now the British were in military control. In Beirut that summer I met an Armenian, a dealer in antiques. Armenians had been third-class citizens, if citizens at all, in the Levant, stateless and detribalized except for massacres and persecutions, for half a century. My friend Dikran's mother had spoken Armenian, Turkish, Arabic, Italian, French and English. She had a stroke at the age of seventy and could then speak only her native Armenian. Dikran spoke most of those languages too, fluently though probably badly. I found his English, hesitant at first, extremely odd. It was laced with bits of slang such as 'old bean' and 'pip-pip'. He used the word 'oofy' for rich – a word I myself hadn't used since schooldays. ('Oof' for 'money' had been, in the 1920s, an obligatory jargon word at Charterhouse, part of the strange private language that we had to learn in our first three weeks and soon came to use without embarrassment.)

I discovered that my friend Dikran had himself been at an English public school, St Peter's, York, just before the First World War. He was, in 1942, for converse with the new master race, groping back to a language he had learnt in an artificial society and had scarcely used at all in the last quarter of a century. Not all of it, but odd bits, came floating, tumbling on to his tongue. The result was the nearest to Wodehouse/ Wooster prose that I have ever heard, and I am sorry that I could not get on to tape our conversations over the arak at the St Georges Hotel. I am also sorry that Dikran so quickly learnt to clean up its anachronisms, and its strange concords of Prayer Book and *Pink 'Un*, Sixth Form and Shell, cockney and cricket, Hollywood and horse-racing. He hadn't, in fact, read much Wodehouse. If his speech then was a linguistic revelation, it would have needed much more study than I was able to give it before it could be presented as a valid contribution to the identification of the root of one of the Wodehouse styles. Certainly a fertilizer of the Wodehouse/Wooster language was the Indian Baboo Jabberjee joke – the florid and idiomatically discordant English spoken or written by 'examination-wallahs' who had learnt from books and who overused and misapplied tags and quotations from the English classics.

Hilaire Belloc, in America in 1936, said on the radio that the best writer of English then alive was Wodehouse, 'the head of my profession'. In particular he praised Wodehouse for creating Jeeves. 'If in, say, fifty years Jeeves and any other of that great [Wodehouse] company – but in particular Jeeves – shall have faded, then what we have so long called England will no longer be.' Strong words, and the fifty years are now up and Jeeves hasn't faded.

1 ~ SUSPENSION OF DISBELIEF

―――――――――― ~ ――――――――――

~ Thirty postulates for relaxed reading of ~
P. G. Wodehouse

1. It is generally hay-harvest weather in England: for fifty-four holes of golf a day, or for a swim before breakfast in the lake, morning in the hammock under the cedars, tea on the lawn, coffee on the terrace after dinner.

2. Money is something you should inherit, get monthly as an allowance from an uncle, win at the races or borrow from Oofy Prosser.

3. All small dogs go for your ankles.

4. All babies are hideously ugly.

5. All small boys are fiends.

6. All aunts are hell, except Bertie's Aunt Dahlia.

7. All butlers have port in their pantries.

8. Old nannies are a menace. They know too much.

9. Drunk men can be very funny.

10. A pig can be housed in an empty cottage, a caravan, a bathroom or a two-seater without danger to the fabric or subsequent trace.

11. Country pubs are open all day long and their home-brew ale is very potent.

12. All decent-sized country houses have cellars, coal-sheds and potting sheds for locking people into.

13. Watch out for girls with two-syllable masculine-sounding shortenings of their Christian names (Bobbie Wickham, Corky Pirbright,

Nobby Hopwood, Stiffy Byng). They get the good man of their choice in the end, but they spread havoc on the way.

14. If a young man has a single-syllable Christian name, is poor and ugly and can stop dog-fights, he is sure to be the hero. He may propose to the heroine at their first meeting and, at their second, waggle her about like a sack of coals, with hoarse cries of 'My mate!' She will love this, though she may kick his shins at the beginning of such an embrace.

15. A hero may get his ring and letters thrown back at him by the heroine, and harsh words spoken about his manners, face and ancestry. But should he contrive to be knocked senseless by a bully, a fall or, as old Sippy, Jeeves with a putter and benevolent aforethought, on waking he will find the adored object showering kisses on his upturned face.

16. Most handsome men have feet of clay.

17. All young men with wavy, marcelled or corrugated hair have feet of clay and worse.

18. No decent man may cancel, or even refuse, an engagement to a girl.

19. Men and girls in love think only of marriage.

20. Rose gardens turn a girl on.

21. A bedroom scene is when you discover someone's made you an apple-pie bed and/or punctured your hot water bottle.

22. Another bedroom scene is when one or more people come and search your room for policemen's helmets, manuscript memoirs, notebooks, jewels or miscreants hiding in cupboards or under the bed.

23. All married couples have separate bedrooms.

24. Chorus girls are all right and Earls (Marshmoreton) and nephews of Earls (Ronnie Fish) are very lucky to marry them.

25. Barmaids are all right and Lords (Yaxley) and Barts (Sir Gregory Parsloe) are lucky to marry them.

26. A country J.P. can call the local policeman and have anybody

arrested and held in a cell on suspicion of anything. At his whim a J.P. can send anybody to prison without the option and without trial, legal representation or redress, for up to thirty days.

27. If, for a country house, you need a secretary, a Harley Street loony-doctor, a butler, a cook, a head gardener, a detective or a valet, you go up to London by a morning train and, without having made any appointment by telephone, you find what you want and come back with him or her by train the same afternoon.

28. The night you go to a nightclub is the night it gets raided by the police.

29. If you are arrested, on Boat Race Night or at a nightclub, give a false name and address and they will be accepted by the magistrate.

30. On Boat Race Night in London a young man always gets a bit tight, and it is then his duty to try to part a policeman from his helmet.

2 ~ NINETY-TWO BOOKS

_____ ~ _____

When a reviewer writes that 'it would be unfair to reveal the plot', it generally means that he has forgotten it. I give the plots here mercilessly, to enable you to remember whether this, or that, is a book you haven't read and must, or that you have read and must read again.

~ The Pothunters ~
1902

It is the Sports term at St Austin's College (600-plus boys; cricket, rugger, fives, racquets). But we start with the Public Schools Boxing at Aldershot. Tony Graham of St Austin's knocks out his cousin, Allen Thomson of Rugby, in the final of the Middleweights. This is a novel, though the episodes hang together loosely as though they started as short stories. The silverware sports prizes disappear from the Pavilion and are cached in a hollow tree in Squire Sir Alfred Venner, M.P.'s pheasant-coverts, out of bounds to the boys. Inspector Roberts comes down from Scotland Yard. In the boys' Houses there are plenty of study frowsts and teas. Charteris ('the Alderman') who talks rot pleasantly, as though he might develop into a Psmith, shares a study with Welch, the all-rounder. Charteris edits _The Glow-Worm_, an anonymous and jovial school monthly magazine.

~ A Prefect's Uncle ~
1903

The summer term at Beckford College. Alan Gethryn is head of Leicester's House, in the Sixth, the XI and the XV. A new boy arrives at Leicester's, Reginald Farnie, who reveals himself to be Gethryn's uncle.

Farnie is a bright lad, but an embarrassment to the nephew set in authority over him. Farnie gets into money trouble (not his fault) and disappears. Gethryn leaves a cricket match, School *v*. M.C.C., to go and find him, and the School loses the match without him. There is a Poetry Prize, entry mandatory to the whole of the Upper Fifth. Lorimer of the Upper Fifth has a kid sister, Mabel, and Pringle, who shares a study with Lorimer, is 'gone on' her. Sex had not reared its innocent head in *The Pothunters* (1902) at all.

~ *Tales of St Austin's* ~
1903

Back to St Austin's College for twelve short stories, eleven of which had appeared in the *Captain* and the *Public School Magazine*. Charteris appears again. In fact 'The Manoeuvres of Charteris' (forty-three pages) may have been the start of a notional novel, with the headmaster's twelve-year-old niece Dorothy as heroine to Charteris's hero. The book ends with four essaylets from the *Public School Magazine*. 'The Tom Brown Question' asks, in dialogue, who can have written the utterly feeble second half of that classic public-school novel. (In fact it was still Hughes. But later biography has shown that he wrote the second half after the loss of a beloved daughter which had badly affected his skill as a novelist.)

~ *The Gold Bat* ~
1904

We are at Wrykyn School now, in the rugger term. The statue of Sir Eustace Briggs, Mayor of Wrykyn, in the recreation ground has been tarred and feathered in the night. And a small gold bat, of the type given to the captain of the team that won the inter-house cricket cup to hang on his watch-chain, is found at the scene of the crime. There is a fight in a fives court and a couple of the boys keep illegal ferrets. Clowes, left wing three-quarter, is a solemn wit, lazy – another potential Psmith.

~ *William Tell Told Again* ~
1904

How tiny Switzerland threw off the yoke of horrid Austria, thanks to William Tell. Hermann Gessler, the Governor, was, with the help of a

Lord High Executioner and his attendant oil-boiler, taxing the poor but honest Swiss down to the nub. But Hermann Gessler got an arrow where it did most good, in the heart. A short, cheerful narrative by Wodehouse, excellent colour pictures by Philip Dadd and excellent captions to the pictures, in verse by John W. Houghton – very much the sort of expert verse Wodehouse himself was already writing, in *Punch* and elsewhere.

The pictures (and perhaps the verse?) were done a year and more before Wodehouse was asked to supply the narrative.

~ *The Head of Kay's* ~
1905

Now we are at Eckleton School, with some chapters of an end-of-term Schools Corps Camp. Mr Kay is an unpopular housemaster and Kay's has gone downhill. Kennedy, 2nd prefect of Blackburn's House and in the school cricket XI, is transferred, not too willingly, to be head boy of Kay's, with encouragement to make it a decent House again. He has to fight a dissident Kayite to assert his authority. There are House matches at cricket and rugger and a five-mile run in which Kennedy, coming second, scores points which win the Sports Cup for his House. Jimmy Silver, head of Blackburn's House and Captain of Cricket, is a near-Psmith talker.

~ *Love among the Chickens* ~
1906

The first five chapters are narrated about, the last eighteen by, Jeremy Garnet, Old Wrykynian, struggling author, verse-writer, ex-prep-schoolmaster, golfer. He is persuaded to join his feckless ex-school, ex-schoolmastering colleague, Stanley Featherstonehaugh Ukridge, and his adoring wife Millie in Lyme Regis, where they are setting up a chicken-farm that is supposed to be going to make fortunes for all of them. In the train from Paddington, Garnet meets a girl, Phyllis Derrick, who is actually reading one of his own (two) novels. She is going to join her father, Professor Derrick, at Lyme Regis. The Ukridge chicken-farm founders. The Professor quarrels with Ukridge and forbids his daughter the house. To win Phyllis's favour Garnet arranges to have her father upset from a boat in the harbour so that he, Garnet, can rescue him. But the Professor only gives his approval to the marriage after Garnet has let him win the final of the local golf tournament. The wedding is told as a short stage play. This book gives us our first view of Ukridge, that great dreamer, idler, schemer, borrower of money and clothes, and general menace.

Wodehouse revised the book and it was reissued in 1921. Now it was all told by Garnet and the playlet of the wedding was removed. For some reason Lyme Regis was changed to Combe Regis. And the price of eggs was changed to allow for inflation.

~ The White Feather ~
1907

Back to Wrykyn School, in the spring term. A mayoral election is pending in the town. St Jude's, a school in the High Street, has a feud against Wrykyn. There is a mix-up fight in the street and Sheen, of Seymour's House, a scholar and a pianist – no boxer – is faced by Albert, a red-haired toughie of St Jude's. Sheen funks fighting him. This gets Sheen despised and virtually cut by the whole school. Sheen takes to going, illegally, to The Blue Boar, where Joe Bevan, ex-world lightweight champion, failed actor, great quoter of Shakespeare, teaches and trains boxers. Sheen, with Joe's training behind him, eventually gets permission from a surprised Sports Master to enter for the Lightweights at the Public Schools meeting at Aldershot. He beats Peteiro of Ripton in the final.

~ Not George Washington ~
1907

A very poor novel, written in collaboration with Herbert Westbrook, who was more than half in Wodehouse's mind for the character of Ukridge in *Love among the Chickens* and many later and more expert short stories. James Orlebar Cloyster is engaged to Margaret Goodwin in Guernsey, and the arrangement is that she shall join him and they'll get married as soon as Cloyster has made a position for himself in London as a writer. Later he tries to conceal his successes so that Margaret won't hear of them and demand marriage. Later still they do marry – or rather, they are left, apparently happy, on the brink of marriage.

I do not understand the title of this book. I do understand why it is such a rarity, and why collectors of Wodehouse pay very high prices when copies emerge at auction sales.

~ *The Swoop* ~
1909

There had been novels in England foreseeing enemy invasion as far back as *The Battle of Dorking*, serialized in *Blackwood's Magazine* in 1870. From 1902, when Germany had decided to build a battle-fleet to equal England's, the idea of a blitz invasion across the North Sea, before the English battleships could get back from the Mediterranean, was a bestselling subject for the popular press, from *Chums* to the Harmsworth journals.

Wodehouse's *The Swoop* is a short squib, taking off these invasion-scare writings as well as the recently-formed, and popular, Boy Scouts. England is invaded by the armies of a multitude of enemies: Saxe-Pfennig, Russia, Afghanistan, China (under General Ping Pong Pang), Turkey, Morocco, Monaco and the distant isle of Bollygolla. England's defences crumble – it's August and everybody is away on holiday. Only the Boy Scouts resist the invaders. Clarence Chugwater, aged fourteen and a junior reporter on an evening paper, is in command of a troop on the Aldwych site, and he leads his men in with catapults and hockey sticks. Eventually the music halls offer the invading generals and princes vast weekly salaries to appear nightly on their stages, Clarence himself topping the bills with £1,150 a week. Some real names occur. Edgar Wallace is a war correspondent, as he was at that time. Charles Frohmann is a theatrical producer, Baden-Powell is head of the Scouts.

In 1915 Wodehouse adapted the book to signal an invasion of America by Germany and Japan in 1916, and sold it for serialization to the smart New York monthly magazine *Vanity Fair*.

Writing to George Orwell in June 1948 (*The Letters of Evelyn Waugh*, edited by Mark Amory, 1980), Waugh seems to ascribe importance to *The Swoop* in the context of the broadcasts Wodehouse made to neutral America from Berlin in 1941. Waugh also says, 'This book is very much funnier than *The Head of Keys* [sic] which preceded it, and in fact forms an important literary link with *Mike* published next year.'

The Head of Kay's is not a funny book in that sense, and there were three books of Wodehouse's published after that one and before *The Swoop*. It is anybody's guess what Waugh thought the important literary link was between *The Swoop* and *Mike*.

~ In this life it is not aunts that matter but the courage which one brings to them.

~ Foggy between the ears.

~ He drank coffee with the air of a man who regretted it was not hemlock.

~ I always bar the sort of story where Chapter Ten ends with the hero trapped in the underground den and Chapter Eleven starts with him being the life and soul of the gay party at the Spanish Embassy.

~ Dark hair fell in a sweep over his forehead. He looked like a man who would write vers libre, as indeed he did.

~ Though he scorned and loathed her, he was annoyed to discover that he loved her still. He would have liked to bounce a brick on Prudence Whittaker's head, and yet, at the same time, he would have liked – rather better, as a matter of fact – to crush her to him and cover her face with burning kisses. The whole situation was very complex.

~ Braid Bates at that time was a young plug-ugly of some nine summers, in appearance a miniature edition of his father and in soul and temperament a combination of Dead End kid and army mule; a freckled, hard-boiled character with a sardonic eye and a mouth which, when not occupied in eating, had a cynical twist to it. He spoke little as a general thing, but when he did speak seldom failed to find a chink in the armour.

~ Any dog will tell you what these prize-ribbon dogs are like. Their heads are so swelled they have to go into their kennels backwards.

~ Mike ~
1909

Of the five Jackson brothers, one plays cricket for England, two others for counties. But Mike, the youngest at fifteen, shows signs of being the best batsman of them all. He goes to Wrykyn School as a new boy. His elder brother Bob is in his last term and they both get their First XI colours that summer. Mike, in the Ripton match, turns disaster into victory with a heroic innings. But two years later Mike's school report is so bad that his father removes him from Wrykyn, when he is just about to be Cricket Captain, and sends him to a minor school, Sedleigh, where they make boys work.

At Sedleigh Mike meets and becomes friends with another elderly new boy, similarly displaced, from Eton, and similarly scornful of his new school – Psmith. The two 'lost lambs' share a study and decide not to take cricket seriously, but to rag. The Sedleigh cricket captain, Adair, dislikes Mike's lack of keenness and it takes a fist-fight (which Mike wins by a knock-out) to cure Mike's antagonism to Adair and to Sedleigh.

In 1953 Herbert Jenkins, Wodehouse's then publishers, split *Mike* into two, *Mike at Wrykyn* and *Mike and Psmith*. They also modernized some of the language.

~ A Gentleman of Leisure ~
1910

Jimmy Pitt, rich, generous, popular American bachelor, has fallen in love with an unknown girl on a transatlantic liner. He bets a friend at the Strollers Club in New York that he can break into a house like any Raffles. He does so and it happens to be the apartment of a crooked New York policeman (English originally, sacked from Eton, and has now changed his name: a bad hat), John McEachern, whose daughter is/was the girl on the boat. The scene changes to Dreever Castle in Shropshire, where 'Spennie', Earl of Dreever, is bossed around by his self-made millionaire uncle, Sir Thomas Blunt, M.P. Lady Julia Blunt has a £20,000 'diamond' necklace (it proves to be valueless white jargoon). Spennie is being sharked at billiards, poker and picquet by one of the house-party. Among the guests are John McEachern, who has made his pile by New York graft and spends it bringing his beloved daughter into good English society. He now hopes to marry her to the 12th Earl of Dreever. Spennie's uncle and aunt also hope this will be a match, because they think Molly McEachern is an heiress. Jimmy Pitt is of the house-party too. He wins the love and hand of Molly.

Dreever Castle, a massive grey pile in Shropshire, built against raiders looming over the Welsh border, is a forerunner of Blandings, and perhaps Lady Julia and her 'diamonds' are forerunners of Lady Constance and her diamonds in *Leave It to Psmith*.

In the two stage versions of this novel Douglas Fairbanks Sr and John Barrymore, neither well known at the time, played the Jimmy Pitt part.

~ *Psmith in the City* ~
1910

Mike Jackson's father has lost 'a very large sum of money' and Mike now can't go to Cambridge. So he goes into the New Asiatic Bank in the City. Psmith's rich and eccentric father thinks that Psmith should go into commerce, so Psmith turns up at the bank too.

Psmith has a comfortable flat in Clement's Inn to which Mike goes to

PSMITH,
of Eton, Sedleigh, Cambridge, the City,
and Blandings Castle.

live. Psmith belongs to the same Club, the Senior Conservatives, as Mr Bickersdyke, crusty Manager of the New Asiatic Bank, who is also running for Parliament for the Conservatives. Psmith decides to harass Bickersdyke and discovers that he had once been a rabid Socialist.

Mike is paid £4 10s. a month. He and Psmith are both bored by the bank. They 'bunk' it together on the same day, Mike because he gets a sudden call to play for his county at Lord's (he makes 148), Psmith to go and watch. Mr Bickersdyke joyfully sacks them both.

Now Psmith's father wants him to go to Cambridge and read Law. And he offers Mike the future agency of his estates, after three or four years at Cambridge which Mr Smith will finance. (Mike's brother Joe, an All-England batsman, is already the agent of a sporting baronet, keen on cricket.)

A good worm's-eye view of City life in banking, and some amusing excursions into politics and political meetings, where you can 'rag' by heckling.

~ *The Prince and Betty* ~
1912

Betty Silver, twenty-four, is stepdaughter of millionaire-tycoon Benjamin Scobell, the nephew and sole male relative of Mrs Jane Oakley, multi-millionairess miser. Some years ago Betty had met a John Maude when he was at Harvard, and he has been her *prince lointain* ever since. Benjamin Scobell virtually owns the Mediterranean island of Mervo and he runs it as a gambling property. He discovers that John Maude's late father had been Prince and ruler of Mervo, deposed when the island elected to be a republic. Scobell decides, for business reasons, to bring John Maude in as Prince and – to keep him in the family – to marry him to his stepdaughter Betty. Betty goes out to Mervo, meets John Maude again but thinks he is courting her simply because her stepfather has ordered him to. She runs away to New York. Her aunt, Mrs Oakley, likes her, tells her to dry her tears and get a job. As Betty 'Brown' she goes as a typist to *Peaceful Moments*, a sleepy weekly. Rupert Smith, ex-Harvard newspaperman, is Deputy Editor, but, when the Editor is ordered away for three months for health reasons, Smith takes over and peps the magazine up. Rupert Smith is clearly a clone of Psmith: very tall, thin and dark, with a solemn face, immaculately dressed, monocle in left eye and calls people 'Comrade'. Helped by good researching, muck-raking and writing by Betty 'Brown', the paper attacks the anonymous owners of the Brosher Street slum tenements in New York. Meanwhile John Maude has quit Mervo, not liking the Scobell methods, and he gets a job at *Peaceful Moments* through his old friend Rupert Smith. Betty, thinking he is pursuing her, disappears and takes a job as cashier in one of Bat Jarvis's (a nice cat-loving gangster) cafés. It transpires that Benjamin Scobell is all the time owner not only of *Peaceful Moments* but of the Brosher Street tenements also. He repents and says he will repair them and run them properly. John Maude, reunited with Betty, wants to marry her. Mrs Oakley gives them enough money to buy a farm out west and make the happy ending.

Not all the material in this first version of *The Prince and Betty* (published by W. J. Watt & Co., New York) went into the English version, published by Mills and Boon in the same year. Some of it went into *Psmith Journalist*, published three years later (1915) in England, never in America.

~ *The Little Nugget* ~
1913

'The Little Nugget' is the kidnappers' name for Ogden Ford, a fat, chain-smoking, rude and badly spoilt American boy, aged thirteen or fourteen. Ogden's mother and father (she rich, he richer) are divorced and each is trying to get the boy away from the other. Meanwhile, professional kidnappers are trying to get him, for ransom from either parent. Elmer Ford, the father, pays double fees for Ogden to go to a snobbish little English preparatory school (boarding), where he thinks the boy will be fairly safe and may even learn some discipline. Peter Burns (rich, a cricket and rugger blue) is persuaded by his fiancée, who is in the pay of Mrs Ford, to go as an assistant master to this school and kidnap Ogden so that his mother can get him on to a yacht and out of his father's reach. But who is White, the new school butler? A professional kidnapper. And others prowl and prowl around. Peter Burns tells the story (except the first twenty-five pages of it) and it makes an excellent thriller, set mostly in the grounds and house of the prep school.

~ *The Man Upstairs* ~
1914

Nineteen early short stories, some fairly good, some fairly bad. Most of them were written in America for the American pulps. 'Archibald's Benefit' is Wodehouse's first golf story. 'The Good Angel' is the first story with a strong butler part (and some very ill-informed comings and goings of a shooting party at a country house). Rollo Finch and Wilson in 'Ahead of Schedule' are a foretaste of Bertie Wooster and Jeeves. Sally, who, in 'Something to Worry About', feuds with a policeman and asks her fiancé to pull the man's helmet down over his eyes, is a foretaste of Stiffy Byng in *The Code of the Woosters*. 'In Alcala' has strands of autobiography in it; its sentimentality is remarkably gooey, but is there, anywhere else in Wodehouse, a heroine who admits to having been a man's mistress?

~ *Something Fresh* ~
1915

The first of the Blandings saga. Aline Peters, daughter of dyspeptic American millionaire scarab-collector J. Preston Peters, is to marry the Hon. Freddie Threepwood, and there is to be a fortnight-long house-party at the Castle, 'a gathering together of the Emsworth clan by way of honour and as a means of introduction to Mr Peters and his daughter'. Lord Emsworth has pocketed one of Mr Peters's valuable scarabs, thinking it a gift. And Mr Peters is determined to get it back, offering a reward too. Ashe Marson, writer of thrillers (*Gridley Quayle, Investigator*), signs on as Mr Peters's valet with instructions to steal back the scarab. And Joan Valentine signs on as Aline Peters's lady's maid with the same quest, and reward, in mind. Ashe and Joan (who are in the same London digs to start with) are to get married in the end and Aline rejects Freddie to elope with George Emerson, of the Hong Kong Police, whom Freddie has asked down casually for the party.

There is more about what goes on below stairs the other side of the green baize door here than in any other book of Wodehouse's.

~ *Psmith Journalist* ~
1915

A good deal of this is material adapted from *The Prince and Betty* (1912). This probably explains the unlikelihood of Mike Jackson going to

America to play for an M.C.C. side, with his friend Psmith accompanying him 'in a private capacity'. While Mike goes off to Philadelphia to play cricket, Psmith stays in New York and becomes the hero of this novel.

There is no heroine. In a New York restaurant Psmith meets the acting editor of the weekly *Cosy Moments* and, through him and the office boy, the cat-loving leader of the Groom Street Gang, Bat Jarvis. As the real editor is away and out of contact, and the proprietor is in Europe, Windsor (the acting editor) and Psmith (amateur sub-editor) decide to jazz up the paper and, amongst other campaigns, to attack the unknown landlord of some dreadful New York slum tenements. The anonymous landlord threatens reprisals to Windsor, Psmith and the paper. With the help of Bat Jarvis and his gang, they fight the gangs that the landlord hires to beat them up. There is some shooting and Psmith has to get a new hat as a result.

Psmith, with the help of a legacy from an uncle and his father in Switzerland, buys *Cosy Moments* from its proprietor. The owner of the slum property turns out to be a politician running for City Alderman. He is made to repent and to make great improvements in the houses for his tenants.

Psmith calls back the old stagnant staff and hands the paper back to them, while remaining owner (apparently) after he and Mike go back to Cambridge.

~ *Uneasy Money* ~

1917

Bill (Lord) Dawlish, twenty-four, is a good footballer, boxer and golfer, has good health, many friends, a beautiful (though hard) fiancée, minor actress Claire Fenwick, and no money except the £400 a year he gets as Secretary to the exclusive Brown's Club. Claire refuses to marry him on that. Then Bill hears he has been left £1m by an eccentric American whose golfing slice he had cured. He also hears that the eccentric's niece, Elizabeth Boyd, who farms bees on Long Island, had expected to inherit the £1m. Bill, without telling Claire, goes to America (as Bill Chalmers) to see that Elizabeth gets at least half of the inheritance. Clare, separately and unknown to Bill, also goes to America, to stay with her ex-chorus-girl friend who is now a successful barefoot dancer calling herself Lady Pauline Wetherby. Claire meets an American millionaire on the boat and makes him propose to her, and she accepts. Then, hearing of Bill's new wealth, she breaks with her American and expects to be taken back by Bill. But Bill now is in love with Elizabeth, though she refuses to marry him with no money of her own.

Well, the eccentric old millionaire had made a later will, and so . . .

This novel is the second in the soon-to-be-common Wodehouse Anglo-American pattern, with Anglo-American marriages. There is some untidy gun-play near the end and Claire's millionaire accidentally shoots a pet monkey.

~ *The Man with Two Left Feet* ~
1917

Thirteen early short stories written in America. One, 'Extricating Young Gussie', is important because it introduces Bertie (though his surname seems to be Mannering-Phipps), Jeeves and Aunt Agatha. Gussie Mannering-Phipps, head of the 'very old and aristocratic' family now that his father, Bertie's Uncle Cuthbert, keen drinker, unsuccessful gambler, big spender, has died, has gone to America and is involved with a girl on the New York vaudeville stage. Aunt Agatha sends Bertie over to extricate Gussie. Bertie is unsuccessful and all ends happily, with Gussie marrying the vaudeville girl, his mother, herself ex-vaudeville, remarrying, this time to an old vaudevillian adorer, and Bertie staying on in New York with Jeeves for fear of meeting Aunt Agatha's wrath.

Otherwise mostly sentimental apprentice work. One story, 'The Mixer' is told by a dog; another is about a cat. One, 'One Touch of Nature', is about a rich American forced by his Society-minded wife to live in England, but longing to see baseball games again. One, 'The Romance of an Ugly Policeman' is about a pretty cook in London courted by the milkman, falsely accused of theft by the lady of the house, being marched off by a policeman and, after doing her thirty days, finding the policeman, not the milkman, waiting for her (see also 'Something to Worry About' in *The Man Upstairs*). 'The Making of Mac's' could almost have been written by 'Sapper'.

~ *Piccadilly Jim* ~
1918

Even in Lloyd George's premiership, would a second-rank American actor, married to an American millionairess forging ahead in London society, be given an English peerage? No, but it's important to the plot of this comedy-thriller that the American millionairess is aiming at just that – to spite her millionairess sister, who has said she married beneath her. Bingley Crocker is the suffering peer-hopefully-to-be, a baseball fan stuck in London (see also 'One Touch of Nature' in *The Man with Two Left Feet*) with an ambitious, snobbish wife, an English butler who is a cricket fan and a son, Jimmy, who is now 'Piccadilly Jim', playboy. Jimmy Crocker, like Jimmy Pitt in *A Gentleman of Leisure*, had, before he became cushioned by money, been a newspaperman and had written a hurtfully ribald review of a volume of heart-felt poetry by Ann Chester – not a good start, because he later finds he wants to marry her.

Here comes young Ogden Ford again, and his mother, widowed and now remarried to, and making life hell for, Peter Pett, New York financier and baseball fan. Ann Chester is Peter Pett's niece and comforter, also governess and supposed to be in charge of Ogden, whom she rightly detests, mainly because he adds to the hell of his stepfather's life. The whole family, Peter Pett, Nesta Pett, Ogden and Ann, comes over to England to persuade Mrs Pett's sister, Mrs Crocker, to let them take her stepson Jimmy back to work in New York rather than be 'Piccadilly Jim', the joy of the columnists (he has had two breach-of-promise cases against him – a barmaid and a girl in a flower shop) in London.

There is far too much disguising and false-naming for even faint credibility. At one stage Jimmy Crocker, pretending to be son of English butler Bayliss, has to *pretend* to be Jimmy Crocker to fool his father. There is a sub-plot about the Secret Service and a new explosive, partridgite.

Jimmy Crocker gets Ann in the end, both agreeing that his hurtful review of her poems five years ago had reformed and toughened her hitherto soppy outlook; and anyway, a fellow like him needs a tough wife.

~ *My Man Jeeves* ~
1919

Four Jeeves stories told by Bertie Wooster staying in New York to avoid the wrath of his Aunt Agatha; four stories told by Reggie Pepper. Six of these eight stories turn up again in *Carry on, Jeeves* (1925), two of them, which had been told by Reggie Pepper, now recast as Bertie/Jeeves stories set in England.

If your textbook is *The World of Jeeves* omnibus, the stories that belong in essentials to *My Man Jeeves* are 'The Artistic Career of Corky', 'Jeeves and the Chump Cyril', 'Jeeves and the Unbidden Guest', 'Jeeves and the Hard-Boiled Egg', 'The Aunt and the Sluggard' and 'Jeeves Makes an Omelette'.

In fact Jeeves had first appeared – though only two lines of him – in 'Extricating Young Gussie' in *The Man with Two Left Feet*.

~ *A Damsel in Distress* ~
1919

This is almost a Blandings novel. Belpher Castle is in Hampshire, but it has an amber drawing-room, a terrace below and a rose-garden. Its widower châtelain is the Earl of Marshmoreton. He is a great gardener; he is bossed by his sister; he has a butler who looks like a saintly bishop and a foolish son and heir. He marries, at the end, a charming (American) chorus girl, a felicity never allowed to Lord Emsworth – only to his nephew Ronnie Fish.

The hero of this book is American composer George Bevan. The heroine is Lady Maud Marsh, the Earl's daughter, a good golfer with a tilted nose. She is a captive at the Castle under aunt's orders because of her 'ridiculous infatuation' for an impossible American. That's not, in fact, George Bevan. Bevan is eminently possible: nice, a golfer with a good line in Psmith talk, and he makes $5,000 a week in a theatre season in a good year, which is not hay even with $5 to the £1. (Italian restaurants in Soho serve *table d'hôte* lunches for 1s. 6d., and you get your top hat ironed in your shaving parlour.)

A good deal of good theatre stuff here and a two-weeks house-party with a ball at the Castle for the son-and-heir's twenty-first birthday. The impossible American who has been a threat to George Bevan's courtship of Maud comes on stage only briefly at the end. When she had fallen for him he had been a 'slim Apollo'. Then he had gone out of her life but not her heart for a year – during which time he had, incidentally, been toying, under an assumed name and the nickname 'Pootles', with the affections of a nice chorus girl (is there ever a nasty chorus girl in a story or novel of Wodehouse's?) to the tune of £10,000 for breach of promise – and now he returns, thirty pounds overweight and talking about food, not love. It is easy for Maud to make the big decision and say yes to George.

~ *The Coming of Bill* ~
1920

It was all the fault of Lora Delane Porter, rich American widow, eugenist, writer and lecturer. When Kirk Winfield, an unsuccessful artist but with a small private income and a fine physique, fell in love with Ruth Bannister at first sight, and she with him (she being Mrs Porter's niece and the daughter of a Wall Street millionaire), Mrs Porter said, 'Marry, for the good of the race.' They marry. It is not too happy. Kirk's income isn't enough for two. Ruth objects to his sponging friends and to the friendly model who is sitting for his 'Ariadne in Naxos' and calls him Kirk. Ruth suggests that Kirk go in for landscape painting and, if he must, finish Ariadne with herself as model. She faints on the dais and there's going to be a b-a-b-y. Enter Bill, 9 lbs and with a fine physique. He is instantly, and without much fuss from Ruth, brought up on Mrs Porter's lines of eugenic untouchability. Kirk, in the hope of making money, goes off gold-prospecting in Colombia with his old friend Hank Jardine. Ruth's father dies and she inherits money and becomes a prominent New York hostess, pursued by a rich ex-boyfriend. Kirk returns, having failed to find gold and having lost his friend Hank Jardine (fever). Kirk, with the help of Steve Dingle, the ex-pug gymnasium instructor, and Mamie, Bill's nursemaid, kidnaps Bill and whisks him off to a mountain fastness. Ruth loses her money in the crash of her silly brother's firm, inherited from father, on Wall Street, and she returns to her own family, poor but happy. It's *that* for Aunt Lora. Young Bill *shall* get dirty sometimes, he *shall* fight the neighbour bully child, he *shall* have an Irish terrier puppy to hug. It's happy endings for the Winfields, reunited, and not so happy for Aunt Lora.

All American, except for an English butler in the Bannister house.

~ *Jill the Reckless* ~
1921

Jill Mariner, pretty, young, with plenty of money, lives in Ovington Square (and owns the house) with her raffish Uncle Chris Selby. She is engaged to Sir Derek Underhill, Bart, M.P., a rich, handsome, athletic stuffed shirt who is dominated by his mother, Lady Underhill. At a first night of a very bad play the theatre catches fire and Jill, who is with Derek and his mother, escapes with the help of the man in the next seat, who is Wally Mason. He happens to be the author and backer of the play and to have known Jill in childhood and to have loved her ever since. Jill and Wally go to the Savoy and there they meet Derek and his mother. Uncle Chris loses Jill's money for her, as her trustee, and at the same time Jill gets arrested in London for fighting with a man who is teasing a parrot. Derek, under pressure from his mother, breaks off the engagement because of the arrest and everybody thinks he has done it because Jill's no longer rich. She goes, in poverty, to America, to the place on Long Island of a dour uncle (her father had been American). She joins the chorus of a play being prepared for Broadway. She acquires money and buys the play, which is foundering. Wally Mason doctors it and it is a hit. Jill will marry Wally. Derek has come over to New York to ask her, again, to marry him, but the answer is no. Even Freddie Rooke, Derek's ex-fag (Winchester) and hero-worshipper, turns on him in the end and calls him a rotter.

Good, with knowledgeable chapters about the theatre. Freddie Rooke, Winchester, Bachelors Club, Albany, moneyed (but goes down on Amalgamated Dyes), gets happily engaged to Nelly Bryant, American chorus girl.

~ *Indiscretions of Archie* ~
1921

The silly-ass Englishman, Eton and Oxford, in America during Prohibition, married to the daughter of an American millionaire. Hardly a novel. A stitching together of a series of episodes which started as short stories.

An ex-bankrupt who has married Lucille Brewster without her father's knowledge and is coming to seek his blessing, Archie has a row with the manager of the Hotel Cosmopolis in New York and finds that the proprietor is also his father-in-law. A bad start, but at the end Daniel Brewster accepts his daughter's marriage and even her husband, because they are going to make him a grandfather.

In Chapter 12 there is a very good, long newspaper report of a pie-eating contest *in verse*.

~ *The Clicking of Cuthbert* ~
1922

Nine stories of golf told by the Oldest Member and one Christmas Number fantasy, 'The Coming of Gowf'. Reverent mockery of the game and its votaries in the days when the clubs had proper names – baffy, cleek, mashie and so on. There is generally a pretty girl to play for. In the story that gives the collection its title, Vladimir Brusiloff, the great Russian writer, turns out to be, behind the beard, handicap 18 at Nijni Novgorod and as mad-keen a golfer as Cuthbert Banks, who had won the French Open and often played with Abe Mitchell.

~ *The Girl on the Boat* ~
1922

Sam Marlowe, English, six foot, broad-chested, a stopper of dog fights, a romantic and a buzzer, has been in America to play in the Amateur Golf Championship (beaten in the semi-finals). Wilhelmina (Billie) Bennett, American, is a very pretty redhead with a freckle on the tip of her nose, a Peke, Pinky-Boodles (who bites everybody), and a rich, fat father. Sam and Billie meet on the SS Atlantic heading for England and, although Billie has one if not more other adorers or courtiers, and though Sam makes a damfool of himself at the ship's concert, he wins Billie in the end. Some other characters are Mrs Adeline Horace Hignett, Sam's formidable aunt, a writer and lecturer on Theosophy, a dominant dame who, to prevent her coddled son, Eustace, from going out to get married, steals all his trousers; Jane Howard, the big-game hunter who takes her elephant gun and cartridges with her on a country house visit in England and is longing to find a nice *weak* man to marry and fuss over – so what about Eustace?; and Montagu Webster, Billie's father's stately, ambassadorial 'gentleman's personal gentleman', a flamboyant and haughty sort of Jeeves. The last chapter evokes the midnight scene at Blandings Castle in *Something Fresh*. And Sam boning up on Tennyson to impress the girl will be repeated in the Freddie Widgeon story 'Trouble at Tudsleigh'. Long quotations from poets written as prose – quite a habit in this book. A very yeasty light novel.

~ *The Adventures of Sally* ~
1922

Like *Jill the Reckless*, an Anglo-American novel largely about the theatre. American Sally Nicholas has inherited $25,000. She is engaged to a very good-looking English unsuccessful artist, who is a would-be playwright too, Jerry Foster. Her brother Fillmore has also inherited, but his new money makes him fat and pompous. Sally is forgiving of his faults and foolishnesses and encourages the good-hearted and simple Gladys Winch, show-girl, to marry Fillmore and look after him. Jerry, like almost all good-looking young men in Wodehouse, is a heel. He marries, behind Sally's back, a girlfriend of Sally's who has become a rising star in the theatre. The marriage is headed for failure and Jerry for the bottle. Sally, a game little friend of all the world, has Ginger Kemp as a constant adorer. Ginger is English. He was doing well at Oxford – boxing and rugger blues – when his father 'failed' in business and Ginger had to go and work for his uncle. That was a failure; then schoolmastering, also failure. He meets Sally on the beach at Roville, stops a dog-fight and asks her to marry him. He follows her to America and does eventually marry her, when she has lost her money. They set up, happily, a sort of dog-farm, which is enjoyable and is going to be successful. Sally rumples Ginger's hair, a sure sign of connubial love and contentment in Wodehouse.

A jerky, choppy book. Mrs Meecher's lodging house in New York is Dickensian. Several short-story themes are tied up untidily together and there is a scrambling of loose ends to finish up.

~ *The Inimitable Jeeves* ~
1923

Ten short stories, eight set in England, one in New York, one in Roville-sur-Mer. Seven of them feature Bertie's friend Bingo Little, in love successively with a tea-shop waitress, Honoria Glossop, Daphne Braythwayt, Charlotte Corday Rowbotham, Lady Cynthia Wickham-mersley, Mary Burgess and, for marriage and keeps, Rosie M. Banks, the bestselling novelist. We also meet Claude and Eustace, Bertie's twin cousins, reading for, at, or sent down from, Oxford. 'The Great Sermon Handicap' is one for the anthologies.

Trial sprint for the young favourite

~ *Leave It to Psmith* ~
1923

Psmith's father has died and the estate has been broken up. Mike Jackson, married to Phyllis, stepdaughter of Joe Keeble, husband of Lady Constance of Blandings, is a schoolmaster and not liking it. Lady Constance had wanted Phyllis to marry rich Rollo Mountford, with 'horrid swimmy eyes', but she had eloped with Mike. Mike wants to buy a farm in Lincolnshire. Psmith advertises himself to go anywhere, do anything, and Freddie Threepwood asks him to come to Blandings Castle to help him help Joe Keeble to steal Constance's £20,000 diamond necklace. Freddie wants, as a reward from Uncle Joe, money to set himself up in a bookmaking business. Psmith goes after the reward in order to help Mike. He goes down to Blandings Castle pretending to be Ralston McTodd, Canadian poet, author of *Songs of Squalor*. Cataloguing the Library at Blandings Castle is Eve Halliday. Psmith pursues her for marriage and succeeds. Freddie has been pursuing Eve too. A crook, Eddie Cootes, turns up, intending to pass *himself* off as Ralston

McTodd. There is some minor gun-play. The necklace is stolen successfully and hidden – by whom? The Efficient Baxter is locked out of the Castle in his pyjamas, throws flowerpots at Lord Emsworth's windows and is sacked. Connie will get another nice necklace (she and Joe have a joint bank account; she won't mind seeing £20,000 on the debit side for a new necklace – but she has refused to have Joe spend money helping Phyllis Jackson). Mike Jackson gets the money for his farm. Eddie Cootes finds his old card-sharping partner, Aileen Peavey, at Blandings Castle and they are going to team up again. Psmith will marry Eve Halliday and take the job of Lord Emsworth's secretary.

This is the first of many times that Wodehouse uses the husband-and-wife joint bank account as a way to stop even a millionaire (Joe Keeble) from writing a £3,000 cheque when his wife says no.

N.B. Wodehouse and his wife Ethel had a joint bank account, with Ethel in total control.

~ Ukridge ~
1924

We first met Ukridge in *Love among the Chickens*, 1906 and 1921. He was then married to his beloved and loving Millie. In these ten stories he has gone back to bachelorhood and he meets Millie and gets engaged to her only in the last story.

These stories are told by 'Corky' Corcoran, who had been at Wrykyn with Ukridge and to whom Ukridge was always a threat – borrowing money and clothes. Here we meet 'Battling' Billson, the soft-hearted heavyweight boxer whom Ukridge is promoting; Ukridge's rich Aunt Julia; George Tupper of the Foreign Office, another school friend of Ukridge's; Evan Jones, the Welsh revivalist whose preaching makes Battling Billson think fighting is wicked; Bowles, Corky's ex-butler landlord in Ebury Street; Flossie, the barmaid, Billson's fiancée; Mabel Price of Clapham Common to whom Ukridge becomes perilously engaged; and finally, Lady Lakenheath, Millie's Aunt Elizabeth with the multilingual parrot, Leonard.

These are some of the best stories that Wodehouse ever wrote.

~ *Bill the Conqueror* ~
1924

Bill West is an athletic young American living on an allowance from a millionaire uncle. The uncle sends him to London to see why his, the uncle's, business interests there are going downhill. Bill takes with him his best but hard-drinking friend Judson Coker, to whose beautiful sister Bill aspires to be engaged. She had wanted Bill to take Juddy away and keep him off the drink.

In London Felicia ('Flick') Sheridan, twenty-one, is engaged to Roderick Pyke, son and heir of Sir George Pyke, founder and proprietor of the Mammoth Publishing Company. Flick had, as a schoolgirl in America, fallen in love with a Harvard footballer who had dragged her out of a lake in which she was foolishly beginning to drown. This was Bill West, and Bill and Flick meet again in London just when Flick has broken her engagement to Roderick and, fearing reprisals, has run away from home and disapproving elders. Flick goes to America. Bill's uncle comes to London. Flick helps Bill find the man who is robbing his uncle's London till, Wilfred Slingsby. So . . .

Here is Wodehouse's first use of Mario's Restaurant, where Society dines and has fracas and where – as at the old Café de Paris – diners downstairs (Must Dress) cannot see the diners upstairs (Needn't Dress) who *can* see *them*.

~ *Carry on, Jeeves* ~
1925

This collection of ten short stories contains five that appeared first in *My Man Jeeves*. 'Jeeves Takes Charge' goes back in story-time to Jeeves arriving from the agency at Bertie's flat, curing his hangover and being instantly taken on, soon sacked and soon retaken on. Bertie is engaged to Florence Craye here, not for the last time in the annals. We meet, for the first and last time, Bertie's Uncle Willoughby of Easeby, Shropshire, and, for the first time, Florence's disastrous kid brother, Edwin the Boy Scout. We find that Jeeves had once worked for their father, Lord Worplesdon. Bertie's forgetful friend Biffy is engaged to Honoria Glossop in 'The Rummy Affair of Old Biffy'. We meet Bertie's Aunt Dahlia Travers ('Clustering Round Young Bingo') and her paper *Milady's Boudoir*, for which Bertie has written a 'piece'. And here are Bingo and Rosie Little, whose chef Anatole joins the Travers staff for many books and excitements to come. The last story, 'Bertie Changes His Mind', is the only one in the canon told by Jeeves.

~ *Sam the Sudden* ~
1925

Sam Shotter (Old Wrykynian, his father English, mother American), roughing it in a log-hut in Canada, has fallen in love with a girl in a picture – a photograph from an English weekly that his predecessor in the log-hut had stuck up. Sam comes to England with his disreputable friend and servant Hash Todhunter, late cook on the tramp-steamer *Araminta*. Sam's American uncle, in process of a business negotiation with Lord Tilbury (as he now is – Sir George Pyke as was) gets Lord Tilbury to give Sam a job in Mammoth Publishing. He now writes the 'Aunt Ysobel' page ('Chats with My Girls') in the *Home Companion* magazine, and finds that the girl in the picture is the niece of his editor and that she lives with her uncle in the house in Valley Fields next to the one that he himself has rented. And one of those semi-detacheds contains a $2m stack of bearer bonds that had been stolen from a bank and hidden away by a thief who had died before he could cash them. So here come Soapy and Dolly Molloy and Chimp Twist (alias J. Sheringham Adair). This is our first meeting with that crooked trio; also horrible Percy Pilbeam, now editor of *Society Spice* for Mammoth. And this is our first visit to Wodehouse's beloved Valley Fields, the West Dulwich of his boyhood.

Sam Shotter is a good specimen of the Wodehouse buzzer hero: no laggard in love and quick to rescue kittens stuck up in trees. He kisses the heroine at their first meeting and gets a furious rebuff. But she is ruffling his hair enjoyably in the last chapter. Sam had found the missing bonds and will get the 10 per cent reward from the bank. He has also had the privilege of calling Lord Tilbury 'you pompous little bounder!'

~ *The Heart of a Goof* ~
1926

Nine more golf stories told by the Oldest Member. In two of them, set in America, we meet a fine couple of fat multi-millionaires who are rivals at golf (both very bad, and arrant cheats) and rivals as collectors of golf treasures (such as J. H. Taylor's shirt stud). They play each other for high stakes. Bradbury Fisher has a baffy Bobby Jones had used in the Infants

All-In Championship of Atlanta, Georgia, and he is prepared to trade it for Gladstone Bott's English butler, Blizzard, the finest on Long Island. And then back from England comes Mrs Bott, with Vosper, the butler supreme lured from the Duke of Bootle's establishment. In two stories we watch the romance of William Bates and Jane Packard, golfers, result in marriage and the birth of young Braid Vardon Bates. We meet this lot again in *Nothing Serious*.

~ The Small Bachelor ~
1927

George Finch, shy young man from Idaho, inherits money and goes to New York to try to be a painter. He is a rotten painter. He goggles with love at a cuddly girl. She turns out to be Molly Waddington, daughter of a 'synthetic Westerner', Sigsbee Waddington, who is tied to New York by his snobbish and rich second wife but dreams of the open-air life as depicted by Zane Grey's novels and Tom Mix's films. To get money for an investment which he thinks will make him rich and free of dependence on his bossy wife, Sigsbee Waddington has stolen the pearls from his daughter's valuable necklace, sold them and replaced them with fakes. George Finch has a 'man', Mullett, a reformed (?) convict. Mullett is engaged to Fanny Welch, pickpocket, and both are trying to go straight. Place, New York. Time, Prohibition. There is a poetical policeman, Garroway, a phony English Lord ('Willie the Dude') Hunstanton, J. Hamilton Beamish, incorrigible writer of advice booklets, and a displaced English butler looking back wistfully from service with the Waddingtons in New York to Brangmarley Hall in Shropshire, where he had been footman and then butler in his day.

The whole thing is a farce, as near a Ben Travers imbroglio as any of Wodehouse's books, and its plot and dialogue show that it started as a play. The first good Wodehouse drunk scene – Sigsbee drunk on alcohol and George Finch drunk on love.

~ Meet Mr Mulliner ~
1927

Dedicated to the ex-Prime Minister Lord Oxford and Asquith, a constant fan, this is a collection of the first nine stories told by that irrepressible bar-parlour raconteur, that mellifluent man of many nephews, Mr Mulliner. Among the best of the nine are two, 'Mulliner's Buck-U-Uppo' and 'The Bishop's Move', showing the effect on the higher clergy of a certain tonic invented by Mr M.'s chemist-brother, Wilfred. One, 'Portrait of a Disciplinarian', is about a pensioned-off old family nanny who has not outgrown her nursery strength; and 'Honeysuckle Cottage' is a warning of what can happen to a contented bachelor, writer of wholesome bloodstained thrillers (revolvers, cries in the night, mysterious Chinamen and dead bodies – with or without gash in throat) when he inherits a cottage from a deceased aunt, in her day a bestselling author of squashily sentimental love stories.

~ Money for Nothing ~
1928

A very good light novel. In the sleepy Worcestershire village of Rudge-in-the-Vale John Carroll is in love with Pat Wyvern. But John's uncle, fat, rich, miserly Lester Carmody, squire of Rudge Hall, and Pat's damn-your-eyes father, Colonel Wyvern, long friends, are now feuding. Lester Carmody's other nephew, and heir, Hugo Carmody, wants his uncle to unbelt £500 for him to go shares in a London nightclub with Ronnie Fish, Eton and Cambridge friend.

Dr Alexander Twist (it's that crook Chimp again) is now running an expensive health farm not far from Rudge. And enter Soapy Molloy and his 'daughter' Dolly. Lester Carmody can't sell his Rudge Hall heirlooms, so why not fake a burglary and diddle the insurance? (The first heirlooms/burglary plot.) Lester Carmody, Chimp, Soapy and Dolly collude to do so. Everything goes wrong. John Carroll and Chimp are given knock-out drops. Briefly, Hugo is engaged to Pat. But it ends happily, of course, with John and Pat engaged, Hugo released, Lester Carmody and the Colonel friends again and Chimp, Dolly and Soapy foiled and ejected.

~ Mr Mulliner Speaking ~
1929

Nine more 'stretchers' told by Mr Mulliner about relatives near and far. In 'Those in Peril on the Tee' Mr Mulliner becomes, to all intents and purposes, the Oldest Member, and introduces us to Agnes Flack and Sidney McMurdo, stalwart golf-addicts. And 'Something Squishy' (a snake in the bed), 'The Awful Gladness of the Mater' (poor Dudley

~ '*I'm a Justice of the Peace. I sit on the Bench at our local Sessions and put it across the criminal classes when they start getting above themselves.*'

~ Bridmouth-on-Sea is notorious for its invigorating air. Corpses at Bridmouth-on-Sea leap from their biers and dance around the maypole.

~ Imagine how some unfortunate Master Criminal would feel, on coming down to do a murder at the Old Grange, if he found that not only was Sherlock Holmes putting in the week-end there, but Hercule Poirot as well.

~ Rodney Spelvin was in for another attack of poetry . . . He had once been a poet, and a very virulent one, too; the sort of man who would produce a slim volume of verse bound in squashy mauve leather at the drop of a hat, mostly on the subject of sunsets and pixies.

~ . . . that inevitability that was such a feature of the best Greek tragedy. Aeschylus once said to Euripides 'You can't beat inevitability,' and Euripides said he had often thought so, too.

~ Freddie experienced the sort of abysmal soul-sadness which afflicts one of Tolstoy's peasants when, after putting in a heavy day's work strangling his father, beating his wife, and dropping the baby into the city reservoir, he turns to the cupboard, only to find the vodka bottle empty.

~ Beach the butler was a man who had made two chins grow where only one had been before, and his waistcoat swelled like the sail of a racing yacht.

Finch!) and 'The Passing of Ambrose' (two splendidly repulsive school-boys) are about the heartless and delightful Bobbie, red-head daughter of novelist Lady Wickham, who is, of course, a Mulliner cousin.

~ *Summer Lightning* ~
1929

The third Blandings novel. The Hot Spot nightclub, run by Ronnie Fish and Hugo Carmody, has failed and Ronnie has got Hugo the job of secretary to Lord Emsworth at Blandings Castle. Ronnie is in love with sweet chorus girl Sue Brown, but what are Ronnie's mother and aunt going to say about a chorus girl, even if her father had been an officer in the Irish Guards? If Ronnie is to marry Sue, he must get his trustee, Lord Emsworth, to unleash the money required. Then there's this rich American girl, Myra Schoonmaker, whom the aunts want Ronnie to marry. And the loathsome Percy Pilbeam is sending Sue flowers and mash notes to the theatre. And Hugo (secretly engaged to Millicent, Lord Emsworth's niece) had known Sue for years – one of his favourite dancing partners. Small, pink, jealous – poor Ronnie. On an impulse he makes Sue come to the Castle *as* the rich Myra Schoonmaker. And Sue meets Galahad Threepwood, who finds she is the daughter of his long-ago dearly beloved Dolly Henderson. So he is determined to get Sue into the family, even if it means her marrying his pink little nephew – nothing like good enough for her. Meanwhile the Efficient Baxter surfaces in a caravan, and the Empress disappears and neighbour and rival pig-enthusiast Sir Gregory Parsloe is suspected of having abducted her.

Lord Emsworth sends to London for a detective and that's how Percy Pilbeam, now proprietor of the Argus Agency, joins the guests at the Castle.

Ronnie gets his money and is set to marry Sue. Galahad sees to that. This is our first meeting with that *beau sabreur* of the Threepwood clan.

~ *Very Good, Jeeves* ~
1930

Eleven short stories. Jeeves saves Bertie from being secretary to a cabinet minister, and saves both from a nesting swan on a lake-isle in a rainstorm. He destroys an offensive vase that Bertie has bought and takes

BERTIE WOOSTER,
stranded over the Drones Club
swimming pool.

away an offensive suit of plus-fours new from his tailors. He knocks out
Oliver Sipperley with a putter to the back of the head, annuls Bertie's
love for Bobbie Wickham, ditto for Gwladys Pendlebury, rescues Bingo
Little and Tuppy Glossop twice each, and saves Bertie's Uncle George
from a *mésalliance*.

We're into the long *floruit* period of Wodehouse's enormous output –
every story a winner. In this lot, if Bertie's worst predicament was the
cabinet minister and the swan, his next worst was having, on his Aunt
Agatha's orders, to go to East Dulwich to buy off a young girl at whose
feet foolish old Uncle George was throwing his superfatted heart and
unexpected title. Lady Yaxley now is that far, far better thing, the young
girl's aunt, widowed ex-barmaid at the Criterion (see, later, Maudie
Stubbs, Beach's niece, now Lady Parsloe).

~ *Big Money* ~
1931

Berry Conway, saddled with his ex-nannie, now over-motherly and gossipy housekeeper, Mrs Wisdom, lives in Valley Fields and works in the City as secretary to dyspeptic American millionaire (Torquil) Paterson Frisby. Berry's school-friend Biscuit (Lord Biskerton) is engaged to Frisby's niece, beautiful, rich Ann Moon. To baffle his creditors Biscuit goes to live in the house next to Berry in Valley Fields and calls himself Smith. To prevent his fiancée from following and Discovering All, he pretends he has mumps. Next door, on the other side from Berry's house, is staying a diminutive American girl, Kitchie Valentine. Biscuit falls for her across the fence. Meanwhile Berry has fallen for Ann Moon and she for him.

Berry has, from an aunt, inherited a lot of worthless-looking shares, including the ownership of the Dream Come True copper mine, next door to the Horned Toad mine owned by Frisby. After a lot of good legal and financial skulduggery the Dream Come True justifies its name.

All very fizzy. Biscuit is an amiable buzzer, Berry a nice simple hero. And they are going to marry delightful American girls. Extra dividends are: Biscuit's indigent and sponging father, man-about-town, sixth Earl of Hoddesdon; a fine conference between sharp financiers and their lawyers; an Old Boys' dinner; and Lord Hoddesdon's visit to Valley Fields in a grey topper, which causes derision, disgust and a chase up Mulberry Grove.

This book is a *locus classicus* for Valley Fields.

~ *If I Were You* ~
1931

Obviously fleshed out from a play-script. Act I, Country House; 2, Barber shop in Knightsbridge; 3, Country House. This time the old Nannie is chief trouble-maker and flywheel for the plot. Mrs Price, something of a drunk, sister of Slingsby the butler, had been Nannie to the fifth Earl of Droitwich and is mother of Syd, who runs a successful hairdressing establishment in Knightsbridge. Or is it the other way round? Was there a cradle-swap? Is cockney Syd the rightful earl and charming aristo Tony the rightful barber? Ma Price knows the answer and Tony's relatives have, behind Tony's back, bribed and pensioned her to keep her mouth shut. But alcohol opens it and Syd is going to take his case – backed by a strong likeness to one of the early earls in the portrait gallery – to the House of Lords. Tony is happy enough to lose the earldom, because it will free him of his engagement to Violet, haughty daughter and heiress of Waddington's Ninety Seven Soups. He has fallen in love with sweet Polly Brown, American, manicurist in Price's Hygienic Toilet Saloon of Mott Street, Knightsbridge.

Well, who is the fifth Earl of Droitwich today? And who's the Countess? And who's making a million out of Price's newly patented Derma Vitalis Hair Tonic?

~ *Doctor Sally* ~
1932

This is a novel made from the play *Good Morning, Bill*, adapted by Wodehouse from the Hungarian. Doctor Sally Smith is an American apparently practising in London, with hospital rounds too. Small, pretty and with handicap 6 at golf. She doesn't realize till the end that Bill Bannister, who has fallen for her in a big way from the first moment, works hard at his farming in Woollam Chersey. When she discovers that he does, she is able to respect him and to respond to his love. She will now be an American country gentlewoman in England who plays very good golf and practises medicine on the side. Fancy all that being first written in Hungarian!

~ *Hot Water* ~
1932

It is mid-July, fête-time at the French seaside resort of St Rocque. The château up the hill has been rented by the Gedges from America: she rich from a previous marriage, ambitious and dominant, he downtrodden and poor. Her plan is to get him (whether he likes it or not, and he does *not*) made the next American Ambassador to France. She is blackmailing Senator Opal, the great 'Dry' campaigner, to exert his influence. By muddling envelopes, he had posted to her a letter to his bootlegger. News has also got around to 'Oily' Carlisle, ace con-man, and to 'Soup' Slattery, ace safe-blower, that Mrs Gedge has some good diamonds, which make St Rocque worth a visit.

Packy Franklyn, young American athlete and millionaire, is engaged to Lady Beatrice Bracken, who, wanting him to become cultured, orders him to consort with Blair Eggleston, the Bloomsbury novelist. Blair somehow gets taken on as Senator Opal's valet and Packy falls in love with Senator Opal's daughter Jane, who is secretly and foolishly engaged to Blair. Packy rents a yawl and sails it across to St Rocque. There too is Old Etonian French playboy, Vicomte de Blissac ('Veek'). Almost all the males, in the absence of their ladies, get plastered at the fête. Mrs Gedge's maid and her secretary turn out to be under aliases, and Mrs Gedge herself – well, she never did become wife of the Ambassador to France, that's for sure. But Packy got Jane, who has promised never to make him go to lectures or meet Bloomsbury novelists again.

~ *Mulliner Nights* ~
1933

Nine short stories, two of them about the bishop's cat, Webster, whose whole outlook and life has been changed by alcohol and who rescues the bishop from marrying an unsuitable widow. Augustine Mulliner's Buck-U-Uppo helps another bishop, dressed as Sinbad the Sailor, to hit a policeman raiding a nightclub in the eye. Yet another bishop, once a headmaster, cures hitherto timid young Sacheverell Mulliner of offensive self-confidence produced by a correspondence course.

But the other five stories are of the laity. There is evidence that Wodehouse had difficulties with 'The Knightly Quest of Mervyn', but that's the only one here that possibly scores less than an alpha.

~ *Heavy Weather* ~
1933

It is ten days after the events of *Summer Lightning*. Ronnie Fish is engaged to chorus girl Sue Brown and his mother, Lady Julia, is determined to prevent the marriage. Sue was once briefly engaged to Monty Bodkin. When she hears that Monty is to come to the Castle as Lord Emsworth's secretary she is very worried that dear Ronnie will get to know and squirm with jealousy. She rushes up to London to tell Monty they must meet as strangers, and Ronnie's mother sees them lunching at the Berkeley before all three take the train to Market Blandings.

Gally has undertaken not to publish his Reminiscences. But Lord Tilbury had a contract with him and is determined to publish them if he can get at them by hook (Monty) or crook (Pilbeam). Sir Gregory

Parsloe is worried silly that Gally's book will tell about his scandalous younger days, and he wants to be the Unionist candidate for the local election to Parliament. Ronnie's mother is considerably jolted to learn that Gally will tell about her late husband's scandalous younger days. Lord Tilbury comes down to reason with Gally and, a pig-enthusiast himself, he covets the Empress.

The book becomes a fast and complicated doubles game – Hunt the Reminiscences and Steal the Pig – with Beach the butler involved much more than he likes on both counts. Pilbeam gets drunk again (see *Summer Lightning*) and makes an ass of himself. Lord Tilbury is rolled in the Empress's sty. Gally's manuscript adds healthy paper-weight to the omnivorous pig. Ronnie and his Sue drive off into the night with a big cheque from Lord Emsworth for honeymoon expenses, and they will be married in the morning. It is Gally's finest hour. Sue is the heroine. The villain is Pilbeam. The enemy is mothers and aunts. It is a very good book.

N.B. Lord Emsworth and Gally still think it was Baxter, working for Sir Gregory, who stole the Empress in *Summer Lightning*.

~ *Thank You, Jeeves* ~
1934

This, the first full-length Bertie/Jeeves novel, starts with a clash of wills about Bertie's banjolele and Jeeves giving notice. The banjolele has produced complaints from the neighbours in Berkeley Mansions, so Bertie proposes to take a country cottage somewhere and devote himself to mastering the instrument. His friend Lord Chuffnell (Chuffy) has a large country house (which he would like to sell) near the sea and lots of cottages. He rents one to Bertie (with his new 'man', Brinkley) and snaps Jeeves up as his own 'personal gentleman'. At Chuffnell Regis there arrives off-shore a large yacht containing American J. Washburn Stoker, multi-millionaire, his beautiful daughter, Pauline (to whom Bertie was once, in New York, engaged; but Sir Roderick Glossop had easily convinced the girl's father that Bertie was a near-loony), and his young son, Dwight. Chuffy thinks Stoker may buy the house to be a clinic for Sir Roderick's patients. Chuffy and Pauline fall in love, but Chuffy, 'penniless', cannot, by the code, speak his love to heiress Pauline – to her fury. Chuffy's aunt lives at the Dower House near the Hall. Sir Roderick is courting her. Pauline's father thinks Pauline is still pining for Bertie and he tries to keep her on board the yacht. In order to see Chuffy she swims from the yacht at night and arrives at Bertie's cottage (Bertie and Brinkley are both out) and gets into Bertie's pyjamas and bed. Chuffy discovers her and there is a great quarrel between them. Pauline's father, thinking that Bertie has done her wrong, decides that they must marry quickly. He kidnaps Bertie on to the yacht. There is a birthday party for Dwight on board, with minstrels. Jeeves does heroic work as a treble-agent, to release Bertie from the yacht, blacked up as a minstrel, to bring Chuffy and Pauline together and to quench Pauline's domineering father. At one stage both Bertie and Sir Roderick are going round with blacked-up faces and unable to find butter or petrol to clean up with. Brinkley sets fire to Bertie's cottage. The banjolele dies with it. Jeeves agrees to come back to Bertie if he gives the instrument up for lost for ever. (We shall meet Brinkley, the Communist valet, again in *Much Obliged, Jeeves*. There he becomes Rupert Bingley, a sort of propertied squire in Market Snodsbury.) Bertie sacks Brinkley. It looks as though Sir Roderick and Myrtle, Lady Chuffnell, are going to marry and Chuffnell Hall will become a clinic after all.

Two nice, silly policemen – Sergeant Voules and his nephew Constable Dobson.

~ Right Ho, Jeeves ~
1934

Jeeves disapproves of the white evening mess-jacket that Bertie has brought back from Cannes. Bertie disapproves of all his friends taking their troubles direct to Jeeves, by-passing him. Newt-loving teetotaller Gussie Fink-Nottle is in love with soupy Madeline Bassett and fears to speak. Tuppy Glossop has quarrelled with his fiancée Angela Travers. Aunt Dahlia has lost, at baccarat, money that Uncle Tom gave her to pay the bills of her magazine, *Milady's Boudoir*. And she has to find someone to give the prizes at Market Snodsbury Grammar School, of which she is a governor. Bertie, funking it himself, persuades her to make Gussie do the prize-giving, and he and Jeeves lace Gussie's orange juice with gin, and more gin, to get his courage up. The prize-giving is a riot, probably the best-sustained and most anthologized two chapters of Wodehouse. Bertie's attempt to tell Madeline of Gussie's love for her convinces her that he is pleading his own cause. Bertie's recommendation to Gussie, Tuppy and Aunt Dahlia to seek sympathy from their loved ones by going off their feed causes Anatole to give notice. Bertie's idea of ringing the fire-alarm bell at Brinkley (in order to get Tuppy to rescue Angela and thus show his love) results in the whole household being locked out in the small hours and Bertie's having to bicycle eighteen miles without lights to get the key. See page 1.

Not Bertie's finest hours, these. But Jeeves solves all the problems in his own ways and Bertie forfeits the mess-jacket.

You can feel a three-Act plot and pattern here similar to that of *Thank You, Jeeves*. Wodehouse, knowing he's got it right, will do it again and again, with only minor variations of names, places and time, in the five or six subsequent Bertie/Jeeves novels. It's vintage Wodehouse.

~ *Blandings Castle* ~
1935

The six Blandings stories that make the first half of this book were, with one exception, published in magazines before the publication of *Summer Lightning* (1929). 'The Custody of the Pumpkin' appeared in 1924, 'Lord Emsworth Acts for the Best' in 1926, 'Pig-Hoo-o-o-o-ey!' in 1927, 'Company for Gertrude' and 'Lord Emsworth and the Girl Friend' in 1928. 'The Go-Getter' first appeared in 1931. Not that this strict chronology matters much. But 'The Custody of the Pumpkin' shows Lord Emsworth, in Wodehouse's words, 'passing through the brief pumpkin phase which preceded the more lasting pig seizure'. And, until (between 'Pig-Hoo-o-o-o-ey!' and 'Company for Gertrude') Sir Gregory Parsloe basely lured – with a higher salary – the gifted pig-man Wellbeloved away from the Castle sty to tend his Matchingham competitor, Sir Gregory was a friendly fellow-J.P. of Lord Emsworth's and dined at the Castle. In *Summer Lightning* Sir Gregory starts as an enemy and is prime suspect in the disappearance of the Empress.

The other half of *Blandings Castle* contains one Bobbie Wickham story, told straight, not by Mr Mulliner (an uncle of hers) or by Bertie Wooster (an admirer, once ardent). In fact this Bobbie Wickham story, 'Mr Potter Takes a Rest Cure', is more than a little reminiscent of 'Saki'. The last five stories here are told by Mr Mulliner in the bar parlour of The Anglers' Rest, but they are all about Hollywood, 'Dottyville-on-the-Pacific', and its humanoid inhabitants.

~ *The Luck of the Bodkins* ~
1935

The central character here is a stuffed Mickey Mouse doll, the head of which screws off in case you want to fill it with, say, chocolates. Monty Bodkin bought it in the shop of the SS *Atlantic* as a *douceur* for his on-again, off-again fiancée, Gertrude Butterwick. Gertrude had cut up rough when, seeing, in a snapshot Monty had sent her from Antibes, a spot on his chest, she had had the photograph enlarged and the spot spelt 'Sue' with a heart round it: a tattoo. Gertrude (centre forward) is travelling to America with an All-England ladies' hockey team. Also aboard are Ivor Llewellyn, President of Superba-Llewellyn Motion Pictures of Hollywood, who has been, to his horror, ordered by his wife to smuggle a pearl necklace past the New York Customs for her; Reggie and Ambrose Tennyson, brothers, Reggie an amusing drone of the type that the ravens feed, Ambrose a serious spare-time novelist, who has been hired away from his job at the Admiralty to write for Superba-Llewellyn for $1,500 a week (Llewellyn had been told that he was *the* Tennyson, who had written 'The Boy Stood on the Burning Deck', which of course was by Shakespeare). Ambrose is engaged to Lottie Blossom, Hoboken Irish red-head movie-star with a pet alligator, the most turbulent of all Wodehouse's hell-raising heroines. The staterooms (or 'sheds') of all these passengers are served by steward Albert Eustace Peasemarch, tubby, talkative and, if, as seems likely, this was once a play or film-script, a fat part for Eric Blore.

Another Anglo-American novel, 90 per cent of it afloat, long and one of the best.

~ *Young Men in Spats* ~
1936

Eleven short stories, three of them told by Mr Mulliner, all eleven about Dronesmen (Freddie Widgeon, Archibald Mulliner, Pongo Twistleton-Twistleton, Barmy Fotheringay-Phipps and such). Two of the best ('The Amazing Hat Mystery' and 'Uncle Fred Flits By') were based on ideas supplied to Wodehouse by his friend Bill Townend.

It's our first meeting with Pongo's irrepressible Uncle Fred, Lord Ickenham, least haughty of earls. He will get star-billing in *Uncle Fred in the Springtime* (1939), *Uncle Dynamite* (1948), *Cocktail Time* (1958) and *Service with a Smile* (1962).

A loaf of bread for the Dronesman

In another of the best stories, 'Tried in the Furnace', there is a heart-breaking girl, a country vicar's daughter, Angelica Briscoe, loved at first sight by two Dronesmen, engaged to somebody else, who turns up again, still young and inexplicably unmarried, thirty-eight years later in the last Bertie/Jeeves novel *Aunts Aren't Gentlemen* (1974).

~ *Laughing Gas* ~
1936

Reggie (Earl of) Havershot, twenty-eight, ugly, boxing Blue at Cambridge, goes to Hollywood to rescue his cousin Egremont (Eggy), a souse, and bring him back unmarried. Reggie had been engaged once to Ann Bannister, an American newspaper girl. He finds that she is now engaged to Eggy and has a job looking after Joey Cooley, child film-star with golden curls, idol of American motherhood, pride of the Brinkmeyer-Magnifico Motion Picture Corp. T. P. Brinkmeyer is a simple, globular multi-millionaire who is bossed by his sister, Beulah, and wishes he was back in the cloak and suit business. The Brinkmeyers have an English butler, Chaffinch. All the servants in the household are hoping to be star actors if they can only get a start by impressing Brinkmeyer.

Reggie meets April June, film-star, very keen to be a countess. He is just about to propose to her when his wisdom tooth gives him gyp. At the I. J. Zizzbaum/B. K. Burwash dentists' surgery, his identity passes, under gas, into the patient under gas in the next room, Joey Cooley. They wake up with swapped personalities.

Joey, now fourteen stone, six foot one inch and a good boxer, enjoys his new-found ability to poke his former enemies (e.g. Beulah Brinkmeyer, whom he chases into the swimming pool, April June and Orlando Flower and Tommy Murphy, rival film-stars) in the snoot, to eat pancakes, drink and smoke cigars. He paints the nose of a statue of T. P. Brinkmeyer red and misbehaves generally.

Reggie Havershot, now a boy with golden curls, gets a kick in the pants from April June, and she kidnaps him so that she can hit the headlines by rescuing him. Chaffinch sells Joey's tooth for £5,000. Eggy Mannering gets engaged to a girl who is an enthusiast for the Temple of the New Dawn and teetotalism. And when the identity switch-back comes (a motor-bike accident with Joey and Reggie thrown together), Reggie will make nice Ann Bannister his countess.

Wodehouse does not bother much about language and accent differences between Reggie and Joey. But he is always funny about Hollywood and Joey must be the only boy with golden curls in all the books of whom Wodehouse approves.

~ *Lord Emsworth and Others* ~
1937

Nine short stories. 'The Crime Wave at Blandings', more than twice as long as the usual P.G.W. short story, is the only Blandings one in this collection. Three others are about Ukridge. Three are told by the Oldest Member about golf, one by Mr Mulliner and one, about Freddie Widgeon, by a Crumpet at The Drones. In 'The Crime Wave at Blandings' the Efficient Baxter returns to the Castle, much to the annoyance of (a) Lord Emsworth, who had hoped never to see this, his first secretary, again and (b) Lord Emsworth's grandson George, who finds himself threatened with an unexpected tutor plumb spang in the middle of his holidays. But Baxter leaves, and hurriedly, after being shot

LORD EMSWORTH
and his prizewinning Black Berkshire sow,
Empress of Blandings.

at, unerringly, with an airgun by (a) George, (b) Beach the butler and (c) Lord Emsworth himself, twice. Meanwhile Lord Emsworth's pretty niece Jane gets the man of her choice, poor, nice George Abercrombie, and rejects the man of Aunt Constance's choice, rich, boring Lord Roegate.

~ *Summer Moonshine* ~
1938

Sir Buckstone Abbott, Bart, has no money and is saddled with a large, ugly and impossible Victorian country house, Walsingford Hall. He is taking paying guests and hopes to sell the house to a very rich and horrid Princess Heloise von und zu Dwornitzchek. Joe Vanringham is the Princess's stepson and they have parted brass rags. Joe, a good buzzer and obviously the hero, works for a dishonest publisher, Mortimer Busby, who has published Sir Buckstone's *My Sporting Memoirs* at Sir Buckstone's expense (£500) and is now trying to charge him an extra £96.3.11 for 'incidental expenses'. Joe has written a play in which his stepmother is the scarcely concealed villainess. It has got good notices for its first night in London and Joe is going to leave Busby's. Sir Buckstone's daughter Jane (obviously the heroine) has gone up to London to plead with Busby's to reduce the bill. Joe meets her, falls in love, gets the bill cancelled and takes her to the Savoy for lunch and proposes marriage. Jane is foolishly engaged (secretly) to wet Adrian Peake, who thinks she will inherit a lot of money. He is the Princess's gigolo currently and secretly engaged to her too. The Princess sees Joe's play, recognizes herself and has it taken off. This leaves Joe without a play, without a job and without money. Sir Buckstone's easygoing (American) wife has an unexpected brother, Sam Bulpitt, a retired 'plasterer' (process-server). His last job is to plaster Tubby Vanringham (Joe's foolish younger brother) for breach of promise and heart-balm to Prudence Whittaker, Sir Buckstone's secretary – very Knightsbridge ('quate').

The Princess goes off with Adrian and won't buy the Hall. Joe and Jane will marry. Then Sam Bulpitt turns out to be very rich and a fairy godfather. He buys the Hall and gives Jane $500,000 as a wedding present – *pecunia omnia vincit.*

Bulpitt the plasterer is a rather surprising Wodehouse character. The Princess, wicked stepmother and not a bit funny, is the most un-Wodehousian character in all the books. The rest of the cast here are from Wodehouse stock and Joe Vanringham is a really good buzzer.

~ *The Code of the Woosters* ~
1938

The Code says that if a girl says to a man, 'I'm going to marry you,' he can't say, 'Oh no, you're not!' So here's poor Bertie *twice* having to face Sir Watkyn Bassett as a prospective relation-by-marriage: once when his daughter Madeline gives Gussie the air and claims she will marry Bertie; and once when his ward Stiffy Byng uses Bertie as a shock-absorber in her determination to get Sir Watkyn to approve her marriage to the Rev. 'Stinker' Pinker. And Sir Watkyn, before his retirement as the Bosher Street magistrate, had fined Bertie £5 for trying to steal a policeman's helmet on Boat Race Night.

Sir Watkyn has treacherously bought a silver cow-creamer that Aunt Dahlia insists ethically belongs to her husband, rival collector, Bertie's Uncle Tom. So, on threat of his never getting another meal of Anatole's cooking, she tells Bertie to go to Totleigh Towers and steal the cow-creamer for Uncle Tom. Gussie Fink-Nottle, scared at the thought of having to make a speech at his wedding breakfast in front of such people as Sir Watkyn and Spode, the amateur dictator (Sir Watkyn is hoping to marry Spode's aunt), takes Jeeves's advice and makes notes in a little book of all the despicable points about Sir Watkyn and Spode, the idea being that this will enable him to face them calmly, despising them for, e.g., the way they eat asparagus. Well, of course, Gussie loses this explosive notebook and of course it gets into the hands of Sir Watkyn and Spode. Meanwhile, Sir Watkyn wants Anatole and Uncle Tom is briefly prepared to trade the super-chef for the cow-creamer, and Aunt Dahlia is briefly prepared to trade him for Bertie's release from a likely thirty days in prison. And Stiffy is feuding with the local policeman and gets her curate fiancé to pinch his helmet. And Jeeves learns Spode's dark secret from the Junior Ganymede Book of Revelations. It's our first meeting with this man of wrath, leader of the Black Shorts, and we wonder what Oswald Mosley made of the loud and sustained raspberry this book delivered to him and his Movement.

A Wodehouse plot more complicated than any yet, clockwork with a hundred moving parts, interdependence absolute and a patter of verbal felicities, five or six to a page. Stiffy Byng is possibly the fizziest of all Wodehouse's fizzy girls, quick to anger, tears and revenge – deplorable, adorable. We assume that Jeeves got Bertie off on that world cruise – he had bought the tickets, though the young master had said no.

~ Uncle Fred in the Springtime ~
1939

The Duke of Dunstable has invited himself, plus secretary Rupert Baxter, to stay indefinitely at Blandings Castle. Notorious for laying about the furniture with a poker if thwarted, he demands eggs for throwing at whichever gardener keeps singing or whistling 'The bonny, bonny banks of Loch Lomond' outside his window. And he tells Lord Emsworth that his pig Empress of Blandings (twice in succession winner in the Fat Pigs Class) needs exercise and diet. He says, 'Give her to me. I'll have her slimmed down and you'll be less potty without her.' And Lady Constance insists that the dangerous Duke be given anything he asks – or else.

Lord Emsworth must take steps to save the Empress and decides to rope in Lord Ickenham, his brother Gally's friend, to help him. Lady

Constance, thinking that the dangerous Duke is going round the bend, has told Lord Emsworth to go to London and get Sir Roderick Glossop, the loony-doctor, to come and keep the Duke under observation.

There are bustling sub-plots. Lord Ickenham's nephew Pongo owes a vindictive bookmaker £200. He tries to borrow it off Horace Davenport, who is engaged to his sister, Valerie. Horace, unable to go to The Drones' Le Touquet golfing weekend, has sent 'Mustard' Pott, private investigator, to tail Valerie up in case she becomes enmeshed with licentious Drones males at golf or casino. Meanwhile, Polly, 'Mustard''s pretty daughter, is engaged to Ricky Gilpin, poet, boxer, nephew of the Duke of Dunstable. He needs £500 to buy into an onion-soup bar and marry Polly.

Sir Roderick won't come to Blandings. Lord Ickenham seizes his chance and comes *as* Sir Roderick, and he brings Pongo as his secretary and Polly as his own daughter. The idea is that Polly shall fascinate the Duke so that he will provide the £500 for onion-soup bar and marriage. But Baxter sees through the impersonations. For his pains, he gets orders to steal the Empress for the Duke. He also gets, literally, egg on his face and a Mickey Finn in his drink.

Uncle Fred Ickenham is in his element. He brings the right couples together and a proper redistribution of other people's wealth. A masterly mix-up, suavely sorted out.

This is our first and only close view of George Viscount Bosham, Lord Emsworth's son and heir. He is, triumphantly, the most blithering idiot in the whole rich Wodehouse canon.

~ *Eggs, Beans, and Crumpets* ~
1940

Nine short stories: four told by a Crumpet about Bingo Little, Editor of *Wee Tots*, his wife, Rosie M. Banks, the bestselling novelist, and his overlord, Purkiss, proprietor of *Wee Tots*. There are three Ukridge stories, and one about Freddie Fitch-Fitch getting caught up in, and getting a fiancée out of, the fearful snobberies of well-to-do invalids at a fashionable spa. The gem of the collection is the solitary Mulliner, 'Anselm Gets His Chance'. Anselm Mulliner is a country curate whose selfish vicar always preaches at Sunday Evensong in summer, prime time for maximum audience appreciation, as every selfish country vicar knows. But the vicar in this case gets a juicy black eye in a midnight scuffle with Joe the ex(?)-burglar who sings in the choir. So Anselm preaches his long-hoarded 'Brotherly Love' sermon that Sunday evening and he preaches as he has never preached before. Result – his engagement to a financier's daughter and a £10,000 cheque from said financier (who is also a philatelist) for a stamp-album for which his first shrewd bid had been £5.

~ *Quick Service* ~
1940

J. B. Duff, dyspeptic head of Duff and Trotter, London's classiest provision-merchants, was once in love with a girl called Beatrice, who gave him the air because even by moonlight he could only talk about Duff and Trotter's Paramount hams. Joss Weatherby, second-rate artist and first-rate buzzer, is on Duff's staff, designing advertisements for the hams. He recently did a portrait of the above Beatrice, now Mrs Chavender, widow. The portrait hangs in Claines Hall in Sussex, where Mrs Chavender lives with her rich sister-in-law, Mabel Steptoe, who is married to an ex-pug, small-time Hollywood actor whom she is still trying to civilize, hiring valets to make him dress properly, etc. Mrs Chavender's pretty secretary, Sally, is engaged to Lord Holbeton, who sings 'Trees' but can't marry her unless he can get some of the money held in trust for him. And who's his sole trustee? Dyspeptic J. B. Duff, of whom he is much afraid. Sally says she will go and tackle J. B. Duff for him.

Mrs Chavender, revolted by slices of a new ham at breakfast at Claines Hall, learns that it's a Duff and Trotter Paramount, so she goes up to London with a box of slices to show Jimmy Duff, her erstwhile courtier, how disgraceful his product is. Joss instantly falls in love with Sally. Duff decides that Joss's painting of Mrs Chavender would make a good advertisement, saying, 'Take this stuff away. Bring me a Paramount ham!' Duff fires Joss and tells Sally he'll give Lord Holbeton his money if Lord Holbeton will steal that portrait and bring it to him at an inn near the Hall where he is going to stay, wearing a false moustache. Sally hires Joss as the new valet for Steptoe. He ('Mugsy') wants to raise enough money to get himself back to Hollywood.

Duff eats sticky cakes and mixes them with brandy and hell breaks loose inside him. So Mrs Chavender cures him (most nice male dyspeptics in Wodehouse are cured by nice women) and love reburgeons. There is an all-night scrambling of people trying to cut the painting out of its frame in order to get money from Duff. Also two suspects locked in the coal cellar by the butler.

Lord Holbeton gets enough of his money to go to Italy to have his voice trained. Duff rehires Joss to be head of the Duff and Trotter Art Department. Joss will marry Sally. Mrs Steptoe, loathing English weather (which has ruined her garden party), is happy to go back to California with her husband. Perhaps this is Wodehouse admitting that the weather he has always given England is Californian and here now he is trying to tell the truth.

~ *Money in the Bank* ~
1946

Lord Uffenham, sixth Earl, is pear-shaped, with huge feet and a tendency to go on about his gallant youth, Boat Race Nights revelry and being thrown out of Victorian music-halls. He has rented his ancestral Shipley Hall to rich, big-game-huntress widow Mrs Cork, and she is running it as a vegetarian, teetotal Health Farm. Lord Uffenham stays on in the guise of butler, Cakebread. He has hidden some diamonds away and cannot remember where. He worries because they are all he can give his niece Anne as dowry. If he can't find the diamonds, he will have to make the supreme sacrifice for Anne's sake and marry Mrs Cork for her money. It turns out that the diamonds, which have given the book its treasure-hunting, with Chimp Twist, Dolly and Soapy Molloy at it again, are in the bank at the other side of the pond.

Jeff Miller, like Romeo and so many Wodehouse heroes, is engaged to the wrong girl at the start. Anne Benedick, heroine, is likewise engaged, to handsome, silky-moustached, feet-of-clay Lionel Green, interior decorator. Anne, at the end, says, 'I never want to see another beautiful man as long as I live.'

Wodehouse wrote this novel while interned by the Germans. Probably all-male camps account for the use of some brave words: 'fanny', 'bloody awful', 'too bloody much' and 'lavatory inspector'. Such modernisms must be balanced against Wodehouse's dreamy return to an England where telephones hardly exist. At one stage in this story Jeff goes up to London from the Hall to send a message to Chimp at Halsey Court in Mayfair by district messenger. The Cork Health Farm, filled with clients longing for square meals, may have got an impetus from internment camps.

Here Jeff Miller is a buzzer. Not the first, but it's the first time Wodehouse has used the word for the type. Chimp says here that he wishes he had thought of starting a Health Farm, forgetting that in the earlier *Money for Nothing* he had been running one.

~ Joy in the Morning ~
1947

Bertie's friend Boko Fittleworth, the popular writer, had been engaged to Florence Craye, as had Bertie in his day. Now Boko wants to marry Nobby Hopwood. Florence being his daughter and Nobby his ward, Lord Worplesdon objects to Boko as a flitter-and-sipper, half dotty and financially unsound, and won't give his okay to Nobby's marrying him. Lord Worplesdon is on the edge of a big shipping deal with American Mr Clam and wants a private place in which to meet him for final talks. On Jeeves's advice Lord Worplesdon provides a cottage on his Steeple Bumpleigh estate for Bertie. It is here that Clam is to nest for the secret pourparlers. Boko has a cottage near by and Stilton Cheesewright is the local policeman and now engaged to Florence. Edwin the Boy Scout, trying to catch up on his Good Deeds, burns Bertie's cottage to the ground. Luckily, Bertie's Aunt Agatha, now Lady Worplesdon, is away, ministering to young Thos at prep school: he has mumps.

Stilton is furious with jealousy when he hears that Florence was once engaged to Bertie. Boko locks Clam in the potting-shed thinking him to be a burglar. There is a fancy-dress dance at a neighbouring village. Lord Worplesdon goes as Sinbad the Sailor, with ginger whiskers, Clam goes as Edward the Confessor, Bertie goes in a policeman's outfit pinched by Jeeves from the riverbank where Stilton is bathing. Boko, not knowing that Lord Worplesdon is asleep, tight, at the back of his car, locks him in the garage overnight. But Jeeves organizes forgiveness and some happy endings. Boko and Nobby are off to Hollywood with Lord Worplesdon's hard-won blessing. Jeeves rescues Bertie from his second (but by no means last) engagement to the dread Florence. Lord Worplesdon, his business deal completed at great profit, is relieved that his wife has been away and may never hear of the dire doings of the last forty-eight hours.

The idiocies of Boko here, the vituperations he gets from his beloved Nobby and the head-shakings of his friend Bertie – 'You can never trust a writer not to make an ass of himself' – may remind us that Wodehouse finished his novel after he had made an ass of himself, with those talks on the radio from Berlin in 1941.

~ *Full Moon* ~
1947

Two new Emsworth nieces need help towards the altar. Veronica, daughter of Lord Emsworth's cook-like sister Lady Hermione Wedge, is the dumbest and most beautiful of the tribe, and she and her parents long for a rich suitor. (All three are staying at the Castle.) American Tipton Plimsoll, friend of Freddie Threepwood, could fill that bill. Prudence, small, pretty daughter of another sister, Lady Dora Garland, in London, is caught trying to elope with big, ugly Bill Lister, a rather bad artist and a godson of Galahad. Prue is sent to the Castle to cool off. Lord Emsworth is trying to find an artist to paint the Empress's portrait for the gallery. Thanks to Galahad, Bill Lister infiltrates the Castle three times, in three guises: Messmore Breamworthy, an artist (Lord Emsworth sacks him as soon as he sees his rough for the Empress's portrait), an under-gardener (McAllister has been bribed to silence) and Landseer, another artist. The portrait is never done, but, largely as a result of the Empress being shoved in her bedroom, Veronica and Tipton are paired off successfully. And, under threat that his son Freddie's marriage will come unstuck and he, Lord Emsworth, will be stuck with Freddie haunting the Castle again, Lord Emsworth gives the green light and a cheque for £5,000 to Prue and Bill to get married and take over The Mulberry Tree pub near Oxford.

This novel is too episodic for comfort, and unevenly paced. In patches Gally, its real hero, acts and talks more like Lord Ickenham than himself. 'Spreading sweetness and light' is Lord Ickenham's specific role, but here, Wodehouse, seeming to forget, applies these words to Gally. It strikes an odd note.

N.B. 'Sweetness and light' is a phrase from Matthew Arnold, who was related by marriage to the Wodehouse family.

~ *Spring Fever* ~
1948

Another impecunious widower earl (of Shortlands, family name Cobbold) with a money-eating stately home, Beevor Castle. His

~ There was a good deal of mud on the policeman's face, but not enough to hide his wounded expression.

~ The house was a frothing maelstrom of dumb chums.

~ 'Don't blame me, Pongo,' said Lord Ickenham, 'if Lady Constance takes her lorgnette to you. God bless my soul though, you can't compare the lorgnettes of today with the ones I used to know as a boy. I remember walking one day in Grosvenor Square with my aunt Brenda and her pug dog Jabberwocky, and a policeman came up and said the latter ought to be wearing a muzzle. My aunt made no verbal reply. She merely whipped her lorgnette from its holster and looked at the man, who gave one choking gasp and fell backwards against the railings, without a mark on him but with an awful look of horror in his staring eyes, as if he had seen some dreadful sight. A doctor was sent for, and they managed to bring him round, but he was never the same again. He had to leave the Force, and eventually drifted into the grocery business. And that is how Sir Thomas Lipton got his start.'

~ In New York detectives' hats don't take off.

~ South Kensington . . . where sin stalks naked through the dark alleys and only might is right.

~ All the Wellbeloveds have been as mad as March hatters. It was his grandfather, Ezekiel Wellbeloved, who took off his trousers one snowy afternoon in the High Street and gave them to a passer-by, saying he wouldn't be needing them any longer, as the end of the world was coming that evening at five-thirty sharp.

~ The lamp-and-mop room at the station was a dark and sinister apartment, smelling strongly of oil and porters.

ambition is to raise £200 somehow, marry Mrs Punter his cook and buy her the pub on which she insists. He has three daughters, two bossy, one nice. One of the bossy daughters, Adela, is married to very rich American, Desborough Topping. But they have a joint bank account and Adela is in charge of it, so her father gets no £200 from her. Ellery Cobbold is another very rich American, distantly related. His son Stanwood has fallen for a Hollywood star, Eileen Stoker. To distance Stanwood from Eileen, Ellery sends him over to England, where, as it happens, Eileen Stoker has just arrived to make two pictures. Sent over by Ellery Cobbold to keep an eye on his son is manservant Augustus Robb, cockney ex-burglar, 'saved' by attending a revivalist meeting. He is a snob and a Bible-quoter.

Lord Shortlands looks like a butler. His butler, Spink, looks like an earl, and is also courting Mrs Punter. The question is, which suitor will first get the £200 for the pub? Courting Lord Shortlands's nice daughter, Terry (Lady Teresa Cobbold), is American Mike Cardinal, very good-looking, prosperous Hollywood agent and a good natural buzzer. Terry, having once been in love with, and let down by, a very good-looking musical comedy juvenile lead, refuses very good-looking Mike for that reason. But Mike gets involved in a fracas with drunk ex-burglar Robb, and his face, much bashed about, then looks very good to Terry. Spink gets Mrs Punter. Stanwood gets Eileen Stoker. Mike takes Terry and her father to Hollywood, the latter to play in butler roles.

The novel splits obviously into three Acts and must have been a play-script on its way to hardback print. Once again Wodehouse uses the rich man's joint bank account with a dominant wife for sour comedy. Once again he makes the hero ugly, by force this time.

~ *Uncle Dynamite* ~
1948

Dotty doings in distant Hampshire. His Uncle Fred (Lord Ickenham) wants Pongo to marry American Sally Painter, a not very successful sculptor in Chelsea. They had been engaged, but she had broken it off when Pongo refused to smuggle jewellery into America for a friend of hers. Now he has got engaged to Hermione Bostock, a bossy, bookish beauty whom Bill Oakshott, just returned from Brazil, had hoped to marry. Bill is the real owner of Ashenden Manor, but his uncle, Sir Aylmer Bostock, ex-Colonial Governor, is a short-tempered cuckoo in the nest, proposing to stand for Parliament. As a J.P. he sentences Pongo and Sally to thirty days' jug without the option, her only tort being pushing the local cop into a duck-pond.

Pongo is *not* a success with Hermione's parents. And Bill Oakshott, disappointed lover, sees Pongo kissing the housemaid, who is engaged to the local policeman, who is bossed by his sister. Wouldn't you know it – Potter the policeman had arrested Pongo and Uncle Fred that day at the dog-races and remembered them by sight and their false names.

Since Lady Ickenham is away, Lord Ickenham wades in gratefully to spread sweetness and light. He had been at school with 'Mugsy' Bostock and had given him six with a fives bat then for bullying. Blackmail, lying, impersonation, knock-out drops, arrests; stealing, breaking and substitution of busts, one of which contains jewellery for smuggling. Preparations for the Ashenden fête and a Bonny Baby Competition. The curate gets measles and spreads it around.

This is our first meeting with the eccentric Major Brabazon Plank, leader of the Brazilian expedition of which Bill Oakshott was a member. (Here Plank is a cricketer; in *Stiff Upper Lip, Jeeves* (1963) he is a rugger fanatic; in B.B.C. Radio 4's adaptation of that book he was a soccer fanatic.) He had been at school with 'Barmy' (Uncle Fred) and 'Mugsy' and his name had been 'Bimbo'. Barmy and Bimbo talk Mugsy into dazed humility and repentance, and the right couples kiss and make up: policeman Potter and housemaid Elsie Bean, Pongo and Sally, Bill and Hermione. Uncle Fred had taught Bill the 'Ickenham Method' of wooing (polite violence and overt ardour) and when Bill sees a man kissing Hermione and goes into action, Hermione gives the memorable yowl, 'Don't kill him, Bill. He's my publisher!'

A brilliantly sustained rattle of word-perfect dialogue and narrative topping a very complicated and well-controlled plot.

~ *The Mating Season* ~
1949

Gussie Fink-Nottle goes wading for newts in a Trafalgar Square fountain at 4 a.m. and is sentenced to fourteen days in prison. This is awkward because he, as Madeline Bassett's fiancé, is due to present himself at Deverill Hall, where Madeline's godmother, Dame Daphne Winkworth, lives and wants to meet him. Bertie is due there too, to star in a village concert organized by the Vicar's niece, Corky Pirbright, Hollywood star, sister of 'Catsmeat'. Corky is in love, and vice versa, with the squire, rich, handsome Esmond Haddock. Deverill Hall is his home, but full of his disapproving aunts, Dame Daphne being one. Corky says she won't marry Esmond until he defies his aunts and tells them to get off his back.

Bertie must at all costs prevent Madeline knowing that her fiancé is doing time, since, whenever she rejects Gussie, she reaches for the man who can't say No, Bertie Wooster. So Bertie goes to Deverill Hall saying he *is* Gussie. Then Gussie's sentence is remitted and he arrives saying he is Bertie Wooster, and Corky ropes him too into the concert. He falls in love with her. Madeline, who could explode this double imposture, announces that she is coming to the Hall, and she must be kept away. Aunt Agatha, who could also blow all gaffs, threatens to come. Jeeves goes to her son, Young Thos's, prep-school and easily lures him into doing a bunk and coming to stay with Corky at the vicarage – so that his mother will go safely to Bramley-on-Sea to join the search for him in Sussex.

Jeeves's uncle, Charlie Silversmith, is butler at Deverill Hall. And there is an atheist village policeman who harasses the Vicar and who's in love with the housemaid at the Hall. Jeeves converts Constable Dobbs to theism with a cosh. Catsmeat elopes with his beloved Gertrude, daughter of Dame Daphne.

The big scene is the village concert, at which Esmond comes out strong and poor Bertie, alias Fink-Nottle, has to recite Winnie-the-Pooh verses.

~ *Nothing Serious* ~
1950

Ten short stories, five of them about golf, told by the Oldest Member. But in three of them the O.M., the club and the course are American. 'Rodney Has a Relapse' pulls A. A. Milne's nose. 'Birth of a Salesman' has Lord Emsworth temporarily in America and jealous of his son Freddie's success as a mini-magnate in the dog-biscuit business. 'How's That, Umpire?' is the story of the salvation of Conky Biddle, obliged to go to cricket matches (which he loathes) with his uncle Lord Plumpton, who provides his allowance and is dotty about the game. A beautiful American girl with a millionaire father rescues Conky from unemployment and cricket. Two stories are about Bingo Little and one of them brings back, to be nanny to young Algernon Aubrey, the nanny who had

nannied Bingo in infancy: a resurrection that Bingo would not recommend now to any *pater familias*. The other Bingo story brings the
disruptive Freddie Widgeon into the Little family's lives. 'Success Story'
is Ukridge at his best, outlying and outsmarting his aunt's crooked butler
Oakshott. But Corky still has to pay the bill for the lordly celebratory
lunch.

~ *The Old Reliable* ~
1951

This is *Spring Fever* (1948) again, put through the theatrical mincing
machine and emerging in Hollywood as a second novel. The only
English characters are the ex-safeblower butler, Phipps (see Augustus
Robb in *Spring Fever*), and Lord Topham, scrounging hospitality from
the aristos of the film colony.

Ex-star of silent films Adela Shannon Cork's late millionaire husband
had said, 'Take care of my brother Smedley', so Smedley gets board and
lodging at the big house in Beverly Hills, and nothing more. He longs to
go on a toot and tries to borrow the wherewithal from Adela's butler.
Adela's sister, 'Bill' Shannon, loves Smedley and lends him $100 and he
goes on a bender and invites to stay *chez* Adela for several weeks Joe
Davenport, who is in love with the Shannon niece Kay.

Adela's house once belonged to Carmen Flores, passionate Mexican
film-star now dead. Everybody is looking for the diary she must have
written and left somewhere in the house. It's sure to be a red-hot property
for a publisher. 'Bill' Shannon is ghost-writing her sister's Memoirs. She
had been on a jury which had sent Phipps to prison. She has been a crime
reporter, sob sister, press agent, minor actress. She quotes a lot from
Shakespeare and explains that she had been a stewardess on a fruit-boat
and *The Plays of Shakespeare* had been the only book on board. (N.B.
Wodehouse in 1940 had packed only one book, *The Complete Works of
Shakespeare*, when he went off to internment.)

Pretty Kay Shannon, the niece, works on a New York magazine. She
calls her Aunt Wilhelmina 'The Old Reliable'. Writer Joe Davenport has
been blacklisted in Hollywood because he once threw a heavy book at
Ivor Llewellyn. But he has recently won a radio jackpot. He is a good
buzzer. He wants to marry Kay. Kay says no, thinking he is not serious
about her. But when she sees him lying on the floor, apparently knocked
out with a bottle by the drunk Phipps, she showers kisses on his upturned

etc., etc. In fact 'Bill' had slipped Joe a Mickey Finn to achieve exactly this effect. Joe will marry Kay. 'Bill' will marry Smedley and Phipps will play butler parts for Medulla-Oblongata-Glutz.

~ *Barmy in Wonderland* ~
1952

'Wonderland' is the American theatre world. Cyril ('Barmy') Fotheringay (pronounced Fungy) Phipps, Eton, Oxford and Drones Club, is attracted by Dinty Moore, secretary of a Broadway producer, Joe Lehman. Film-star, buzzer and boozer Mervyn Potter, due to appear in a Broadway play, burns his cottage down and is rescued by Barmy. He persuades Barmy to put up his little all, $22,000, to buy 25 per cent of his play, *Sacrifice*, producer Joe Lehman. Potter is engaged to Hermione (page 55) or Heloise (page 128) Brimble, daughter of a tycoon. * She swears him off drink and puts a detective on to report if he drinks. Potter owns a Tanganyika lion-dog, Tulip, dangerous when Potter is drunk and argumentative.

Potter will *not* marry Miss Brimble. Barmy Phipps will marry Dinty. The play is 'fixed' to be a success. Lehmac Productions buy Barmy out for $100,000. Fanny, wife of Joe Lehman of Lehmac Productions, 'a man of the great indoors', had been a famous juggler. She is a very good wisecracker. Peggy Marlowe, showgirl, is based, surely, on Marion Davies, mistress of William Randolph Hearst, American newspaper tycoon, owner of, and host at, San Simeon.

It's a return to the backstage world of *A Damsel in Distress*, *Jill the Reckless* and *The Adventures of Sally*. It is loosely adapted from George Kaufman's play *The Butter-and-Egg Man*. Some critics said Wodehouse's American dialogue, especially the slang, was all wrong, but he said that he took it verbatim from the Kaufman script. So there!

~ *Pigs Have Wings* ~
1952

Gally, Beach and others have bet their savings on the Empress for a third win in succession in the Fat Pigs Class at the Shropshire Show. Now Sir

---

* There is another Hermione Brimble, English and daughter of a bishop, in 'The Right Approach' in *A Few Quick Ones*.

Gregory Parsloe, having already lured Wellbeloved away from Lord Emsworth for higher wages as pig-man, has *bought* a super-fat pig, Queen of Matchingham – legally, but unethically – to run against the Empress. Monica Simmons, Lord Emsworth's new pig-girl, turns out to be Sir Gregory's niece. Gally and Lord Emsworth are sure Sir Gregory will try to nobble the Empress so that the Queen may win the Silver Medal. Beach's widowed niece, Maudie Stubbs, once barmaid at the Criterion, had been going to marry young 'Tubby' Parsloe, but they had missed each other at the wedding. Now Sir Gregory is engaged to Gloria Salt, a lithe tennis player who has ordered him to diet drastically, or else . . . Penny Donaldson, younger sister of Freddie Threepwood's wife, Aggie, is at the Castle. Lady Constance wants her to marry Orlo, Lord Vosper, handsome, serious, rich, a tennis player (who had been engaged to Gloria Salt, but they had quarrelled about poaching on court). Penny is in love with Jerry Vail, writer of thrillers, and they need £2,000 for Jerry to take over a Health Farm. Gloria, asked by Lady Constance to find Lord Emsworth a secretary, produces Jerry Vail, who used to be something of a boyfriend of hers.

Sir Gregory's butler goes to the village chemist to buy half a dozen bottles of Slimmo for his master. Gally hears of this and is sure it is meant for thinning the Empress. The battle-lines are drawn and it develops into snatch and counter-snatch of pigs, the Castle Commando being Gally, Penny and Beach. They bring Maudie Stubbs, who has inherited a detective agency from the late Stubbs, down to watch over the Empress's cause, and they infiltrate her into the Castle as a friend of Penny's millionaire (American) father. Lord Emsworth's foolish heart goes out to Maudie in a letter (which has to be retrieved quick when Lord Emsworth discovers she is an ex-barmaid and, more embarrassing, niece of his butler – he'd have to call his butler 'Uncle Sebastian'). Well, Lord Emsworth, thinking that Jerry has restored the Empress to her sty, writes the necessary £2,000 cheque for him and Penny to start in on the Health Farm. Orlo Vosper and Gloria Salt become a mixed double again and Sir Gregory proposes again to dear Maudie, who will become Lady Parsloe and will work on the principle that the way to a Bart's heart is through his stomach. Beach, having been in the Market Blandings police lock-up for half an hour, gets £500 hush-money from Lady Constance for his pains. The Queen consumes six bottles of Slimmo and the Empress wins the Silver Medal for the third time running. The local newspaper celebrates the event in expert verse.

~ *Ring for Jeeves* ~
1953

Guy Bolton 'borrowed' Jeeves from Wodehouse for a play. And here is Wodehouse making a novel from the play-script. Jeeves is now a butler who helps his master, 9th Earl of Rowcester, make the money he badly needs for white-elephant, leaky, 147-room stately home, Rowcester Abbey. They set up as bookies – Honest Patch Perkins (Lord Rowcester disguised) and his clerk (Jeeves disguised). And Bertie Wooster is explained away as having gone off to a post-war school that teaches the aristocracy to fend for itself 'in case the social revolution sets in with even greater severity'.

The bookie-firm is in trouble and has to welsh over a flukey double pulled off (£3,005 2s. 6d.) by Captain Biggar, white hunter, in love with Mrs Rosie Spottsworth, widow of two multi-millionaire Americans. (But she is nice. She had written *vers libre* in Greenwich Village before she started marrying millionaires.) Biggar's code says, 'A poor man mustn't make advances to a rich lady', but he ends up satisfactorily engaged to marry Rosie.

Bill Rowcester will marry small, pretty Jill Wyvern, freckled local vet, ex-hockey outside right. Her father is Chief Constable of Southmoltonshire. Bill sells the Abbey to Mrs Spottsworth, who, not liking its dampness, will have it transported brick by brick and rebuilt in California, to dry out at last.

Jeeves as a butler, in disguise, acting as a bookie's clerk and hamming it up, is not the Jeeves we know. He overdoes the quotation thing. . . Pliny the Younger, the Psalms, Whittier, Kipling, Omar, Tennyson, Shakespeare (eighteen times), Maugham, Marcus Aurelius, Milton, Byron, Congreve and (slightly inaccurately) Montrose. Latin: '*fons et origo mali*', '*ne quid nimis*', '*rem acu tetigisti*', '*retiarius*'. And French: '*faute de mieux*'. It is odd that this should ring so false. But it does.

~ *Jeeves and the Feudal Spirit* ~
1954

Once more Bertie grows a moustache and again Jeeves disapproves. But Florence Craye thinks it's beautiful, and that infuriates Stilton Cheesewright, who is engaged to her (he is no longer a policeman). Florence orders Stilton to grow a moustache too. Stilton would beat Bertie up in his jealousy, but he has drawn the Wooster ticket in the Drones Darts

Tournament sweep and Bertie's tipped to win. Naturally Stilton does not want to have his man throwing darts with bunged-up eyes and a twisted neck.

Florence, needing atmosphere for her next novel, gets Bertie to take her to a low London nightclub, the Mottled Oyster. Of course it is raided by the cops. The magistrate next morning happens to be Stilton's uncle and Stilton finds out. Stilton has to lie low in London while his moustache is growing, so Bertie gratefully drives, with Jeeves, to Brinkley Court, where Aunt Dahlia is entertaining the ghastly Trotter couple from Liverpool She wants L. G. Trotter to buy *Milady's Boudoir* for his stable of magazines. She hopes that a week or two of Anatole's cooking will soften Trotter up to sign for a generous price.

The ghastly Mrs Trotter is trying to get her husband knighted, so that she, 'Lady Trotter', may queen it over Mrs Alderman Blenkinsop, her rival in Liverpool society. The Junior Ganymede Book of Revelations reveals to Jeeves that Mr Trotter has actually been offered a knighthood but has turned it down, without telling his wife, because he is ashamed of his Christian names. 'Sir Lemuel' or 'Sir Gengulphus', in knee breeches and with a sword between the legs walking backwards, would make him the laughing stock of the Palace, the press and his friends. And now, if he is to buy *Milady's Boudoir*, Mrs Trotter insists that Anatole comes to her servants' hall in Liverpool as part of the deal.

Aunt Dahlia yells for Jeeves, who fixes everything. He spots that Mrs Trotter's pearls are false – not the ones her husband gave her. He provides a cosh for Aunt Dahlia to fell Spode/Sidcup, an expert, just as he is about to spot that *her* pearls are false too. Enter Daphne Dolores Morehead, bestselling writer and very beautiful. Stilton falls for her. Florence briefly is re-engaged to Bertie, but then changes to Percy Gorringe, side-whiskered poet who has dramatized her novel *Spindrift* and writes successful thrillers under another name. Jeeves cures L. G. Trotter's dyspepsia with one of his miracle mixtures, and Trotter buys the *Boudoir* and refuses to consider taking Anatole – all that nasty continental cooking. Bertie calls for soap and a razor and forfeits the lip-fungus.

All very fresh and fizzy.

~ *French Leave* ~
1956

The Wodehouses had lived in France, on and off, for about six years. This is the most French of the novels. It is set mostly in the holiday resort of Roville. Jeff, the hero, is Jefferson Comte d'Escrignon, now a writer. He had been in the Resistance. His mother had been American. He has fallen in love at first sight with American Terry Trent, but he won't court her because he isn't rich and he thinks she is. (Actually she and her sister are pretending to be a rich girl and her maid.) Jeff's father, Marquis de Maufringneuse and a lot more, has had two American wives. He is a sort of feckless Uncle Fred/Ukridge/Mr Micawber combined with Jill the Reckless's Uncle Chris and Lord Hoddesdon. He sponges cheerfully on his son, Jeff. He is called 'Old Nick' and his best friend is a Prince, an old reprobate with three breach-of-promise cases against him.

This novel is distantly related to an idea Guy Bolton sold to Hollywood of three attractive sisters (in this case, Terry, Josephine and Kate, who are running a hens-and-bees farm on Long Island) setting out to blow a small legacy and find husbands and happiness.

If Wodehouse is trying to say something in this novel (and he stoutly denied that he ever had a message), it is that the fringes of the French nobility are just as lunatic as the English ditto; and perhaps not only the fringes.

~ *Something Fishy* ~
1957

Pre-October 1929, New York. A bunch of American millionaires amuse themselves making a secret tontine: $50,000 each into a kitty that will provide about a million dollars for whichever is the last of their sons to get married. Summer 1955, Valley Fields, London S.E. Keggs, once butler to, amongst others, the multiest of those millionaires, is now living in one of the houses he owns in Mulberry Grove, with, as lodgers, Lord Uffenham, another of his previous employers, and Lord Uffenham's niece, pretty Jane Benedick (sister of Anne in *Money in the Bank*). Jane's dowry is, Lord Uffenham hopes, to come from the profitable sale of his pictures at his ancestral Shipley Hall. The Hall is now rented to Roscoe, unpleasant, grossly rich son of the above (late) multiest. Jane is, at first, engaged to a sculptor with marcelled hair. Anyone who has read more than half a dozen Wodehouse novels knows that the engagement of a pretty girl called Jane to a chap with marcelled hair called Stanhope Twine who addresses her uncle as 'Ah, Uffenham' will soon be broken up by a fresh young buzzer called Sam, Jeff or, in this case, Bill (Hollister). It proves that grossly rich Roscoe and rather poor Bill are the only survivors in the race for the tontine loot.

Roscoe had bullied Jane as a girl. He is very mean. He is afraid of dogs and prepared to feed drugged meat to a harmless bulldog. He had been sacked from school for usury. Remember 'Battling' Billson? Remember the barmaid Flossie whom he married? Well, Flossie is Keggs's sister. And the Billson daughter, Emma, is the beautiful actress 'Elaine Dawn'. And Roscoe had proposed marriage to 'Elaine Dawn', with letters to prove it. It is the work of a moment for hired sleuth Percy Pilbeam (that two-timing rat again!) to steal them back for Roscoe. But Emma Billson's parents have a word with welshing Roscoe and an immediate wedding has been arranged. Two, in fact. Emma gets rich Roscoe. *Nouveau riche* Bill gets Jane.

We wonder whether the Billsons invited Ukridge to their daughter's wedding.

~ *Cocktail Time* ~
1958

Opposite the Drones Club is the Demosthenes Club. A brazil nut from the Drones window, from a catapult in the hands of Lord Ickenham, bashes the topper of pompous barrister Sir Raymond Bastable, Lady Ickenham's half-brother. Sir Raymond blames it on the young, and furiously writes a novel fearlessly attacking that generation of vipers. But, not wanting his name on its spine, he gives it to his sister Phoebe's scrounger son Cosmo to claim authorship. It becomes a scandalous bestseller, *Cocktail Time*.

It's a pity about 'Beefy' Bastable. He used to be a very proper young gentleman: had eaten seven vanilla ices on the trot at school, followed by only three days in the San; he was an Oxford rugger Blue; he was often thrown out of the Empire. Now he's a stuffed shirt: he bullies his sister and proposes to stand for Parliament for Bottleton East. Just the man for Lord Ickenham to get to work on.

Peasemarch had been a transatlantic ship's steward in *The Luck of the Bodkins*, his constant talk laced with pleasant malapropisms. Now he is 'Beefy's' butler, and a friend of, and ex-Home Guards warrior with, Lord Ickenham. Lord Ickenham's godson, Johnny Pearce, writer of suspense thrillers, has rented a country house to 'Beefy'. Barbara Crowe, once engaged to 'Beefy', works at the literary agency that handles *Cocktail Time*. So, as end products of Lord Ickenham's spreading of sweetness and light, a nicer, more spiritual 'Beefy' will marry Barbara, Peasemarch will marry Phoebe, Johnny will marry his Belinda and Johnny's limpet-like ex-nannie will be taken off his back and marry a policeman.

Three elderly romances, one younger. We meet, briefly, Sir Roderick Glossop again, a second (or is it third?) Bishop of Stortford (he preaches against *Cocktail Time* in the pulpit of the church of St Jude the Resilient), crooks Oily and Sweetie Carlisle again, and an eminent literary agent, Barbara's boss, who knits socks to keep himself from smoking. Also the policeman, Cyril McMurdo, who wins £500 in a football pool, which delays Nanny Bruce's acceptance of his courtship. And we learn that Lord Ickenham's nephew, long-suffering Pongo, is safely married now to Sally Painter.

Wodehouse is seventy-seven and his vintage years are nowhere near ended.

~ *A Few Quick Ones* ~
1959

Ten stories: four of them from The Drones Club, all with happy endings, three of them of tight-wad Oofy Prosser losing money and (pimply) face, one of Bingo and his boss Purkiss lying like mad to preserve their marital honours, another of Bingo putting little Algernon Aubrey Little up for The Drones in gratitude to him for saving his father's marital honour; two Mulliners, two Oldest Members, one Ukridge and one Bertie/Jeeves (originally, long ago, a Reggie Pepper story). In publishing dates this is the final Ukridge, and Ukridge, last seen, is in the soup.

In 'Oofy, Freddie and the Beef Trust', told by a Dronesman, the dialogue of everybody – greasy cockney Jas Waterbury, Oofy, two plug-ugly professional wrestlers and Freddie Widgeon – converges into a single slush-parody style, e.g. 'purged in the holocaust of a mighty love'. Perhaps the golden heart of Wodehouse's linguistic humour *is* slush-parody. In their weaker and most wonderful moments all his best fat-heads seem to show that they've been to too many silly silent films and absorbed their captions complete.

~ *Jeeves in the Offing* ~
1960

In Jeeves's *Times* Bertie sees the announcement of his engagement to Bobbie Wickham. Panic! But this is Bobbie's way of softening up her mother to accept her engagement to Bertie's friend 'Kipper' Herring.

And, of course, Bobbie had forgotten to warn either Bertie or Kipper that she was going to do this. Staying at Brinkley is Aubrey Upjohn, *quondam* H.M. of Bertie's and Kipper's prep school of the filthy food of which Kipper tells horror stories. Kipper, on the staff of the *Thursday Review*, scathingly and anonymously reviews a book about prep schools by this Upjohn. And dear Bobbie, reading the final proof, sees that he has left out the splendid stuff about the Malvern House food and puts it in, again without asking or warning Kipper. So Upjohn will see the *Thursday*, and know who wrote the piece.

With Upjohn at Brinkley is his stepdaughter Phyllis, rich (inherited from her late mother), 'a well-stacked young featherweight' who is Aunt Dahlia's goddaughter. There is a rich young American pursuing her and reading poetry to her. He is believed to be the much-marrying playboy 'Broadway Willie', and Sir Roderick comes down to 'observe' him and becomes a butler for the purpose. Kipper will marry Bobbie, after a quarrel which drove both of them in pique to get engaged to others (Phyllis and Bertie, for the record).

Jeeves is away shrimping at Herne Bay for most of the novel and Bertie has to drive there and fetch him to solve all the problems, which he does, finally, by putting the blame on the young master and labelling him as a loony and kleptomaniac – not the first or last time for this drastic way out in a last chapter. The plots creak a bit. Some of the writing is 'short'. Many of the images, quotations and verbal handsprings are recognizably old. New and surprising is that Jeeves has taken Bertie to the Louvre to see the *Mona Lisa*. Now, at last, they get that quotation from Walter Pater right – it's 'ends' of the world that come on that head, not 'sorrows' as so often before.

~ *Ice in the Bedroom* ~
1961

Here we must say goodbye to Freddie Widgeon. * He's off to Kenya with Sally (*née* Foster), whose tip-tilted nose twitches like a rabbit's, with a £3,000 loan from old Mr Cornelius of Valley Fields and the blessing of Sally's boss, bestseller Leila Yorke, who has found a long-lost husband too.

* He appears in 'Bingo Bans the Bomb' in *Plum Pie* (1966), but that's the Widgeon of old, bachelor and butterfly.

But let's start at the start. Freddie, who has a lowly job in the solicitors' office of Shoesmiths (four of them), shares Peacehaven in Valley Fields with a policeman who was a college friend. Sally and Leila normally live in Sussex, where 'Leila Yorke' turns out very successful 'predigested pap' (her own phrase) novels. Irked by the critics, who refer to her stuff in much the same phrases, she decides to show them she can write a Hardy/Gissing type of novel too, 'grey as a stevedore's vest', if she can only find somewhere grey to live for a while, for atmosphere. Bottleton East? No, says Freddie, they live for pleasure alone in Bottleton East. Come to grey, grey Valley Fields – the house next to mine is vacant, etc., etc. So Leila and Sally come to Castlewood, which, as it happens, Soapy and Dolly Molloy had rented previously and where they had stashed some nice diamonds that Dolly had lifted off Mrs Oofy Prosser. (Wait a minute. Aren't we back to *Sam the Sudden*? Well, yes, but you should have forgotten that in the last thirty-six years.)

Soapy has been selling his dud 'Silver River' oil stock regardless of age or sex – to Leila, to Lord Blicester (Freddie's uncle), to Oofy Prosser (twice) and to Freddie. Lord Blicester as a young man, Rodney Widgeon, has been engaged to Leila, but she had broken it off because he got so fat. Oofy Prosser has the majority of the shares of Popgood and Grooly, the publishers of Leila's books. And so it goes, round and round. And it's just as well that Leila brought her shotgun to Valley Fields with her. *Bang, bang*, and Chimp Twist regrets he has taken up burglary again.

Wodehouse wrote that he thought *Sam the Sudden* was 'darned good'. So is *Ice in the Bedroom*. And Leila Yorke is a great addition to Wodehouse's beloved female bestsellers. She has been making £15,000 a year for the last fifteen years, has saved most of it and has sold her last novel to Hollywood for $300,000. And she is very funny about it all. The Aunt Dahlia of the book world.

N.B. Popgood and Groolly (with two ll's) were the publishers waiting to be offered the never-ending *Typical Developments* book in *Happy Thoughts*, by F. C. Burnand, serialized in *Punch* in 1866 and onwards.

~ *Service with a Smile* ~
1962

Lord Emsworth is sorely tried. He has got Wellbeloved back as pig-man, but Constance has got him, as secretary, Lavender Briggs, who irritates him. The horrible Duke of Dunstable has invited himself to stay at the

Castle again. And Constance has allowed the Church Lads' Brigade to camp in the Castle grounds, squealing, throwing crusty rolls at his top hat, making him jump into the lake fully dressed to save a boy, who turns out to be a log of wood. And Constance has brought Myra Schoonmaker, daughter of an American millionaire, down to the Castle as, left in her care in London, Myra has fallen in love and tried to elope with a penniless curate, Rev. 'Bill' Bailey. Constance invites the Duke's nephew, Archie Gilpin, down to keep Myra company and help her to forget her curate.

At the opening of Parliament Lord Emsworth meets Lord Ickenham, who says he will come and sort things out, bringing with him a young friend, Cuthbert Meriwether, from Brazil (*alias* of the Rev. Bill Bailey, Myra's beloved).

Keep an eye on Lavender Briggs. She needs £500 to start her own secretarial bureau, and blackmail comes easy to her to that end. Keep an eye on the horrible Duke. He's out to steal the Empress and sell her to Lord Tilbury, who has long coveted her for his farm in Bucks. The plots thicken so fast now that at one stage Lord Emsworth, whose grandson has secretly photographed him secretly cutting the guy-ropes of the Church Lads' tent and who is now held to ransom for his crime, is prepared to buy his own thrice-medalled pig back from the Duke, his guest, for £3,000. Wellbeloved is sacked and re-reinstated. Myra's widower father will marry widow Lady Constance Keeble. Bill Bailey will marry Myra. Lavender Briggs has got her £500. Archie Gilpin, who needs £1,000 to buy into his cousin Ricky's onion-soup bar, gets that and rejoices.

All thanks to Lord Ickenham's virtuoso counter-plotting. He has spread sweetness and light all around except to the horrible Duke.

You will remember that, in *Summer Lightning*, Lord Emsworth's brother Galahad had known Myra's father, Jimmy Schoonmaker, in America. In *Service with a Smile* Lord Ickenham proves to have known Myra when she was a child, and to have been a dab-hand at soaping her back in her bath. Galahad and Lord Ickenham tend to act similar parts in Blandings novels. In *Galahad at Blandings* you will find that Jimmy Schoonmaker has married Lady Constance Keeble . . . her second millionaire husband.

~ *Stiff Upper Lip, Jeeves* ~
1963

Bertie has bought himself a jaunty little Tyrolean hat and Jeeves dislikes it. Gussie still hasn't married Madeline, so Bertie is still in danger of having to do it himself. The Rev. 'Stinker' Pinker begs Bertie to get Madeline to invite him down to Totleigh as there is something his fiancée Stiffy Byng wants Bertie to do. (*They*'re not married yet, either. Sir Watkyn hasn't come across with that vicarage for Stinker which would enable them to marry.) And Gussie, on his way to Totleigh, speaks to Bertie of Madeline in a way no fiancé should. 'Madeline makes me sick!' he says and buzzes off.

So Bertie, silly ass, decides to go to Totleigh and try to heal the Gussie/Madeline rift, plus Alpine hat, plus Jeeves. Madeline has put Gussie on a meatless diet and he is being fed steak and kidney pie at midnight by the sympathetic young cook – a temp.: in fact Emerald, kid sister of that Pauline Stoker, now Lady Chuffnell, who had led Bertie such a dance in *Thank You, Jeeves*. A guest at Totleigh is Roderick Spode, now Lord Sidcup, always keen to break Gussie's neck if he thinks he's not treating his beloved Madeline right. When Spode sees Gussie kissing the cook, he feels that the neck-breaking cannot wait. First to Gussie's rescue is Stinker (who has boxed heavyweight for Oxford. One day

Bertie Wooster's two-seater, probably a Sunbeam, with Jeeves at the wheel. The car occasionally goes wrong, but only for purposes of the plot.

someone must count the number of Wodehouse characters, mostly heroes, who have boxed for their universities. I'm sure I could find twenty-five without a small-tooth comb). He knocks Spode out with a sweet corkscrew left. Then Emerald does it again, with a kitchen basin. Gussie elopes with Emerald. Madeline says she is going to marry Bertie. Spode says, 'Oh no you're not. You're going to marry me!'

There has been a sub-plot. What Stiffy had wanted Bertie to come to Totleigh for was to steal a black amber statuette that Sir Watkyn had acquired by apparently dirty-dog methods from Major Brabazon Plank, that explosive explorer who had operated in *Uncle Dynamite*. Jeeves, pretending to be Chief Inspector Witherspoon of the Yard, rescues Bertie from Plank's threatened knobkerrie. And he rescues Bertie from imprisonment by Sir Watkyn, J.P., by agreeing to become Sir Watkyn's valet ('*psst* . . . only temporarily, sir'). But Bertie must forfeit that hat. Sir Watkyn's butler is glad to have it to add dash to his courtship of a widow in the village.

It's marvellous the way Wodehouse can get the same actors into new imbroglios using the same scenery; and the way innocent Bertie has only to see a noose to stick his fat head into it. It is comforting to know that, in the tea-tent at the School Treat at Totleigh, Sir Watkyn received a well-aimed hard-boiled egg on the cheek-bone from an anonymous donor.

~ *Frozen Assets* ~
1964

Two years ago English journalist Jerry Shoesmith had met American journalist Kay Christopher on the *Mauretania*. And now they meet again in a Paris police station – a very good scene this, for openers: Wodehouse was obviously remembering how he and his wife had been pushed around by the Paris police in 1944. Kay is engaged to a stuffed-shirt Englishman at the Paris Embassy. Her brother Biff had saved the life of Lord Tilbury's brother and will inherit a million pounds on condition he is not arrested before the age of thirty. Only a week to go, but the urge to drink is strong and, when drunk, he finds the urge to sock cops strong. And working for Lord Tilbury, who thinks *he* should have his brother's million pounds, is Percy Pilbeam, who tries to get Biff drunk and seeking cops to sock. Lord Tilbury's secretary is Gwendoline Gibbs and he is in love with her and will marry her. Lord Tilbury's niece, who is his hostess in the Wimbledon

Common mansion, Linda Rome, will marry Biff. They had been engaged years before. Jerry will marry Kay.

There is a sequence of de-baggings in Valley Fields. Henry Blake-Somerset (he's the mother-dominated stuffed-shirt Embassy chap) had twice been de-bagged by rowdies at Oxford. Now he is de-bagged by the de-bagged Pilbeam, and Lord Tilbury and Biff Christopher make up the chain, each clothing himself in the bags of the next comer. Surprisingly funny as told here, but hasn't Lord Tilbury been de-bagged in Valley Fields before? Yes, in *Sam the Sudden.* And Pilbeam de-bags himself, doesn't he, in *Summer Lightning?* A proper privation for prodnoses and pompous asses.

We find in this book a whole new list of authors from whom Wodehouse quotes: Shelley, Du Maurier, Robert Service, Alexander Woollcott, Theodore Dreiser, Horace (in Latin), Shakespeare (*Henry IV*), Malory, Burke, Defoe, Raymond Chandler and Mickey Spillane.

~ *Galahad at Blandings* ~
1965

In which Lord Emsworth finds Dame Daphne Winkworth being shoved at him as a prospective second Countess; in which Dame Daphne's horrible son Huxley is determined to release the Empress for cross-country exercise; in which the Empress gets pie-eyed on whisky and bites Huxley's finger; in which Dame Daphne hears Lord Emsworth calling the vet to ask if biting Huxley can have done the Empress any harm; in which Gally introduces a pseudo-Augustus Whipple to the Castle and the real one wants to visit too; in which beefy Monica Simmons, the Empress's current guardian, is wooed and won by little Wilfred Allsop; in which Tipton Plimsoll and Veronica Wedge head for the registrar's office.

Lady Hermione Wedge is in the chair as hostess now that Constance has become Lady Constance Schoonmaker, married in New York. Tipton still hasn't married Veronica and when Lord Emsworth mistakenly announces that Tipton has lost all his money, Veronica's parents find he has lost all his charm as a prospective son-in-law.

At this late stage Wodehouse ravels as tangled a plot as ever, but he unravels it with a rather unseemly rush. Gally has to 'tell the tale' (i.e. lie) briskly in all directions to get the right endings.

~ Jerry had never been snubbed by a butler before, and the novel experience made him feel as if he had been walking in the garden in the twilight and had stepped on a rake and had the handle jump up and hit him on the tip of the nose.

~ On the short fourteenth hole she got one of those lucky twos which, as James Braid once said to J. H. Taylor, seem like a dome of many-coloured glass to stain the white radiance of Eternity.

~ Now, seeing her weeping and broken before him, with all the infernal cheek he had so deprecated swept away on a wave of woe, his heart softened. It has been a matter of speculation among historians what Wellington would have done if Napoleon had cried at Waterloo.

~ Freddie's views on babies are well defined. He is prepared to cope with them singly, if all avenues of escape are blocked and there is a nurse or mother standing by to lend aid in case of sudden hiccoughs, retchings and nauseas. Under such conditions he has even been known to offer his watch to one related by ties of blood in order that the little stranger might listen to the tick-tick. But it would be paltering with the truth to say that he likes babies. They give him, he says, a sort of grey feeling. He resents their cold stare and the supercilious and up-stage way in which they dribble out of the corner of their mouths on seeing him. Eyeing them he is conscious of doubts as to whether Man can really be Nature's last word.

~ In places like Bottleton East, when you are having a scrap and your antagonist falls, you don't wait for anyone to count ten – you kick him in the slats. This is the local rule.

~ *Plum Pie* ~
1966

Nine stories here. In the first, 'Jeeves and the Greasy Bird', Bertie, engaged again to Honoria Glossop, tries to get out of it by compromising himself with Trixie, actress niece of greasy Jas Waterbury. Jeeves and Aunt Dahlia perjure themselves to get Bertie out of that mess, and he and Jeeves are now off to Florida, where Jeeves hopes to catch tarpon. We must suppose that Honoria will now marry Blair Eggleston and be off her father's hands so as to let him marry Myrtle, Lady Chuffnell (as he seemed to have done already, six years ago, in *Jeeves in the Offing*; you can't win trying to equate publishing dates with Wodehouse's calendar). In 'Sleepy Time' hypnotism produces strange golf scores. 'Sticky Wicket at Blandings' isn't about cricket, but about Freddie Threepwood giving away his wife's beloved Alsatian dog to an attractive neighbouring girl. 'Ukridge Starts a Bank Account' finds Ukridge (so does his aunt) selling Aunt Julia's antique furniture. Corky as usual pays for the lunch. There are two Bingo Little stories. In one he gets arrested for sitting in Trafalgar Square at a Ban-the-Bomb rally with a beautiful red-head who he had last met in a water-barrel. Her father, Lord Ippleton, is a good buzzer. 'George and Alfred' is a Mulliner story about twin brothers and Jacob Schnellenhamer and his yacht at Monte Carlo. Only so-so. 'Life with Freddie' is about the dog-biscuit salesman supreme again. And its length and course suggest that it might have been planned to go to a full novel. Ditto 'Stylish Stouts', which ends with a surprising clang. There is a fine drunk scene in 'Stylish Stouts' and the first paragraph of 'Sleepy Time' is a gem even among what might be a slim anthology of Wodehouse's best opening paragraphs.

~ *Company for Henry* ~
1967

Wodehouse is eighty-six now and this is a tired book, especially at the finish. My first-edition hardback has several glaring misprints in the last chapter. There is a highly suspect poesy-paragraph in it which might have come in, or from, something fairly gooey he'd have written before the First World War. And I strongly suspect that about ten pages have actually dropped off at the end. *Did* Stickney buy Henry Paradene's awful old mansion? Surely some nice, competent girl would have come and taken nice, incompetent Algy Martyn in hand. What about that flock of extra staff, hired for Ashby Hall in the early chapters in case Stickney came to stay? Did the broker's man marry Mrs Simmons the cook, or run away from her hymn-singing?

Henry Paradene could sell Ashby Hall if anybody would buy it. But he isn't allowed, by the entail, to sell a rare French eighteenth-century paperweight, an heirloom, which Mr Stickney covets. Henry's pretty niece is engaged to interior decorator, silky-moustached Lionel Green (what, him again?), and when Bill Hardy (who looks like a plug-ugly gangster until he smiles, and who wants to chuck his job and write thrillers in a country cottage somewhere) comes along, you know he'll get Jane in the end, if the end hasn't dropped off. He rescues a cat up an elm in Valley Fields (we're back to *Sam the Sudden* yet again) and he gets into Ashby Hall by impersonating the Duff and Trotter bailiff.

There are some good items, verbal 'nifties' and incidentals. 'Bill' Hardy's real name is Thomas. As he can't use Thomas Hardy on the spines of his books, he calls himself Adela Bristow, hoping this might sound, to a bookseller, like 'Agatha Christie' and make him stock up with a lot. Otherwise it's deckchairs on the lawn, swims in the lake, gazing at a girl's bedroom window in the moonlight, going up to London to hire an instant valet, going for a walk 'to think' and going to a bedroom to search it. Even though Lionel Green is a stinker and breaks his engagement to Jane (she is delighted, but no gentleman breaks an engagement), it is good news that he may marry the daughter of an American millionaire client of his shop, Tarvin and Green.

~ *Do Butlers Burgle Banks?* ~
1968

This novel feels as though it may have started out as a light comedy play-script, with all characters on stage for the finale of the last act. A privately owned Worcestershire bank, insolvent through bad management, is now inherited by Mike Bond, Cambridge boxing blue, once third in the Grand National, etc. The pretty nurse-companion of Mike's aunt, who lives with him and has broken her leg, is daughter of an impecunious country squire and she is in love with Mike. The butler says his father is ill and a temp. takes his job. This is Horace Appleby, head of the Appleby Gang, late of Chicago, now active in England, robbing country houses. Appleby, sharing house with Ferdy the Fly (porch-climber) as his bedmaker/cook, likes to get into country houses first as a butler and then plan the burglary in comfort. Appleby was one of the Duplessis mob on the Riviera. He plans to marry Ada Cootes, Mike Bond's secretary, and retire to the South of France to a house where he has done a burglary job. This time he has bribed the Mallow Hall butler to say his father is ill and leave the post vacant.

Appleby's safe-opening expert, Llewellyn ('Basher') Evans, colossal in size, soft in heart, gets 'religion' at a revivalist meeting (Ukridge's 'Battling' Billson did the same thing) and opts out of the burglary at a critical moment. Charlie Yost, gunman from Chicago, is angry because Appleby has docked his wages for carrying a gun against orders.

Mike's bank is saved when its debts are paid by investments in it by three rich ex-burglars.

Happy endings for all.

~ A Pelican at Blandings ~
1969

In *Uncle Fred in the Springtime* (1939) Lord Emsworth, weighed down in a sea of troubles (the Duke of Dunstable being the worst), had enlisted Lord Ickenham's help in taking arms against them. Now, with remarried Constance back for the summer and the disgusting Duke once more self-invited, Lord Emsworth summons his brother Galahad to his aid. Galahad is more and more doubling his part with Lord Ickenham these days: spreading sweetness and light; mornings in the hammock; the great sponge in the bath (Lord Ickenham's was 'Joyeuse', Gally's is not named); blackmail; telling the tale; godsons; unsundering young hearts; ringing in impostors.

The Duke has brought his pretty niece Linda with him and of course John Halliday, her ex-fiancé (there had been a flaming 'take back your ring' row), is one of Gally's godsons. And sundered hearts make Gally sick, so he'll have to bring Linda and John together again. For instance, why, when the call comes, shouldn't John come to the Castle as Sir Roderick Glossop's junior partner, to keep an eye on the suspected pottiness of Lord Emsworth? Meanwhile, there's this American heiress (is she an heiress?), Vanessa Polk, whom Lady Constance met on the boat. And Wilbur Trout, much-married American playboy. And the painting (is it a forgery?) of the reclining nude that the Duke has bought, brought with him and hung in the gallery. It's up to Gally to find answers to all these problems. He does.

You learn in this book that the oak staircase at the Castle is slippery. And if you're trying to work out what rooms were on which floor of the Castle, and how to get on to the roof over the semi-detached West Wing, this is required reading. It leaves even architects as baffled as ever. Remember, Wodehouse, after years of living in America, could make 'first floor' mean the ground floor. And so on up. Or not.

Wodehouse was eighty-eight when this book was published. The writing is now thin and tediously stretched in places. The ribs of the plot often stare out gauntly with too little flesh on them. Just for a laugh poor Lord Emsworth falls face down into the Empress's sty in the small hours and dressing-gown and pyjamas. Many of Gally's old Pelican stories are repeated, often verbatim, as though from notebooks. But there are some lovely plums in the duff still.

~ *The Girl in Blue* ~
1970

Crispin Scrope, middle-aged bachelor, has inherited vast, decrepit Mellingham Hall (not the same one as in *Pearls, Girls and Monty Bodkin*). He runs it as a guesthouse and he hasn't enough money to pay the repair bills. His butler is really a broker's man. His younger brother Willoughby is a prosperous London solicitor, from whom Crispin has to borrow. Willoughby passes on to Crispin some rich Americans as double-paying guests: Homer Pyle, corporation laywer and (slightly) a poet; Barney Clayborne, Homer's sister, widow, a sort of Aunt Dahlia and, actually or seemingly, a shoplifter/kleptomaniac.

Willoughby is trustee for young Jerry West, but refuses him his money if he intends to marry gold-digging and imperious Vera Upshaw, daughter of Dame Flora Faye, actress. Jerry, on a jury-duty, falls in love with Jane Hunnicutt, air-hostess, also on jury-duty. She hears from Willoughby Crispin that she is inheriting one or two million dollars from someone she was kind to in a plane. So Jerry can't now ask her to marry him – he has scruples about seeming to be a fortune-hunter.

Willoughby has just bought a Gainsborough miniature. It disappears from his office and the fingers of suspicion point to Barney. Several people, for rewards, search her bedroom at the Hall for the picture. Vera Upshaw, thinking that Homer Pyle is going to propose to her (she is a writer), ditches Jerry. Then she hears that Jerry has got his money and she tries to switch back. But Jane's legacy doesn't materialize, so Jerry can

marry Jane. And rich Barney will marry Crispin Scrope and take over the
management of Mellingham Hall. Willoughby warns Homer against
Vera Upshaw and Vera remains single and discomfited while all the
others rejoice in happy endings. (The Gainsborough turns up, and it
wasn't Barney who took it.)

Plotting and narrative are rather lack-lustre. But there's some excellent dialogue, very crisp for an eighty-nine-year-old. And there is a good
situation moment when the broker's man/butler blackmails his master,
Crispin, J.P., into agreeing to push the local cop into a stream while he is
dabbling his hot feet after the day's duty. In fact Crispin funks it, but
Barney does it for him.

One idea for making Barney disclose the Gainsborough, if she had it,
was to sound the fire alarm – the principle being that, in a fire, everybody
grabs the thing most dear to him/her to escape with. Not new (see *Right
Ho, Jeeves*), but funny here.

~ Much Obliged, Jeeves ~
1971

This is the one in which we learn Jeeves's Christian name; in which
Bertie is Jeeves's guest at the Junior Ganymede Club; in which Bertie is
unwillingly, briefly and almost simultaneously re-engaged to Madeline
Bassett and Florence Craye; in which Spode, 7th Earl of Sidcup, gets hit
in the eye with a potato in an electioneering fracas and is thus cured of his
idea of renouncing his title and standing for Parliament.

We're back at Brinkley and the house is full of guests for the Market
Snodsbury by-election. Bertie's, and Aunt Dahlia's, friend Ginger
Winship is standing as Conservative candidate and has asked orator
Spode to speak on his platforms. Spode's fiancée, Madeline Bassett,
comes too. Winship is engaged now to Florence Craye and she comes, a
very bossy fiancée as usual. Ginger falls in love with his new secretary and
will do anything to get Florence to break their engagement. A final guest
at Brinkley is financier L. P. Runkle, who became rich on something that
Tuppy Glossop's late father, a research chemist, had invented. But
Runkle had not rewarded the inventor and Aunt Dahlia is determined,
by Anatole's cooking, theft or blackmail, to get Runkle to give the
long-owed money to Tuppy so that he can marry Angela.

A newcomer to Market Snodsbury is Bingley, once Brinkley, Bertie's
valet in a period (*Thank You, Jeeves*) when Jeeves had left him. Now,

Bertie Wooster's fearsome AUNT AGATHA.

thanks to a deceased grocer uncle, he is a man with a house, property and a butler; though still a country member of the Junior Ganymede. He was once also Ginger Winship's 'man', and Runkle's. And he has 'borrowed' the Junior Ganymede Book of Revelations, containing facts about Ginger which, if published, would turn the strait-laced electors of Market Snodsbury against him. Just what Ginger would now hope, since it would turn Florence against him too. But Jeeves, with a knock-out drop, steals the book back from Bingley. The book contains stuff about Runkle also. Ginger, on Jeeves's advice, makes a speech advising the electors to vote for his opponent. Florence's self-willed re-engagement to Bertie after that lasts for a single page and she is still unattached, a proud and bossy beauty, when we hear of her, here, for the last time.

When the Book of Revelations goes back to the Junior Ganymede, it will not contain the seventeen pages Jeeves had contributed over the years about Bertie.

My first edition hardback of this book has many misprints and misprisions – e.g. Bertie says that Arnold Abney, M.A., was the H.M. of his prep school (of course he meant the Rev. Aubrey Upjohn, H.M. of Malvern House, Bramley-on-Sea), Jeeves misquotes Lucretius, ruining sense and scansion, and Brinkley has changed his name arbitrarily and without explanation. Wodehouse is writing very short now.

~ *Pearls, Girls and Monty Bodkin* ~
1972

Rich Monty (Montrose) Bodkin must put in another year's employment with Ivor Llewellyn, the Hollywood tycoon, if hockey-international Gertrude Butterwick's father is to allow him to marry her. Now he is Llewellyn's secretary and pint-sized Sandy Miller, who had been Monty's secretary in Hollywood, is now Mrs (Grayce) Llewellyn's secretary, and the Llewellyns have taken Mellingham Hall in Sussex, furnished, for a season. Sandy has long been in love with Monty, but has let conceal-ment, like a worm i' th' bud, etc., as she knows he's engaged to that beefy English girl. Grayce has a valuable ($50,000) pearl necklace, and you know what that means – a detective to watch it (Chimp Twist, of course) and that nice couple they met in Cannes, the Molloys, Soapy and Dolly, soon to be watching Chimp and their own opportunity. And, wouldn't you know (Ivor Llewellyn does, because he did the switch – poor chap, he has a joint bank account with Grayce, so how else can he get spending money for gambling? See Sigsbee Waddington in *The Small Bachelor*), the pearls are fake. Besides which Grayce has put Llewellyn on a diet and Chimp is disguised as his valet with orders to report if he eats or drinks anything he shouldn't. Grayce makes Chimp shave off his moustache for the part.

The old problems: (a) a tycoon shackled by a joint bank account with his wife and (b) an English gentleman (Monty) wanting to get out of his engagement with a girl. Monty, you see, is now in love with Sandy. When he saw her pull a dustbin full of bottles down over a policeman's head in a raid on a nightclub, he knew that there was the girl he must marry. It all ends happily, with Grayce divorcing Ivor Llewellyn, Monty and Sandy teamed up and Gertrude to marry the dustbin-crowned cop, who is an Old Etonian and also a hockey international. And Chimp, Dolly and Soapy are stuck with a lot of dud pearls.

There is an affinity between this story and *Money in the Bank*.

~ *Bachelors Anonymous* ~
1973

Her former employer, Laetitia Carberry, of the Anti-Tobacco League, has left to journalist Sally Fitch a Park Lane flat and £25,000 if she doesn't smoke for two years. And a detective, Daphne Dolby, must share the flat and keep an eye on her and report.

In Hollywood a number of businessmen form 'Bachelors Anonymous', to save friends, clients and themselves from matrimony. The prime mover is Ephraim Trout, lawyer who has handled Ivor Llewellyn's five divorces. Trout always carries Mickey Finns as a last resort to save a soul. He is determined to save Llewellyn from a sixth marriage. When Llewellyn goes to London, Trout arranges for a firm of solicitors there to provide a man to dog his footsteps and save him, especially from Vera Dalrymple, who has just wrecked the chances of Joe Pickering's first play, in which she took the lead. Joe meets Sally Fitch and falls in love with her when she comes to interview him. Sally had once been engaged to Sir Jaklyn Warner, 7th Bart and a no-good sponger. Hearing about Sally's legacy, Sir Jaklyn courts Sally again and, in pique because she thinks Joe has stood her up on a dinner date, she accepts him. Sally smokes and loses her £25,000.

Ivor Llewellyn buys Joe's play for $250,000 for a movie. Joe will marry Sally. Daphne Dolby, the detective, drags Sir Jaklyn to the altar, or registry office, and will probably make something of him. Ephraim Trout is bitten by a dog in Valley Fields and the dog's owner, a widow and ex-nurse, bandages him up and feeds him tea and home-made scones and strawberry jam, and Trout will marry her. Happy bachelor Ivor Llewellyn, having escaped Vera Dalrymple, will join Bachelors Anonymous enthusiastically when he gets back to Hollywood.

A most benign, autumnal novel, formulaic but much simpler in plot than Wodehouse in his long summer would have thought fair to his cash customers.

~ *Aunts Aren't Gentlemen* ~
1974

Plots now run so much in grooves that the fun is almost 100 per cent linguistic. Bertie and Co. get into fun situations – he is tied up and gagged, horsewhipped, made to fall in a middenish puddle and later a swimming pool. But it's the narrative grammar and syntax murdered by Bertie that is the main strand of humour. When it's fresh and new, it's good. But there is quite a lot of old, cold stuff too. Sad but, dash it, Wodehouse is rising ninety-three.

Bertie, with spots on his chest, is told by a doctor to go to the country and live a quiet, fresh-air life. He goes, with Jeeves, to Maiden Eggesford, to a cottage on the estate of a Colonel Briscoe, brother of the vicar. Aunt

Dahlia is staying at the Colonel's house. Jeeves has an aunt in Maiden Eggesford too. Colonel Briscoe has a racehorse, Simla, which is hotly rivalled by his neighbour Mr Cook's Potato Chip for an important local race. Potato Chip pines in his stable if his friend the cat isn't there. Aunt Dahlia and all the Briscoes, including the Vicar's daughter Angelica (remember her from the fizzing short story 'Tried in the Furnace'?) have their shirts on Simla and Aunt Dahlia thinks to safeguard their investments by stealing the cat from Potato Chip, so that he'll pine and lose the race. Of course she expects Bertie to house the hijacked cat until after the race.

The young love interest is Orlo Porter; an Oxford Union Communist, who yearns to marry Vanessa Cook, whose father, Mr Cook, above, is Orlo's sole trustee and who won't unbelt Orlo's money to let him marry his daughter. Vanessa (to whom Bertie had proposed marriage some time previously) quarrels with Orlo because he hasn't the guts to go and thump the table with her fierce horsewhipping father. At one stage she says, 'Right, Bertie, I will marry you.' This would be for Bertie worse even than Florence Craye. Vanessa is dominant and disapproving and proposes that Bertie shall, when they are married, give up smoking, his silly laugh and The Drones.

Simla wins the race on a technicality. Orlo and Vanessa elope. Mr Cook and his friend (Bertie's enemy in the last book) Major Plank are made to look silly. Why Plank, and Jeeves's aunt for that matter, are there at all is a mystery. Aunt Dahlia wins a lot of money and Bertie and Jeeves escape to the quiet life in New York, far from aunts.

~ *Sunset at Blandings* ~
1977

Wodehouse (at long last Sir Pelham Wodehouse) died before he had finished this novel. It was in the form of a rough typescript (he had typed it himself as usual) of the barebones narrative and dialogue of the first sixteen chapters of a planned twenty-two. Its story keeps to the Blandings formula: a pretty niece brought to the Castle to separate her, and cool her off, from an 'impossible' (i.e. poor) suitor in London; suitor infiltrated under an assumed name by Gally, as artist come to paint the Empress for the Portrait Gallery; Lord Emsworth innocently blowing the gaff to an angry sister. But there is a lot of good fresh stuff, even in this first-draft précis. Two new sisters (that gives Lord Emsworth ten in all) appear, one formidable as usual, the other, uniquely, nice. The formidable one is separated from a 'weak' husband. The Chancellor of the Exchequer, Sir James Piper, wants to propose to the nice one, but cannot do so with his Scotland Yard bodyguard always hovering. It goes practically without saying that Jimmy Piper had been a Pelican and a bit of a lad when young and indigent. But now he too needs Gally's help.

The sixteen chapters at this stage run to scarcely 30,000 words. At that rate the whole novel would have worked out at about 40,000. A finished Wodehouse novel is minimum 60,000. Which shows – and it shows when you read it – that the sixteen chapters would all have been considerably fleshed out. When he was young Wodehouse wrote long and, in the last stages of a novel, enjoyed cutting and simplifying. In his old age he wrote short and enjoyed, but less, the fleshing-out process.

To Wodehouse's 30,000 words of draft narrative have been added illustrations of some pages of his autograph notes and the typed scenario they led to, suggested explanations on some of the difficult passages in the narrative, a discussion of the times of trains between Paddington and Market Blandings in all the Blandings novels and stories, and, as endpapers, a fine map by the artist Ionicus of the Castle and its surroundings.

~ *Autobiography: Wodehouse on Wodehouse* ~
1980

This three-part heavyweight was put together by Hutchinson after Wodehouse's death. It contains most of *Bring on the Girls*, which he wrote with Guy Bolton and published in 1954; *Over Seventy*, which had been published in England in 1957, a version differing somewhat from his *America, I Like You*, which had been published in America in 1956; and *Performing Flea*, 1953, which was his letters to his schoolfriend Bill Townend between 1920 and 1952, with Townend's commentaries. Parts of this were incorporated into *Author! Author!*, published by Simon and Schuster in America in 1962.

Each part of this collation, *Wodehouse on Wodehouse*, has been changed, to a greater or lesser degree, from its earlier issues. For a start, the English *Bring on the Girls* (Herbert Jenkins, 1954) differs in several sequences from Simon and Schuster's version of the same title published in 1953. Then, when *Wodehouse on Wodehouse* was being put together by Hutchinson for 1980 publication, the aged Guy Bolton cut some pages that had been in both the English and the American versions, and added new stories, mainly about Wodehouse and a beautiful showgirl, which Wodehouse would have disallowed (or anyway written much better) had he been alive. Always a good raconteur, Bolton was not, at the end of his life, so good at the writing desk. Bolton's telling here of 'Plum's One Wild Oat' is a muddle. Its sequel, Plum and lovely Fleur meeting again on the overnight train, I have heard Bolton tell with a more dramatic ending and with John Barrymore as the trapped lover.

But *Bring on the Girls* was, was intended to be and still is the theatre and Hollywood careers of Bolton and Wodehouse threaded with boisterous stories of their sockos and floperoos, and, all good if not true, of the producers, moguls and stars for and with whom they so profitably worked. Alas, the publishers of *Wodehouse on Wodehouse* have had to dispense with the pages of photographs that enlivened the first *Bring on the Girls*. Nor have they put in those excellent drawings from the American version (*America, I Like You*) of *Over Seventy*. That again is Wodehouse autobiography leavening a few score of meditations of a mind pleasantly loose in the socket. Here you will find a version of that tale of young Wodehouse disfiguring the new ledger at the Bank, thus ending his City career. Some of the essaylets appeared in the New York magazine *Vanity Fair* during the First World War, some are to be found in *Louder and Funnier*, some in old copies of *Punch*. They are written in the mood that made the *New Yorker* reviewer call Wodehouse a 'burbling pixie'. They are lovely stuff.

The originals of the Wodehouse to Townend letters which made *Performing Flea* are in the P. G. Wodehouse Library at Dulwich College. They would show a bookworm how extensively Wodehouse doctored the originals for publication. But this part of *Wodehouse on Wodehouse* remains (a) a first-class guidebook for beginners in the trade of fiction, one that any headmaster or parent might give to any aspirant literary sprout, as a combined fertilizer and weedkiller – it shows a determined, inexhaustible and always benign writer with his hands temporarily behind his head, but mostly on his typewriter – and (b) the longest public statement Wodehouse ever made about his internment in 1940–41 and the five broadcast talks he gave (and wished, as all his friends did, that he hadn't) to still-neutral America on the radio from Berlin after his release from camp.

The whole three-part book is essential reading if you are interested in the reclusive man behind almost a century of books. A giant of English letters.

~ Lord Emsworth had one of those minds capable of accommodating but one thought at a time – if that.

~ Inherited wealth, of course, does not make a young man nobler or more admirable, but the young man does not always know this.

~ I admit that Madeline Bassett is pretty. Any red-blooded Sultan or Pasha, if offered the opportunity of adding her to the personnel of his harem, would jump to it without hesitation, but he would regret his impulsiveness before the end of the first week. She's one of those soppy girls, riddled from head to foot with whimsy. She holds the view that the stars are God's daisy-chain, that rabbits are gnomes in attendance on the Fairy Queen, and that every time a fairy blows its wee nose a baby is born, which, as we know, is not the case.

~ The question of how authors come to write their books is generally one not easily answered. Milton, for instance, asked how he got the idea for Paradise Lost, would probably have replied with a vague 'Oh. I don't know, you know. These things sort of pop into your head, don't you know,' leaving the researcher very much where he was before.

~ Bobbie Wickham was a one-girl beauty chorus.

~ 'Last night this Englishman was explaining the rules of cricket to this American girl and answering all her questions on the subject, and, as he didn't at any point in the proceedings punch her on the nose, one is entitled to deduce, I consider, that he must be strongly attracted by her.'

~ The butler loomed in the doorway like a dignified cloudbank.

3 ~ AUNTS, SCHOOL AND
THE SCHOOL STORIES

———————— ~ ————————

The Pothunters (1902), *A Prefect's Uncle* (1903), *Tales of St Austin's* (1903), *The Gold Bat* (1904), *The Head of Kay's* (1905), *The White Feather* (1907), *The Luck Stone* (published pseudonymously, as a serial in *Chums*, 1908, but never republished), *Mike* (1909) (which, in 1953, had been divided into *Mike at Wrykyn* and *Mike and Psmith*), *The Little Nugget* (1913).

If the sons of a judge in Hong Kong were going to be educated in England, there had, in the days before aeroplanes, to be long separations from the parents. In school holidays the Wodehouse boys were much in the care of aunts and under the jurisdiction of aunts. Plum Wodehouse squeezed some of his best copy out of aunts, and schools provided him with seven or eight complete books.

The best aunt cannot wholly fill the gap left by an absent mother; still less can a plurality of aunts. Wodehouse finally came to know his mother only when he had outgrown his need for her lap and love. He regarded her more as an aunt. He said that his proper aunts were very good to him as a boy and he wished that, as a boy, he had been nicer to them. His Aunt Mary (Deane) harried and harassed him a good deal, and he exaggerated her later into Bertie's Aunt Agatha. Aunt Mary honestly considered that her harrying and harassing of the young Pelham was for his good; and the older Pelham thought she could have been right.

Thackeray, Kipling, Saki, Kenneth Grahame and other sensitives, dispossessed too early of their proper complement of parents, looked back in anger and indulged in revenge fantasies against the Olympians whose proxy parentage had chilled their childhoods. Wodehouse blew out the perilous stuff in profitable, plot-fertile mockery. To others their Aunt Gonerils; Wodehouse made his all Aunt Sallies. When he found his feet on solid ground in farce, he adopted aunts and aunthood as good comic business.

The aunt represents authority and interference. The nephew owes her a duty. But there is no absolute necessity for love on either side. A monstrous aunt can be funny. A monstrous mother would be tragic. In Wodehouse's light novels several personable young men, of an age when they should have shed their mothers, retain them, or are retained by them, with sad results. Their girlfriends or fiancées find them weak of will and laggards in love. But give a girlfriend an opportunity to mother a man she is fond of and all sorts of the right glands start functioning in her. In *A Pelican at Blandings* (1969) it is soon clear that what the stupid, weak, much-divorced American millionaire, Wilbur Trout, needs is a final marriage to sensible, poor, pretty Vanessa Polk, daughter of a long-ago Blandings Castle below-stairs match, a visiting American valet and an English housemaid. In a late-night thieving operation, approved and abetted by Galahad Threepwood, Vanessa, with courage and resource for two, helps Wilbur's courage along with a resourceful flask of strong drink. At the critical moment, when Wilbur should be at his keenest and most alert, Vanessa finds him slumped in a chair, his head lolling, asleep at his post. 'She stood watching him, and was surprised at the wave of maternal tenderness that surged over her . . .' There, Wodehouse has got over that awkward little hump in the scenario – to make the nice girl fall in love, love for the man, not his money. Vanessa comes over all motherly, with pity and love. Desdemona fell for Othello that way, you recall.

Wodehouse in his books has ten aunts to every one mother, and of the many middle-aged females who are both mothers and aunts all are more important as aunts than as mothers. The function of Mrs Spenser Gregson, later Lady Worplesdon, is to be Bertie's Aunt Agatha. It is only incidentally that she is Young Thos's mother. It is Mrs Travers's function to be Bertie's Aunt Dahlia. It is only incidentally that she is mother of Angela and Bonzo. Wodehouse had to have an older generation as a background to his protagonistic younger set. He chose to make them aunts and uncles rather than mothers and fathers. It gave him much greater scope. It is funny when Bertie slides down drainpipes or sneaks off to America to escape his Aunt Agatha's wrath. It would be sad if he were thus frightened by his mother. It is funny when Squire Esmond Haddock, at the end of *The Mating Season*, finally rounds on his oppressive aunts and puts them in their places. It would have been painful had he rounded on his mother and threatened to cut off her pocket money if he had one more yip out of her. When he so threatens his Aunt Myrtle, it is with the rapturous support not only of his charming fiancée but of the reader.

Nepotism, if that is the word I want for the state of being a nephew, is rife in the Blandings, as in the Wooster, books. Lord Ickenham spends all his best time being Uncle Fred; and Bill Oakshott, the hero in *Uncle Dynamite*, is a version of Esmond Haddock in *The Mating Season*. Bill Oakshott returns to his heritage, Ashenden Manor, to find an uncle irremovably self-installed there, bossing the place, occupying the best bedroom and chairs, and regularly taking the brown egg at breakfast. Bill Oakshott feels like a toad beneath the harrow, and he only lifts the harrow (with Uncle Fred's help) in the last chapter.

By and large all the nice young people in Wodehouse are orphans. No single nice young person of any importance, except Mike Jackson, has both parents alive. Some nice young girls (Bobbie Wickham, Pauline Stoker) have single parents alive and dominant. All the ghastly girls (Madeline, Florence, Honoria) have dominant fathers but no mothers. Stiffy Byng draws ex-magistrate Bassett as an uncle and guardian. Ukridge is an orphan, dependent on his fierce Aunt Julia. Bingo Little is an orphan, dependent on his Uncle Bittlesham until another uncle dies and he inherits his plenty. Freddie Widgeon is an orphan, dependent on his Uncle Blicester. Jeeves himself is an orphan. Nepotism is cardinal to many of Wodehouse's plots.

Wodehouse has so confidently established by repetition his own picture of the state of aunthood that he can use the word 'aunt' to mean 'a bossy, pernickety woman'. Somewhere he describes a bossy and pernickety young girl as 'growing up to be an aunt', and somewhere else he strains the language even more boldly. He is describing a certain type of garden and house as seen over a fence. He says: 'It was the sort of house of which you could say "Someone's aunt lives here."' Wodehouse treats the bossy aunt seriously in his one serious book, *The Coming of Bill*. There Aunt Lora Delane Porter is the villainess of the piece, spoiling her niece's marriage by spoiling her niece's child. There is a satisfactory chapter of aunt-defiance at the end of that book, and the aunt-defiance is a more important resolution of the reader's tensions than the re-establishment of the happiness of the niece with her son and husband.

'In this life it is not aunts that matter, but the courage that one brings to them,' says Bertie philosophically. In his experience aunts create when you try to marry actresses or go on the stage. Aunts create when you break the vicar's umbrella or are fined in court for pinching a policeman's helmet on Boat Race Night. Aunt writes to aunt about your idleness, excessive income, selfish bachelorhood, spinelessness and uppish manservant. There is no decent reticence about aunts, as there may be with mothers. When you annoy one aunt, she tells all the others. Aunt booms to aunt like mastodons across a primeval swamp. Aunts visit your bachelor flat before you've even had your morning tea. Aunts expect you to board their loathsome schoolboy sons in London and take them to see Shakespeare and Chekhov at the Old Vic; also to the dentist and the school train at the end of the holidays.

In an essaylet at the beginning of a chapter in *Right Ho, Jeeves*, Bertie says:

> I remember Jeeves saying on one occasion that hell hath no fury like a woman scorned. And I felt that there was a lot in it. I had never scorned a woman myself, but Pongo Twistleton once scorned an aunt of his, flatly refusing to meet her son Gerald at Paddington and give him lunch and see him off to school at Waterloo, and he never heard the end of it. Letters were written, he tells me, which had to be seen to be believed. And two very strong telegrams and a bitter picture post card with a view of Little Chilbury War Memorial on it.

That is the way aunts behave if you scorn them, and that's the way they behave even if you don't. If you are as angelic as Bertie, *plein de peur et de reproche*, you accept nepotism and make the best of it. But you still chafe.

Aunts are nothing new in light literature. Lady Bracknell and even Betsy Trotwood may exist vestigially in Lady Worplesdon and Mrs Tom Travers. But Wodehouse more than any other author has glorified the state of aunthood by chi-iking at it cordially in more than fifty books.

Dulwich College comprises sixty-five acres of green fields, chestnut avenues and Victorian red-brick buildings. There were 600 boys in Wodehouse's time, mostly day-boys. Dulwich was a rugger school. The fives they played was also the Rugby game, which provides the best sort of court for school fights, having no buttresses, steps or other hazards. Sheen has a fight in a fives court in *The White Feather*. Wodehouse remembered no fights at all during the six years he was at Dulwich. His contemporaries say there were one or two fairly serious ones but that it was typical of Wodehouse to have forgotten them. What he did not forget were cricket and football matches. He wrote to me, when he was in his late seventies:

> I was in the Dulwich cricket team in 1899 and 1900, and I am always proud to think that in 1900 I used to go on to bowl before N. A. Knox (I admit he was a

child of about ten then). If only I could have got Scotty Gibbon, the greatest captain of football ever seen at Dulwich, to see eye to eye with me, I should have been in the football fifteen as early as 1897, but it was not till 1899 that I got my colours. We had a great team that year, not losing a school match, but the season was spoiled by the scratching of both Bedford matches, the first because of fog, the second because of frost. We had played a scoreless draw with Haileybury, who had a tremendous side that year, and as Haileybury had beaten Bedford 9–nil, we were expecting to beat Bedford. I was a forward, weight 12.6. Boxing: I was to have boxed at Aldershot in the heavyweights but illness prevented. Fortunately, I realise now, as I should have been murdered. I was never really much good.

Situated near to London and having good late-night and early-morning trains, Dulwich has, as a dormitory suburb, attracted the stage and press. The school has probably produced a higher proportion of writers and actors than any other great English public school. It was, by all accounts, a happy place. Wodehouse was certainly very happy there. He said that his schooldays went like a breeze. He realized that it was all wrong for a sensitive and spiritual writer to have enjoyed public school. He insisted, too, against all the wishful prying of snoopers hoping to get their hooks on some psychological trauma in the early years, that his father had been 'as normal as rice pudding'. The stubborn psychologist, daunted by finding no trauma at home and that the great writer Wodehouse wasn't a mouse or a misfit at school, ought possibly to study him as, in that respect, abnormal. Look how unhappy their schooldays were for Shelley, Paul Nash and George Orwell! But Wodehouse came through Dulwich smiling, and the Dulwich area is often affectionately remembered for casual addresses or as Valley Fields in his stories.

Wodehouse between the wars went and watched Dulwich cricket and rugger matches as often as he could, and sometimes wrote them up, knowledgeably and seriously, for the *Alleynian*. He wrote of Trevor Bailey on one occasion: 'Bailey awoke from an apparent coma to strike a four', which slightly annoyed Bailey at the time of publication but has amused him since. Bailey remembers that, in his first year in the Dulwich cricket side (1938), they won all their school matches, and Old Boy Wodehouse treated the team to a dinner in the West End, followed by the London Palladium. Bailey, then fourteen, was much impressed. But what Bailey forgot – and another of the conquering team told me – was that Wodehouse himself was not at the dinner or the Palladium.

'Billy' Griffith, who captained the Dulwich rugger side through a season without defeat, told me that he had a letter from Wodehouse (whom he had not met) after the last desperate school match. Wode-house, writing from the Dorchester, said he had tried to see the match through from the touchline, but couldn't bear the tension and had had to go and walk round the outside of the school grounds, waiting for the whistle and the final cheer to make sure that Dulwich had held their slight lead to the end. When he deduced the good news, he walked home to his hotel and found he remembered absolutely nothing of the seven-mile footslog through the streets, as he was thinking only about the match.

A boys' magazine called the *Captain*, then a year old, published in April 1900 the beginning of a public-school serial called *Acton's Feud*. The first sentence was:

> Shannon, the old Blue, had brought down a rattling eleven – two internation-als among them – to give the school the first of its annual socker matches . . .

The eighteen-year-old Wodehouse thought that opening sentence the best of any he had come across in school literature. Victorian public-school fiction, favouring the second, rather that the first, half of *Tom Brown*, had kept to a frowsty formula of Chapel and Sanatorium. This was something new in school stories. Wodehouse decided that he was going to write like this himself, if he could. He anonymously reviewed *Acton's Feud*, when it appeared as a book, in the *Public School Magazine*. He called it a classic and quoted that opening sentence.

When he left Dulwich and went to work in the bank, he wrote in the evenings and on Sundays. He was writing not so much for all time as for money. But the question was, what to write? He saw there was no market in the magazines for prep-school stories, even though a large proportion of the readers of the *Captain* and the *Public School Magazine* were of prep-school age. So he gave the reading world no sustained worm's-eye view of any St Custard's of the late 1880s and early 1890s. He did put the action of one of his early novels (*The Little Nugget*) in the setting of a prep school. Very good the action is, and very well the prep school is described. But it is described from the assistant master's point of view, and Wodehouse's confidence in the subject came to him, not from his own schooldays, but from periods when he used to go and stay and write at his friend Baldwin King-Hall's prep school at Emsworth, on the border of Sussex and Hampshire. *The Little Nugget* is a light thriller, and the school is Sanstead House, Hampshire, where, for fairly nefarious reasons, Peter Burns, the first-person-singular hero, has signed on as assistant master under Mr Abney, the snobbish Head. The pupils number twenty-four, sons of the nobility and gentry.

As a not too dedicated prep-school master, Peter Burns has some good observations to make about prep schools, their smells, their boys and their masters. Of the two other masters:

. . . headmasters of private schools are divided into two classes: the workers and the runners-up-to-London. Mr Abney belonged to the latter class.

And:

Mr Glossop was a man with a manner suggestive of a funeral mute suffering from suppressed jaundice.

Although at one moment an American gunman holds up Peter Burns and his enraptured class with a revolver, you will not, if you have been at a prep school as a boy, find Sanstead House a travesty of your memories. Prep-school masters insist that *The Little Nugget* shows that Wodehouse cared for them too, knew their job and added a small gem to the literature of their calling.

But only an unduly sophisticated boy of prep-school age could properly appreciate *The Little Nugget*. His easier, and preferred, reading would be Wodehouse's seven or eight public-school books. Your best chance today of finding those Wodehouses together, including the one-volume *Mike*, is to look through the locked cupboard of the bookshelves of a prep school (not public school) Mr Chips. He keeps them in the locked cupboard because they are books that cannot easily be replaced, and so must be lent, with care and circumspection, only to favoured boys with fingers guaranteed jam-free.

If old bound volumes of the *Captain* occupy the bottom shelf of the school library, you can even more enjoyably trace the same stories (except *The Pothunters* and *A Prefect's Uncle*) serialized and illustrated there. But while you're looking, and before we discuss the stories that later became books, see if there are any bound volumes of *Chums* on the same shelf. If so, and if the volume starting September 1908 is among them, extract it. The *Captain* can wait for a moment, and the bound books too. In that volume of *Chums* is a serial school story called *The Luck Stone*, by 'Basil Windham', who was P. G. Wodehouse with an assist from W. Townend. *Chums* commissioned the story. Wodehouse paid Townend a tenner for his help. You're fortunate to have discovered *The Luck Stone*. Read it.

It is an off-beat Wodehouse. His other school stories, expertly tailored for the *Captain*, were still of the stuff of his own schooldays. *The Luck Stone* was fiction born of fiction, professionally written and produced from wide and purposeful reading of *Chums*. It is the only story that Wodehouse ever had in *Chums*. *Chums* asked him for a blood-and-thunder school story, and Wodehouse gave it to them. He was twenty-seven then, and had been a successful London freelance journalist for six years. For his official correspondence he had a letter-head printed with his name in red, half an inch deep, at the top, and four lists going just short of half-way down the quarto page: '*Author of:* –; *Part Author of:* –; *Contributor to:* –; *Some Recent Song Successes:* –'. He gave his permanent address as the *Globe* newspaper. He had been to America and was due to go again the next year. Doubtless Wodehouse enjoyed writing *The Luck Stone*. Doubtless he found it pretty easy going too. He had shown, in breezy asides throughout his school novels, and in breezy essays in the *Public School Magazine*, *Punch* and elsewhere, that he had read acres of catchpenny fiction, had enjoyed it all and knew all the tricks of it. *The Luck Stone* shows that he could imitate it too, at the rustle of a cheque. Wodehouse wrote it within months of finishing *Mike*, which is not bilge at all. Never underestimate the power of a professional.

Chums in 1908 was a twenty- or twenty-four-page illustrated weekly for boys: about the size of the *Daily Mirror* of today, but with thicker paper. Its front cover generally gave most of its space to a lurid line-illustration of a lurid episode from one of the lurid stories inside. Its back cover had advertisements for Gamages, offering all sorts of things from bicycles to joke goods, cricket bats to violin outfits ('Violin, extra set of strings, resin and Tutor, lined case: 12/6 complete, carriage 9d. Beginner's full size violin: 5/11'). Inside were a number of illustrated editorial features, mostly instructive ('This is the right way to carry a boa-constrictor. This is the wrong way'), elevating and anti-'frowst'. But the main guts of the magazine were the five or six fiction stories, of which two or three were serials. Captain Frank Shaw's *The Vengeance of the Motherland* had London invaded by the Russians. '*Suppose your home were shelled.* Have you ever considered what you would do? Get next week's *Chums*.'

The illustrations were cheap and bad. Although photography had by then enabled two of their artists in particular, Caton Woodville and Stanley Wood, to draw splendidly animated horses, charging the reader head-on ('The Russian brigade thundered over the bridge, firing at their pursuers'), other artists were less felicitous with Restoration sword duels, express trains bearing down on a prison warder tied to the rails (a 'trusty' risking his life to get the man untied), a boy astride the back of a tiger which has got its forefeet across a little girl ('its teeth began to close on the slim white neck') in an English school playing-field, and Colonel Sir Henry Babcock, Bart, firing pointblank into the mouth of a charging lion.

In *The Luck Stone* ('A Story of fun and adventure at School') the schoolboy hero's father, Colonel Stewart, D.S.O., Indian Army (Rtd), had been political agent to the Maharajah of Estapore and now he is guardian to the Maharajah's heir, of Eton and Cambridge and a century-maker in the Varsity cricket match. When the story opens, Colonel Stewart has been away from England for nine months, big-game shooting in Africa. It means that Jimmy Stewart has to deal with his problems alone at first.

Jimmy ought to be back at Marleigh College for the Christmas term, but he has just had mumps and must stay at home. Then a mysterious sunburnt stranger from India turns up at the Stewart house. Nice chap (he addresses Jimmy as 'Well, matey . . .'), if a bit dazed. Jimmy questions him politely: 'The man opened his mouth to reply, when suddenly something hummed past Jimmy's ear like an angry wasp. The man from India reeled, staggered back, groping blindly with his hands, and fell in a heap.'

'*To be continued next week*' gives only a seven days' interval, and then Jimmy is looking round at the window and seeing a face 'with piercing, cruel eyes, the lower half covered by a beard'. (What had laid out the man from India was a silenced air-gun. He was bringing from India, for Colonel Stewart to give to his ward, the heir, a talisman stone belonging to the Maharajahs of Estapore.) And when Jimmy gets back to Marleigh, he thinks there is something fishy about the new master, Mr Spinder . . . the same piercing, cruel eyes . . .

The Luck Stone story did not come from anywhere deep in the recesses of its author's personality. He had read Wilkie Collins's *The Moonstone*. He had read Conan Doyle's *The Sign of Four*. The sympathetic and comic-talking schoolboy from Calcutta, Ram, shows that he had also read Kipling's *Kim* and Anstey's *Baboo Jabberjee*. He had read *Chums* for years, and knew its needs. It was open-cast mining for him to slice out the story off the top of his brain.

Wodehouse's other public-school stories (republished) are also highly professional jobs, but done for magazines whose demands were less lurid, though no less strict, than those of *Chums*. The first, *The Pothunters*, appeared serially in the *Public School Magazine*. The rest appeared in the *Captain*. The *Captain* was very much about, and supposedly for, public-school boys. The great athlete C. B. Fry was Athletics Editor. After the death of Fry in 1956, a correspondent wrote to *The Times* referring to Fry's 'editorship' of the *Captain*. This correspondent was put in his place by another correspondent, who gave the correct fact (as above), ending his letter with: '*Inter alia*, the *Captain* printed the earliest work of P. G. Wodehouse, school stories of unmistakable quality, in which there appeared for the first time the immortal Psmith.' As a correction to this it should be pointed out that P. G. Wodehouse's earliest work was printed in the *Alleynian*, *Tit Bits*, *Fun*, *Sandow's Magazine*, the *Weekly Telegraph*, the *Universal and Ludgate Magazine*, *Answers*, the *Globe*, *To-day* and (regularly and extensively) the *Public School Magazine* before he sold so much as a short story to the *Captain*.

In the era of Wodehouse's contributions to the *Captain*, the editor was R. S. Warren Bell, and under the title 'The Old Fag' he did an 'Answers to Correspondents' column that is, to the later researcher, one of the most strange, delightful and time-wasting columns in literature. Fry had done a similar column in the first years of the paper's life, and Fry had established the forthright style.

C. S. (Radley)   Fish and cutlet for breakfast, cold beef for lunch and whatever you jolly well please for dinner.

H. C. Lott   I expect you have outgrown your strength. Try leaving off the cold bath.

'Weakling'   You are the first man I've met who measures his chest in feet. You are all right. Time will adjust your ins and outs.

Then came 'The Old Fag', who for years advised, teased, lectured, hectored and snapped at his pen-pals, male and female, without fear or favour.

J. Y. Miller   I do not know of any way of curing knock-knees. I may mention that bicycling will make you more knock-kneed than you are now. There are hundreds of thousands of people who would not be knock-kneed if there were any remedy for it.

A.L.F.   Abandon once and for all any idea of going on the

Stage. I wonder at any fellow of nineteen hesitating between the Army and the Stage. Be a soldier, my friend.

One of My Readers

Of course you can take Holy Orders without going to Oxford or Cambridge.

G.N.E.

Just at present I don't want any photographs of Quebec.

'Dejected'

I should think that if you tried hard and practised constantly, you could soon learn to pronounce your 'r's' properly. I have no particular advice to give you concerning it. But if any other Captainite has conquered this difficulty perhaps he will write to me, as then I will forward his advice on to you.

The Baby

I think a girl might adopt a more profitable recreation than shooting. It is not exactly a pastime that fosters womanliness.

Nellie

The French for iodide of potassium is *iode de potassium. Iode* is pronounced ee-ode.

D.M.F.

Yes, you write abominably. Let me see how you have improved in three months' time.

B.S.

If the Boy Scouts in your neighbourhood are as riotous as you say, they are certainly no credit to that craft, but you must always remember that in a widespread movement there are bound to be some less considerate of their self-respect than others. As a whole, I think the Boy Scouts behave themselves most commendably.

F.R.

Something is wrong either with your friend's digestion or his teeth. A dentist would recommend him a wholesome mouthwash, which would do much to alleviate the unpleasantness you speak of.

Med Student

If you would say what 'monomania' you suffer from, I might be able to give you some advice. Probably your complaint is 'nerves', for which exercise and fresh air are the best cures.

Julius Caesar

Why bother about your ears, Mr C.? I believe elastic bands can be obtained from chemists and surgical appliance manufacturers, but I cannot help repeating . . . Why bother about them?

It is proper that we should know the splendidly unevasive manner of the editor, so that, when he speaks about the stories in his own magazine, we may know he speaks the truth.

'Anxious enquirer', not being a boy, has serious doubts about the *Captain* school stories. 'Are they true to life,' she asks, 'or are they only piffle?' and she waits in trepidation for my reply. How glad I am to be able to assure her that they are the real thing and are written by men who know. 'Anxious enquirer' need be anxious no longer.

From privileged reading of the files of Wodehouse's letters to Townend from which *Performing Flea* was hewn, I deduce that, for a period in 1908–9, Wodehouse himself was doing a clandestine temp. fill-in job as editor of this 'Old Fag' column. I commend this as a field of exploration for some literary dowser with a more sensitive divining rod than mine.

Somerset Maugham tells of rereading the first book of short stories he ever had published, *Orientations*:

It sent so many cold shudders down my spine that I thought I must be going to have another attack of malaria. As a measure of precaution I dosed myself with quinine and arsenic . . . [The stories] had passages so preposterously unreal that I could hardly believe it possible that I had written them.

If Wodehouse reread his public-school books, he did so, I am sure, without needing to run to the medicine cupboard. He would not have agreed with the editor of the *Captain* that they were either true to life or the real thing, but he would not have thought them piffle. They never had, nor were intended to have, any high moral tone, which puts them right out of the class of *Tom Brown*, *Eric* and *The Hill*, to name but three.

In the *Public School Magazine* in 1901 there is an anonymous essay on 'School Stories'. I had noted Wodehouse's style in this even before finding him, in a later piece on 'Fictional Improbabilities' under his by-line, referring back to what he had written in 'School Stories'. In these two contributions he says:

The worst of school life, from the point of view of a writer, is that nothing happens . . . Of course, if you are brazen enough to make your hero fall in love with the Doctor's daughter . . . A time may come when a writer shall arise bold enough and independent enough to retail the speech of school as it really is, but that time is not yet. The cold grey eye of the public-which-holds-the-purse is upon us, and we are dumb. Rudyard Kipling went near it . . . a gallant pioneer of the Ideal; but even the conversation of *Stalky & Co.* leaves something unsaid: not much, it is true, but still something.

Wodehouse referred to a school story called *Gerald Eversley's Friendship*, published in 1895. The book had already drawn the disapproval, in print, of E. F. Benson on the grounds, among others, that its hero 'spends most of his leisure time forming theories of life, and wrestling with spiritual doubts . . . all this at the age of thirteen . . .' Young Wodehouse adds:

Gerald intends to commit suicide, but finally Nature provides him with a galloping consumption and with his death the story ends, as all school stories should, happily . . . Sudden death is always good . . . but to make your hero die on a sunset evening, in a bathchair, placed under a big cedar tree, looking o'er the shining waters of the lake, and quoting extracts from obscure Greek poets, is, I aver, a mistake . . . No, the worst thing that ought to happen to your hero is the loss of the form-prize or his being run out against the M.C.C. There should be a rule that no one under the age of twenty-one be permitted to die, unless he can get the whole thing finished in a space of time not exceeding two minutes . . .

Improbabilities about villains are the worst. The villain always has too much pocket money, and he *will* spend it on gin, billiards and cigars. The man who drinks without getting drunk is unknown . . . He comes to roll-call with the regulation reel and hiccough which we know so well from Dean Farrar's books . . .

One cannot but agree with every word of young Wodehouse's sentiments above. But for the first few lines he must have had a book other than *Gerald Eversley's Friendship* in mind. *Gerald Eversley's Friendship* had a different plot, though it is still an excruciatingly wet novel. The author was J. E. C. Welldon, who was (often called 'a great') Headmaster of Harrow when this, his only novel, was published. It might well be taken as the ultimate in evangelical public-school fiction of a type that got its start in *Tom Brown's Schooldays*, and was by no means dead until Alec Waugh's *The Loom of Youth* gave it its last clout in 1917.

Wodehouse's school stories are good yarns, full of games, ragging and study teas, with occasional sixth-form words ('stichomythics', 'intempestive') and references to the humming watchman in *The Agamemnon* and Nicias's speechmaking in Thucydides – not wholly out of place in serials for a public-school magazine. There is not much reason why anybody should want to read these stories for the first time now, except as interesting Wodehouse *juvenilia*, showing the Santeuil that later became a Swann. But, although schoolboy literature as a rule dates very quickly in sentiment and tends to look, even in short retrospect, soppy or pompous or both, Wodehouse's books carry their years lightly. The slang inevitably dates a little. One of the stories in *Tales of St Austin's* is entitled 'How Payne Bucked Up'. We no longer use the phrase 'to buck up' quite so absolutely today. You can find it in Poet Laureate Alfred Austin's *The Human Tragedy*:

> When with staid mother's milk and sunshine warmed
> The pasture's frisky innocents bucked up . . .

There is a nice period flavour, too, about 'brekker', 'rotting' and 'bar' meaning 'dislike' ('the governor bars Uncle John awfully'). Boys wear nightshirts; a school suit costs 42/-; the Head drives in a carriage and pair; the school doctor prescribes 'leeches and hot fomentations' for practically everything; and cigarettes are 2½d. for twenty.

When, in 1953, Herbert Jenkins reissued the long, single-volume *Mike* (1909) as two books, *Mike at Wrykyn* and *Mike and Psmith*, they did a little modernization on the text. Cricketers Fry, Hayward and Knox became Sheppard, May and Trueman, the indoor game diabolo became yo-yo, 'bunking' (a match) became 'cutting', and 'jingling, clinking sovereigns' became 'crisp, crackling quids'. (But the Gazeka still wore pince-nez and Adair still went for the doctor on his bicycle.)

These were not big changes to ask after forty-four years, and they are already mostly outdated now. The stories themselves are absolutely valid as public-school fiction up, certainly, to the end of Hitler's war. The Code is broadly right. The games blood is more glamorous than the Balliol scholar. In fact, the swot is a figure of mild derision. Ragging and rule-breaking are good things, and a skill in these is the next best thing to eminence at games. But even if you play cricket for your county in the summer holidays, you must not put on side.

Wodehouse refers to 'the public-school boy's terror of seeming to pose or do anything theatrical'. One of the least likely snatches of chatter ever recorded in a public-school novel comes in the first chapter of Horace Annesley Vachell's *The Hill* (1905). The school is unashamedly Harrow.

By this time the boys were arriving. Groups were forming. Snatches of chatter reached John's ears. 'Yes, I shot a stag, a nine-pointer. My governor is going to have it set up for me . . . What? Walked up your grouse with dogs! We drive ours . . . I had some ripping cricket, made a century in one match.'

Mike, a first-chapter new boy at Wrykyn, is told: 'Nothing gets a chap so barred here as side.' Mike faces the problem in a fairly acute form when he becomes a cricket blood while still a new boy; and in an upside-down of that when, going on to Sedleigh at the age of eighteen, he becomes a new boy while a considerable blood.

Wodehouse sold school stories (but no serials) to the *Public School Magazine*, the *Royal*, *Pearson's* and the *Grand*. But the *Captain* was his best market. Its editor never commissioned anything from Wodehouse, but he never rejected anything from him. Wodehouse gave the *Captain*'s readers an extra in humour, much of it at the expense of school stories such as *The Luck Stone*. Almost the first remark that Psmith, in fact an Old Etonian but also technically a new boy, makes to Mike Jackson when they meet at Sedleigh is: 'Are you the Bully, the Pride of the School, or the Boy who is Led Astray and takes to Drink in Chapter Sixteen?' There is a distinct streak of parody already in Wodehouse, and he pulls the leg of the *Chums* type of story for the *Captain* just as easily as he imitates it for *Chums*.

In *Tales of St Austin's* Wodehouse included an essay, which first appeared in the *Public School Magazine*, about and against *Tom Brown's Schooldays*. He doesn't mind the first half of *Tom Brown*, but suggests that the second half of the book was compiled, not by Hughes, but by the S.S.F.P.W.L.W.T.R.O.E.B.A.S.T.H.G.I. (Secret Society For Putting Wholesome Literature Within The Reach Of Every Boy And Seeing That He Gets It). Wodehouse wrote for boys, not for their parents or their schoolmasters. Hughes's *Tom Brown*, Dean Farrar's *Eric, or Little by Little* and *St Winifred's, or the World of School*, and an unfair amount of other school fiction, were written with strong moral purpose or overtones. It was *Eric* and *St Winifred's* that Stalky's aunt gave 'To dearest Artie', and for which Stalky could only get ninepence the pair from the Bideford bookseller. Such books have done well as gifts but can very seldom have been willingly bought, out of his own cash, by a boy intending to read them. Wodehouse wrote, refreshingly, for guineas, sometimes even for half-guineas, but never to do good. In Wodehouse's books there is no piety, no purity, no pathos. There are virtually no parents either. In the *Public School Magazine* for March 1901 the nineteen-year-old Wodehouse had an anonymous contribution, an essay 'Concerning Relations'. It starts with the pithy sentence: 'The part played by relations in school life is small but sufficient.'

In none of Wodehouse's school fiction is a boy shown writing home to his mother. To his father, yes, asking for money; but never to his mother. In *The Luck Stone* the schoolboy hero, Jimmy Stewart, has a fine soldier father but no mother. The absence of a mother isn't even remarked on.

No Wodehouse schoolboy dies, even in the Sanatorium. Ever since Dickens's *The Old Curiosity Shop*, schoolboy mortality seems to have fascinated school-fiction writers, if not their readers; the white angel-face on the pillow, the thin pale hands plucking at the coverlet in fever (Jeeves would have known the technical name for this: carphology), or resting, in near-posthumous blessing, on the head of some kneeling and weeping chum. I think that there is only one death, and one near-death, of boys in *Tom Brown*. But boys in Dean Farrar's books fall off cliff-tops, spend fatal nights on wave-whipped rocks, or just decline and perish. And you may (happily) have forgotten the *Stalky* story in which the great headmaster rested from his canings and saved a boy's life by 'sucking the diphtheria stuff' out of his throat through a tube. That rescue was at least successful.

The death-wish is strong in many subsequent authors of public-school novels, even after Wodehouse had publicly jeered at the propensity. If death in the Sanatorium is avoided, the hero is apt to die young, fair and pure, as though too good for life, in war or warlike adventure. Harry Desmond of *The Hill* is shot through the heart in a hail of Boer bullets in South Africa. The Head preaches about him in Harrow Chapel. Mark Lovell, C. B. Fry's hero in *A Mother's Son* (1907), after many chapters of schools and Oxford, riding the winner of the Grand National, and, off his own batting and bowling, almost winning a Test Match against the Australians at Lord's, marries and then finds that he has heart trouble. It is somehow in keeping with the rules of the Code that Mark should not tell his wife or his doting mother about this, but should enlist, take his heart out to the Boer War and get shot through it. In Wodehouse's books nobody, boy or Old Boy, gets anything worse than a case of mumps.

His boys' main interests are in the school. They like their school and they hope it will win the matches. Their conversation is mostly about games, ragging, other people's rows, who's funking his tackles and, generally, who's bucking up and who's not. There is no bullying, though boys occasionally have fist-fights in bad blood. Their favourite reading is the *Sporter* (otherwise the *Sportsman*), Haggard, Anstey, Doyle, Hornung, Gilbert and Dickens. If a boy is in the Classical Sixth, he writes two Greek and two Latin compositions a week, can 'do' Virgil and Livy unseen, but has to battle, with labour and lexicon, with the apparently maniac speeches in Thucydides. He writes an essay for the headmaster in his spare time. He will get a scholarship of sorts to Oxford or Cambridge. But all this is not considered swotting. Swots are the boys who read their Thucydides and *Paradise Lost* beyond Books 2, translate the choruses of the *Agamemnon* into verse for the Mag., and read Herodotus in the original (little Geordie did this in *Tom Brown* too) with their feet on the mantelpiece. All of which is rather regrettable and frowsty. It will probably end up in a Balliol scholarship or a breakdown.

Mike is Wodehouse's most mature and by far his best school book. There is some sense in comparing it with Ian Hay's school story *Pip*. *Pip* was published in 1907; *Jackson Junior* (as the first half of *Mike* was called in serialization) first appeared in the *Captain* in 1908. Wodehouse had read *Pip* when he was writing *Mike*. He admired Ian Hay as a writer always. But *Pip* is written from a master's-eye point of view. *Mike* is written from a boy's-eye point of view. *Pip* dates; *Mike* dates very little.

In *Pip* there is romance. In *Mike* there is none. In *Pip* the schoolmaster plays the father-figure to the cricketing hero. In *Mike* there is no father-figure. The difference between the books on this is a very wide one. Mike is on his own, he has to consume his own emotional smoke and to pick up his wisdom, in matters of public-school life, from his fellow schoolboys. He has no pigtailed girlfriend to dream of, no cosy clergyman in whose book-lined, tobacco-scented study he can browse on books and blub in bewilderment. But you can read of Mike's triumphs in the cricket field without feeling that they are very surprising. Wodehouse has made you identify yourself with the character and the skill; it is you that he is taking through the fears and perils of the Ripton match. If you have played cricket at all, it is you out there playing Mike's innings with him. But you are not bowling with Pip; you are sitting with Ham, smoking a pipe, watching someone, perhaps your own son, do an extraordinary headline feat of bowling.

It is really very unlikely that a father would remove his son from one public school and send him to another for a single term. But that's what Father Jackson and Father Smith both did, to the great advantage of public-school literature. Mike Jackson and Psmith turned up at Sedleigh together. The two eighteen-year-old new boys teamed up, proposing to devote their attention exclusively to ragging, and thus perhaps to salve the indignity that their fathers had inflicted on them. (As a serialized sequence to *Jackson Junior* in the *Captain*, the second, Sedleigh, part of the story was titled *The Lost Lambs*.) They wouldn't play games and they joined the archaeological group so that they could disappear and hunt rabbits.

'Behave yourself. Don't make a frightful row in the House. Don't cheek your elders and betters. Wash.' Those were the words of advice that the Gazeka had given the new boy Mike at Wrykyn. Doctrinally you won't find Wodehouse burrowing much deeper into the mystique of the English public school than that.

Counting that as a generalized First Commandment, you might construct the rest of the Decalogue as:

2. Thou shalt not put on side.
3. Thou shalt not sneak on other boys.
4. Thou shalt not lie except to get other boys out of trouble.
5. Thou shalt think thine own school the best in England, and thine own House the best in the school.
6. Thou shalt sponge thyself with cold water after a long soak in a hot bath.
7. Thou shalt not smoke: it is bad for fitness. If thou dost smoke, let it be a pipe and not cigarettes.
8. Thou shalt consider games more important than work.
9. Thou shalt not talk about thy parents except in jest.
10. Thou shalt not smarm thy hair with pungent unguents.

And the Eleventh Commandment is for all healthy public-school rule-breakers:

11. Thou shalt not be found out. Otherwise thou mayest get sacked and have to go into a bank.

Tom Brown was enough of a classic for Wodehouse to have been able to laugh at it as such, and as it deserves. But *Stalky* had appeared while Wodehouse was at school and was still among the bestsellers. To a young writer of school stories, not sure which way to turn, *Stalky* must have been a great temptation. It had clearly influenced Ian Hay when he was writing *Pip*. Ham in *Pip* is the Reverend John in *Stalky*: both wise padres, both good with boys. Mr Bradshaw in *Pip* is King in *Stalky*: both Balliol scholars, both fools in their treatment of boys.

You can find evocations of *Stalky* in Wodehouse's schoolbooks too, and an interesting scholarship question might be: 'If Beetle is the stripling Kipling, and Charteris/Mike the stripling Wodehouse, how do they compare in actions and character?' (Notes: Beetle and Charteris both edited a magazine; both were called 'buffoon' by masters. Beetle went off to a job at £100 a year in India; Mike went into an £80 a year job in a bank which would eventually have sent him out East.) One can suggest that there is parallelism between the turning off of the gas-main (*Stalky*) and the ringing of the fire-bell (*Mike*); Sergeant Foxy in *Stalky* and the school sergeant in *Mike* who was 'feeflee good at spottin''; the masters, King and Downing; the angry squire fussing about his pheasants in *Stalky* and the ditto in *The Pothunters*. Perhaps the Wrykyn Head who beat the boys so liberally after the great Wyatt Walk-Out is a memory of 'Prooshian' Bates of *Westward Ho!*, who never stopped beating boys, even when he was being cheered by them for his heroism on behalf of the boy with diphtheria. (Wodehouse checked his admiration for head-masters at a sensible point and in his later books teased them quite a lot.)

Wodehouse always felt that Kipling's schoolboys were not boys; they were at least twenty-five years old. Wodehouse (to repeat) was writing for boys; Kipling for masters, parents and Old Boys. Wodehouse was not trying to teach anybody anything, Kipling was teaching, in a sense, all the time. He was saying: 'What a great school, what a great headmaster, what clever and interesting boys! That's the way other schools, head-masters and boys ought to be.'

Obviously *Stalky* would have been too difficult, allusive, gnomic, sophisticated and painful for the *Captain* (one wonders whether 'The Moral Reformers', the story of bullying and counter-bullying in *Stalky*, read as revoltingly in 1898 as it does today). Perhaps there is a small, symbolic summing-up in M'Turk's remark, 'The Head never expels except for beastliness and stealing.' 'Beastliness' is a purely pi-jaw word, and M'Turk would never have used it, even evasively, to Stalky and Beetle. *Stalky* was written, not for 'boy, just boy', but for grown-ups and for a certain Calvinistic relish of the author's own. The *Captain* offered stories for boys. There is no 'beastliness' in them, mentioned or inferable. It was left to 'The Old Fag' to deal with that in that 'Answers to Correspondents' column of his. Boys (and, at least once, a mother) apparently wrote to him fairly regularly about beastliness; and he castigated it frequently and with enthusiastic commination.

What about girls? If the *Captain* had an official editorial attitude on what a sister wanted her brother to be, it might be deduced from this nerve-racking poem, by Grace Mabel Hudson, printed, with all italics, quotation and exclamation marks, in the *Captain* in October 1910, titled 'My "ideal" brother'.

He is straight as a pine, and as broad as an oak,
And his jokes unto laughter a cat would provoke!
He's not handsome, oh no, but his kind, honest face
Tells you plainly *he*'ll never his people disgrace!

He's a 'dab' both at cricket and 'footer', and yet
When it's tennis I'm wanting he'll put up the net,
And when off for a spin he will pump up my tyres
And help me up hills if occasion requires!

He calls hard work at school 'quite the silliest rot',
But he's head of his class, so he knows how to 'swot'.
Though when *I'm* playing scales he will burst in and shout
'Where's the tune? I say, stop it, kid; let us go out!'

He's a critic of blouses, and really quite wise
In the matter of neckbands and colour of ties,
And I *know* I look nice when *he* says I'm 'all right',
As I know that I *don't* when he says I'm a fright!

He's not *perfect* – his chums call him just 'a good sort' –
And he does not do always the things that he ought,
But he's *sterling good stuff*, and that is to my mind
Quite the nicest ideal for a brother you'll find!

What and when did the Wodehouse schoolboys think about girls? Not much and not often is the answer. There are very few girls about, and I remember only Marjorie Merevale, the housemaster's sporting little daughter (in a story, 'Welch's Mile Record' in the *Captain*, but never republished); twelve-year-old Dorothy who reformed Charteris; and Mike's own sister Marjory, a great admirer of his cricket but hopeless at keeping a secret. It was Marjory Jackson who coolly revealed, in a letter to brother Bob, that Mike, in order not to keep Bob out of the last place in the Wrykyn side, had pretended he had hurt his wrist. Mike, thoroughly embarrassed by being shown up for a martyr by the young squirt, decided that no girl ought to be taught to write until she came of age. Female kids! Pshaw! A rather older menace appears in a story in *Tales of St Austin's*, a Miss Beezley, who marries Dacre, the housemaster. Miss Beezley reads Browning and is a blue-stocking forerunner of Florence Crayė, Honoria Glossop, Heloise Pringle and other over-educated girls who put Bertie Wooster through the mangle in the later years.

In *The White Feather* Wodehouse studied with some interest and seriousness the situation of a boy, of prefect level, shunned by his fellows. He says somewhere in that book that to experience exclusion and loneliness in its deepest sense, a boy should try breaking one of the unwritten laws at a public school. Sheen, in *The White Feather*, had

'I say, can you tell me the way to Limpstone?'

funked a fight with a townee. Everywhere else in his school books, Wodehouse excellently conveys the sense of inclusion, of moving in coveys and thinking in teams. He also gives the other sense of the word 'inclusion', instantly recognizable to anyone who has been at one of the older, and older-fashioned, public schools: the sense of being behind bars and perpetually challenged to climb out.

'Climbing out' is a rag or a crime at a public school in a virtually intransitive sense, without need of any explanation of whence or why you are climbing out. (I still use the present tense, because this was truth in my between-the-wars public-school days as in Wodehouse's.) It is assumed that all windows are barred, as in a prison or a nursery. It is never clear what the outside dangers are from which one is being so scrupulously locked in. It is simply that from the clanging of one bell to

---------------- ~ ----------------

~ 'The moment my fingers clutch a pen,' said Leila Yorke, 'a great change comes over me. I descend to the depths of goo which you with your pure mind wouldn't believe possible. I write about stalwart men, strong but oh so gentle, and girls with wide grey eyes and hair the colour of ripe wheat, who are always having misunderstandings and going to Africa. The men, that is. The girls stay at home and marry the wrong bimbos. But there's a happy ending. The bimbos break their necks in the hunting field and the men come back in the last chapter and they and the girls get together in the twilight, and all around is the scent of English flowers and birds singing their evensong in the shrubbery. Makes me shudder to think of it.'

~ Bill sat down and put his head between his hands. A hollow groan escaped him, and he liked the sound of it and gave another.

~ He strode off into the darkness, full to the brim with dudgeon.

~ It is never difficult to distinguish between a Scotsman with a grievance and a ray of sunshine.

~ Only the necessity of keeping both hands on the handlebars prevented him from patting himself on the back.

~ 'It's an iron-clad contract, and if she attempts to slide out of it, she'll get bitten to death by wild lawyers.'

~ The Captain was on the bridge, pretty sure he knew the way to New York but, just to be on the safe side, murmuring to himself 'Turn right at Cherbourg and then straight on.'

---------------- ~ ----------------

the clanging of another all doors to the outer world are locked. The house is an effective fire-trap. If you take the bars away from windows of public-school houses, you may save a few boys from being burnt to death in each decade when the fire-alarm for once turns out to be genuine. But you also rob schooldays, or rather nights, of one of their immemorial excitements – climbing out.

I said that the postulates of the public school in Wodehouse's early writings were valid for public schools up to the end of the Hitler war. What changes have been brought about by the infusion of girls and other innovations into public-school life and literature I don't know. I haven't come across any novels set in a public school of today. There must be some. As I write this (1986), the Head of the School at Westminster is a Barbadian girl. Surely the current Westminster generation will produce a few novelists, and one or more will do this girl the honour Hughes did to Old Brooke at Rugby or Thackeray to the boy who became Colonel Newcome.

Wodehouse wrote what the *Captain* asked for and wrote it better than anyone else in the magazine at the time. He peddled their dreams back to its readers. He accepted the magazine's formulas and was perhaps saved a lot of bother and thinking by the restrictions that the formulas imposed. George Orwell called *Mike* 'perhaps the best light school story in the English language'. And Rupert Hart-Davis records in his biography *Hugh Walpole* that in 1908 Walpole, then a schoolmaster, started to write a school novel which he planned to be like P. G. Wodehouse's.

Wodehouse in his *floruit* years felt that critics of his works, myself among them, paid too much attention to his school books. He held them to have been apprentice work. If what he called 'orators' were going to sound off with lit. crit. about Author Wodehouse, he would prefer to be judged by periods of his work when he felt he had a better stranglehold on his writing craft.

4 ~ PSMITH

———————— ~ ————————

Enter Psmith (1935) and *Mike and Psmith* (1953), both virtually the same book, made from the second half of *Mike* (1909), *Psmith in the City* (1910), *Psmith Journalist* (1915), *Leave It to Psmith* (1923), *The World of Psmith* omnibus (1974).

Psmith is Wodehouse's first adult hero. At Sedleigh he is already the Old Etonian, the grown-up among boys, the sophisticate among the callow. His eyelids are a little weary and he wears a monocle. In a schoolboy world, where nobody else has done much but play cricket and see the latest Seymour Hicks show at the theatre, Psmith talks and behaves like someone who has swept together ten thousand experiences and is never going to be surprised at anything again. In his first book he patronizes his headmaster, in his last he patronizes Lord Emsworth.

Psmith is like a breath of good, stale nightclub air coming through the healthily open, if precautiously barred, windows of commonroom, study and dormitory. To readers of Wodehouse, he is the link between Awkward Adolescence and the Great After Life. He leads us to the new world of the City, America, gangsters, crooks, clubs, Psocialism and Blandings Castle. Those of us who are unable to dissociate Wodehouse's school books from our own schooldays (a test of their excellence for the market for which they were written) have been, for seven books, moving in the smell of cooked cabbage and old plimsolls, in the sound of bells and whistles and clanging clocks. We have been sitting, if at all, on lockers and benches, with chilblains and spots, red wrists, rude health, huge hungers and bull-calf enthusiasms. Psmith is a lazy man who likes his comforts. He is strongly opposed to missing his sleep and he quotes a learned German doctor's theory that early rising leads to insanity. Psmith offers us late breakfasts, deep armchairs, the smell of cigar-smoke, the folding of the hands in repose after good lunches in clubland, and a lifetime truce to 'training'. Psmith wafts us painlessly from the School Close to Piccadilly.

Psmith does not despise his schooldays. But he is unsentimental about them. He is finished with them. His father hoped that his one term at Sedleigh might 'get him a Balliol', but Psmith avoids anything so swottish. He looks back to his Eton days without regret and without rancour. At Cambridge he is objective enough to decide that his happiest memory of the school whose Old Boy blazer he wears with his sky-blue pyjamas is of a certain hot bath after 'one of the foulest cross-country runs that ever occurred outside Dante's Inferno'. He would have played for Eton at Lord's in his last half; but in the matter of cricket he is more likely to remember that, in a village match, he had been caught at point by a man wearing braces. 'It would have been madness to risk another such shock to my system.'

When Wodehouse went to live in New York in 1909, he was determined to forget, and if necessary disown, his school stories. Admittedly American editors would not want cricket or rugger, and they would choke over 'public school' meaning 'private school'. But Wodehouse in New York proposed to turn over a new leaf and write on it only for adults. A Rupert Smith comes into *The Prince and Betty* and Psmith himself is the hero of *Leave It to Psmith*. But other than Psmith, I think that no character from Wodehouse's eight school books appears in anything that was published in America at the time.

The first adult, Psmith is also the first man of means – a sufficiency of available cash – in Wodehouse. There was 'a tolerable supply of simoleons' and doubloons in the Psmith family old oak chest. Psmith's father, though eccentric, was County, landed and a man of capital. In the Sedleigh period, Psmith's money is immanent, but unimportant to the story. In *Psmith in the City* the Psmith simoleons are useful in softening the asperities of London clericalism, both for Psmith and for Mike. And in *Psmith Journalist*, Psmith's money is cardinal to the plot. In fact, Psmith returns to Cambridge after that book, the owner of a successful New York weekly paper, *Cosy Moments*. Then his father dies, the money disappears and Psmith goes into, and out of, his uncle's fish business. Hence the 'Leave it to Psmith! Psmith will help you. Psmith is Ready for Anything,' etc., advertisement on the front page of the *Morning Globe*. A member of four London clubs, and due to be a member of two more, Psmith is without means of support. He needs that secretary's job at Blandings when Baxter is driven forth.

But the job is, in fact, an afterthought. Psmith has been working for Freddie Threepwood at Blandings, not for personal profit, but to get, by a concatenation of events that would follow if he stole the necklace, the £3,000 that Mike Jackson needs to buy the farm in Lincolnshire. When that is accomplished, Psmith takes the job with Lord Emsworth.

Psmith is not afraid of poverty. But he is afraid of being bored. He prefers danger to being bored. And though this compulsion has produced heroes as innocuous as Ratty in *The Wind in the Willows* and as nocuous as Bulldog Drummond, it needs a little study in the Psmith and Wodehouse context.

Psmith might have developed into a Raffles after *Psmith Journalist*, with gun-play and detection providing breezy excitements. His exploits in *Leave It to Psmith* were mildly in the Raffles vein, and there was gun-play in the last chapters. But Wodehouse veered to farce and away from heroics, and the derring-do in his books veered away from revolver-shooting to pig-stealing and policeman's helmet-pinching. The Psmith-type Wodehouse hero does not have to duck the bullets again after the early 1920s. He does, however, seek to avoid boredom still, and (as Psmith did) he uses his tongue as a weapon in that cause. This is the essence of the 'buzzer' in Wodehouse. He buzzes in the hope that his talk will 'start something'. Buzzing cheers him up and makes him feel better himself. But there is always the possibility that it may also cause someone else to do something exciting that will relieve the monotony.

Although Wodehouse didn't coin the word till *Money in the Bank* in 1946, Psmith is the first integrated 'buzzer' in the books. He emits radiations of sound. What he says may or may not be true. It may have much meaning or none. But it may be reckoned to lift dull reality a notch or two into the air and, if it starts nothing more than a train of thought to play with, it has done a job. 'Comrade Jackson's name is a byword in our literary salons', 'Comrade Jackson is possibly the best known of our English cat-fanciers.' Both these claims are made by Psmith, in New York, in *Psmith Journalist*, to a prominent New York gangster. Neither is true. But this kind of typical buzzer's remark induces two kinds of danger, plays with two kinds of fire. There is the danger that the gangster will realize that Psmith is engaged in persiflage and take steps. And there is the danger that Mike, hearing himself thus described, will switch from surprise to giggles. In that case too the gangster may take steps. By inducing this kind of danger the buzzer staves off boredom from himself. Buzzing is a conversational excitement-inciter. It is a

Wodehouse proprietary patent medicine, and Psmith is its first consistent dispenser. He has many expert disciples in later books.

Wodehouse had been playing with the ingredients of buzzing in his first book, *The Pothunters*. Charteris is 'seldom silent'. Dallas describes his housemaster airily as 'a man of the vilest antecedents' (an echo of Conan Doyle). In later school stories you get Marriott and Jimmy Silver putting their feet up and simply persiflating. These, to change from the chemist's shop to the music-room, are Wodehouse's five-finger exercises which will break into the chords of Psmith, just as soon as that local habitation and name occur. Who is talking now?

> . . . there are stories about me which only my brother knows. Did I want them spread about the school? No, laddie, I did not. Hence, we see my brother, two terms ago, packing up his little box, and tooling off to Rugby. And here am I at Wrykyn, with an unstained reputation, loved by all who know me, revered by all who don't; courted by boys, fawned on by masters. People's faces brighten when I throw them a nod. If I frown . . .

That's Clowes, in the first half of *Mike*, three years, as the fictional calendar goes, before Psmith appears at all: a mere twenty chapters, as the pages of *Mike* turn. Psmithery is there, in the keys of Wodehouse's typewriter, waiting to come out. Wodehouse said he got the character of Psmith handed to him on a plate when a Wykehamist cousin told him about a schoolmate, Rupert, son of the Savoy Opera's D'Oyly Carte. He called his fellow Wykehamists 'Comrade', wore a monocle and was orotund of speech. In the orotundity of speech that Wodehouse gave Psmith I think one can hear, also, Sherlock Holmes, Baboo Jabberjee, Beetle imitating King, Stalky, Dick Swiveller, Mr Micawber and, perhaps, Raffles.

But just because Psmith has emerged, and is going to recur, why should the faithless Wodehouse not go on using some of his ingredients for pleasant characters in the books between? In 1915, midway between Psmith's appearance at Sedleigh and his reappearance, in 1923, in *Leave It to Psmith*, Ashe Marson, hero of *Something Fresh*, goes to Blandings, disguised as Mr Peters's valet, to steal a scarab, much as Psmith later, disguised as the Canadian poet, goes to Blandings to steal Lady Constance Keeble's necklace for her husband. And this is Ashe addressing his employer, the testy millionaire:

> 'I've come to read to you,' said Ashe.
> 'You fool, do you know that I have just managed to get to sleep?'

'And now you're awake again,' said Ashe soothingly. 'Such is life. A little rest, a little folding of the hands in sleep, and then, bing, off we go again.'

Here is Ashe again, describing to Joan Valentine, who is pretending to be a lady's maid, his success in the Servants' Hall:

'Let us look on the bright side . . . the commissariat department is a revelation to me. I had no idea that servants did themselves so well. As for the social side, I love it . . . Did you observe my manner towards the kitchen maid who waited on us at dinner last night? A touch of the old *noblesse* about it, I fancy? Dignified, but not unkind, I think? . . .'

And who's speaking now?

'The advice I give to every young man starting life is "Never confuse the unusual with the impossible!" Take the present case, for instance. If you had only realised the possibility of somebody some day busting you on the jaw when you tried to get into a cab, you might have thought out a dozen crafty schemes for dealing with the matter. As it is, you are unprepared. The thing comes on you as a surprise. The whisper flies around the clubs: "Poor old What's-his-name has been taken unawares. He cannot cope with the situation."'

No, that's George Bevan, who marries the lady named in *The Damsel in Distress* (1919). Bevan is a playwright, and supposed to be an American too. Perhaps he met Psmith in New York in the *Psmith Journalist* period and decided to model his own conversational style on Psmith's.

This business of 'starting something' is recurrent throughout Wodehouse, and in his later years he has made it the mainspring of one of his best girl characters. Bobbie Wickham periodically feels the urge to 'start something' just for the heck of it. Bobbie, a human ticking bomb, is, in that sense, the female of the species Psmith. In the post-school books the Wodehouse male ragger, whoever he may be, from Psmith to Lord Ickenham, has to have a good cause, such as helping a friend, as an excuse for anything more than verbal ragging. The female can start something for the purpose of doing down an enemy (Stiffy Byng *v.* the village policeman) or (Bobbie Wickham) merely through boredom. Lord Ickenham insists that all the best girls are apple-pie-bed-makers, preferably of bishops' beds. In fact, prime movers of misrule.

Psmith's buzzing, and the buzzing of all successors to Psmith in Wodehouse, is a one-man verbal rag. Psmith buzzes, not to call attention to himself: that happens, and must be tolerated. He buzzes in order to attract causes for amusement, to make amusement occur, so that he may be amused.

Psmith, in appearance and, very broadly, manner, is the Knut. The Knut was not a Wodehouse invention. He was a fashion-eddy of late Edwardianism, though his line goes back to the dandy and the fop of earlier centuries. Captain Good, R.N., in Rider Haggard's *King Solomon's Mines*, wore a gutta percha collar, a monocle, matching hat and jacket and impeccable other kit in the African bush, to the amusement of his companions and Rider Haggard's readers, but not to the lessening of his own dignity. *Punch* was making jokes about the Knut at the same time as Wodehouse was using him as part of Psmith.

The Knut was an amiable person. You could laugh at him kindly. He cultivated a 'blah' manner and vocabulary. Some of Psmith's vocabulary was from early Knut sources. 'Oojah-cum-spiff' and 'Rannygazoo', both Knut locutions, were used by Psmith first, and later by Bertie Wooster. In the Wodehouse play *Good Morning, Bill* of which the novel *Dr Sally* is virtually a transcript, Lord Tidmouth, a Knut, says goodbye in six different ways: 'Bung-ho', 'Teuf-teuf', 'Tinkerty-tonk', 'Toodle-oo', 'Poo-boop-a-doop' and 'Honk-honk'.

Knut language, like any other generic slang, substituted for the sake of substitution. It was the manner of the Knut to call a man a 'cove' or a 'stout sportsman'. In *The Lighter Side of School Life* Ian Hay, discussing Dean Farrar's *Eric*, says, 'No schoolboy ever called lighted candles "superfluous abundance of nocturnal illumination".' Psmith could have. Psmith, instead of 'tea' says 'a cup of the steaming'. Psmith, first in Wodehouse, plays variations on the already several-times-removed-from-reality imagist phrase 'in the soup'. Psmith refers to '*consommé* splashing about the ankles' and someone being 'knee-deep in the *bouillon*'. He always prefers the orotund to the curt. Instead of 'shoot a goal' he says 'push the bulb into the meshes beyond the uprights'. 'Archaeology will brook no divided allegiance from her devotees', and 'the dream of my youth and aspirations of my riper years' – these are pleasant enough suggestions of pulpit pomp. In the crowded school study they would certainly be given in a parody voice, adding a specific victim to the general parody. The headmaster or the padre would be the local wax figure for the group to stick their verbal pins into.

'Don't *talk* so much! I never met a fellow like you for talking!' complained Freddie Threepwood to Psmith in *Leave It to Psmith*. Mike Jackson in *Psmith Journalist* simply fell asleep to Psmith's conversation. It is stated of Psmith that 'conversation always acted on him as a mental stimulus', and he was the more attracted to Eve in the last book because she 'let him talk oftener and longer than any girl he had ever known'. The pleasant Psmith buzz, a rich mixture of glancing parodies, quotations, word-muddles and false concords, contained as ingredients three main, separable styles. Wodehouse soon thriftily and successfully isolated them for the individual use of others. The first he developed for the subsequent buzzers, the conscious maestros of racy conversation, invective and persiflage: Galahad and Uncle Fred, and all those chirpy young heroes of whom testy tycoons say in opening chapters that they are 'a darn sight too fresh'. These are clever men who talk that way because it amuses them.

A second ingredient of Psmith's talk has gone, in later books, to those unconscious humorists at the lower I.Q. level, of whom Bertie Wooster is the finest flower. Bertie jumbles his words, phrases and concords through innocence and stupidity; he stumbles on his images; he seems only just to be listening to what he himself is saying; and at occasional pinheaded moments he can stop to be intrigued by something he has just heard coming out of his own mouth, like a kitten intrigued by the flicking of its own tail. Such innocents are vulnerable and lovable. But they are burblers, not buzzers.

The third form in which the Psmith manner was bred out is the Jeeves style. In essence that style is the Ciceronian/Johnsonian. It is the parliamentary or Civil Service style, level, pompous, circumlocutory, didactic. It is the language of leaders, school sermons, toastmasters and treaties. It is funny when used out of place – as by Mr Micawber – and consistently by such as would seem to have no need of it: butlers and gentlemen's gentlemen.

In Psmith this super-fatted style becomes dominant only when he talks to people who would be most dazed by it. In *Psmith Journalist* he is in New York, with a six-inch bullet-hole in his hat after a skirmish with gangsters, and he addresses three cops with a battery of yard-long sentences, polysyllables and subjunctives:

'I am loath to interrupt this very impressive brain-barbecue, but, trivial as it may seem to you, to me there is a certain interest in this other matter of my ruined hat. I know that it may strike you as hypersensitive of us to protest . . .'

Apart from the blah Knut manner, the two strongest influences in the rhythms and locutions of the Psmith language are, first, Conan Doyle's

Sherlock Holmes stories, and, second, 'babu'. Wodehouse recalled to Townend (in *Performing Flea*) the excitement of waiting for new issues of the *Strand Magazine* on Dulwich Station. Schoolboys and paulo-post-schoolboys of Wodehouse's own vintage, and of Psmith's a decade later, were not only steeped in the Sherlock Holmes stories, but they knew that they could recognizably bandy the language of them with anyone else of their age and class. Stalky and his friends dropped into Brer Rabbit language almost as a code. Wodehouse's first major conversational parodist, Psmith, is constantly echoing Sherlock Holmes (indeed, the Conan Doyle *Valley of Fear* influence probably to some extent suggested the plot of *Psmith Journalist*). Psmith has verbal 'lifts' from Sherlock Holmes, with direct quotations of words, and copying of manner. 'You had best put the case in my hands . . . I will think over the matter.' 'Do not disturb me. These are deep waters.' '. . . Omitting no detail, however slight' – these are the parts of the iceberg that appear above the water.

'It is possible that Comrade Windsor may possess the qualifications necessary for the post. But here he comes. Let us forgather with him, and observe him in private life before arriving at any premature decision.'

There, only 'But here he comes' is a direct lift from Holmes. But we could not be sure of that unless the surrounding rhythms were making us us alert for identifications of exact phrases.

The element of Psmith's language that was hived off later for the use of the burblers such as Bertie Wooster is babu-English, and I'd like to take a few minutes here to have a look at F. Anstey's 1897 book, compiled from pieces in *Punch* in 1896, called *Baboo Jabberjee*. (I shall spell it 'babu' from now on.) Wodehouse read all Anstey's stuff as a boy, including, as is obvious from his school stories, *Vice Versa*. But *Baboo Jabberjee* (which is quoted by name in *Love among the Chickens*) was powerfully seminal to Psmith and the quintessential Wodehouse style of false concords.

Anstey's Hurry Bungsho Jabberjee, B.A., is a Bombay law-student in England. He uses the appellation 'Hon'ble' more or less as we say 'Mister' and the *Uncle Remus* characters say 'Brer'. Psmith's appellation 'Comrade' chimes well with Jabberjee. Jabberjee has learnt his English from books. He uses absurdly inflated phrases, and he makes unintentional false concords. He writes, for instance:

'The late respectable Dr Ben Johnson, gifted author of Boswell's Biography, once rather humorously remarked, on witnessing a nautch performed by canine quadrupeds, that, although their choreographical abilities were of but a moderate nature, the wonderment was that they should be capable at all to execute such a hind-legged feat and *tour de force*.'

Some of Jabberjee's false concords are repeated verbatim by Bertie Wooster. Some of his inflated phraseology goes into Jeeves's vocabulary. Isn't that last quotation, apart from its howlers, rather reminiscent of Jeeves when he muffles the furious Pop Stoker with a chloroform mask of verbiage in *Right Ho, Jeeves*? Jabberjee writes: 'As poet Burns remarks with great truthfulness, "Rank is but a penny stamp, and a Man is a man and all that."' This is a pleasant skid on the banana skin of education. Bertie and Jeeves, you remember, get tangled up in this same quotation at a moment of great crisis.

Rem acu tetigisti, non possumus, surgit amari aliquid, ultra vires, mens sana in corpore sano, amende honorable – these are gobbets of education that Jabberjee uses and Jeeves takes over. And (this is sad) we find that it was Jabberjee, and not Bertie, who first made that excellent Shakespeare emendation, only conceivable through the ears, only translatable through the eyes. Jabberjee writes: 'Jessamina inherits, in Hamlet's immortal phraseology, "an eye like Ma's to threaten and command".' There are other trace elements of Jabberjee in the wider Wodehouse. Jabberjee, describing an evening of professional boxing matches in a London hall, mentions the NO SMOKING notice, and says that everybody goes on smoking just the same. This point is made by Corky when describing an East End boxing evening in an Ukridge story. Jabberjee's 'I became once more *sotto voce* and the silent tomb' is a phrase Bertie evokes once or twice, if perhaps with faint quotation marks in his voice. Jabberjee's mystification at Stratford, on finding that all the portraits of Hon'ble Shakespeare are unalike, and that none bears any resemblance to the bust, is a point which Wodehouse sharpens in an essay. Jabberjee who, like Bertie Wooster *passim*, is plagued by being engaged to a girl he wishes he were not engaged to, speaks of a 'manly, straightforward stratagem' for oiling out of the commitment. Wodehouse gets variations on this happy phrase into the mouths of Ukridge, Bingo Little, Tuppy Glossop and Bertie on separate occasions. Jabberjee, like Dick Swiveller, sucks the knob of his cane. So does Bertie. So does Freddie Threepwood. So does Motty, Lord Pershore, in the early Jeeves story.

Jabberjee introduces himself to 'Hon'ble Punch' as 'one saturated to the skin of his teeth in best English masterpieces of immaculate and moderately good prose extracts and dramatic passages'. Take your line through Ram, an actual babu schoolboy who appeared in *The Luck Stone*, into Psmith the buzzer, Bertie the burbler and Jeeves the orotund, and you may feel inclined, as I do, to pay a passing tribute to F. Anstey for planting a seed in the rich soil of young Wodehouse's burgeoning mind. Or, if you prefer the image, for putting a piece of grit into the Wodehouse oyster shell, so that Wodehouse built it into a pearl, richer than all his tribe of humorous writers.

Psmith has a large vocabulary and wide range of imagery. Many of his quotations, verbal images and conceits pass into the Wodehouse language, free for all later pleasant characters to use: restoring the tissues; *solvitur ambulando*; making us more spiritual; of all sad words of tongue or pen; Patience on a monument; couldn't find a bass drum in a telephone booth; this tendency . . . fight against it; it would be paltering with the truth; not so but far otherwise; I have my spies everywhere; the man who discovered that alcohol was a food long before the doctors did.

Psmith is the first runner in the Wodehouse Non-Stop Quotation Stakes: the recitation, printed as prose, of gobbets from the better-known poets. At one moment he feels like some watcher of the skies, and keeps the feeling going accurately for three and a half lines of Keats. This stands as the record distance, until he beats it himself with four lines of uninterrupted Omar. Wodehouse appropriated this trick, I suspect, consciously or unconsciously, from Dick Swiveller in *The Old Curiosity Shop*:

'An excellent woman, that mother of yours, Christopher,' said Mr Swiveller. 'Who ran to catch me when I fell, and kissed the place to make it well? My mother. A charming woman . . .'

This is one of Psmith's own quotations, and Jeeves's and Bertie's. And that typographical manner of quoting poetry as prose became a pleasant habit of Wodehouse's. (Mr Cornelius of Valley Fields holds the record with sixteen lines of Scott.)

Psmith had been 'resting' for eight years after *Psmith Journalist*. In those eight years Wodehouse had written the first of the Blandings saga, the book and the play of *Piccadilly Jim*, *Jill the Reckless*, his first book of golf stories and two books of Jeeves. For a Wodehouse who had turned so many corners and advanced so far as a writer, it must have been a little difficult to keep the revived Psmith exactly in register with his previous self. Wodehouse said that he had had trouble with the last half of *Leave It to Psmith* and, indeed, had to rewrite it after it had appeared serialized in the *Saturday Evening Post*. It is not the most successful Psmith book or the most successful Blandings book. Its main interest to us in these days is for its attempt, even if not too happy, to develop Psmith as a Raffles and at the same time make him fall in love.

Wodehouse wrote that he had dropped Psmith as a character because he couldn't think of anything new for him to do. We readers may feel that Psmith had earned his retirement and his reward. He was going to marry Eve, 'straight and slim', with 'a cheerful smile', 'boyish suppleness of body', 'valiant gaiety' and 'a golden sunniness'. Few of Wodehouse's young clubmen survive marriage. Bingo Little, yes. Freddie Threepwood, yes. Oofy Prosser, marginally, yes. Marriage is generally the happy ending, 'ending' being the operative word. Psmith had been a splendid find as a schoolboy, good as a wage-slave in the bank, less good as a crusading journalist in America or a Raffles at Blandings. But he opened the door on to some excellent buzzers in subsequent books and certainly helped to produce the excellent middle-aged 'Uncle Fred' Lord Ickenham.

5 ~ UKRIDGE

———————— ~ ————————

Love among the Chickens (1906 and, somewhat rewritten, 1921), ten short stories in *Ukridge* (1924), three short stories in *Lord Emsworth and Others* (1937), three short stories in *Eggs, Beans, and Crumpets* (1940), one short story in *Nothing Serious* (1950), one short story in *A Few Quick Ones* (1959), one short story in *Plum Pie* (1966).

Ukridge spans sixty publishing years, starts as a married man, and then goes backwards in time into previous bachelorhood. He is a handier property when he can be single-mindedly selfish, and when the reader's relish of his knavery is not edged with pity for his wife, the adoring little Millie.

The Times wrote the following of Tony Hancock in 1958:

Mr Hancock is a comedian governed by the basic humours of vanity and greed. The odds are heavily weighted against his satisfying either, but all disasters are effaced from his memory by invincible egoism. Action springs either from his delusions of orientally voluptuous grandeur or from his taste for ludicrously elaborate conspiracy. There is constant alternation between fantasy and realism.

Defeat, indignity, physical cowardice, and moral turpitude are constantly recurring, but they are saved from embarrassment by the aggressiveness of the comedy. Mr Hancock is not a clown to be trampled on: he is a belligerent grotesque who engulfs all surrounding characters, who never descends to pathos, and who speaks an idiom all his own that is a compound of vehement slang, satirised cliché, and extreme literacy.

It would be a fairly faithful description of Ukridge.

His friend Bill Townend gave Wodehouse, in a letter, the background material – the desperate chicken-farm and its bellowing owner – for *Love among the Chickens* in 1906. Townend knew the real chicken-farmer, who had been a master at a prep school where Townend had boarded after leaving Dulwich. Wodehouse never met Ukridge's real-life prototype, then or later, and he built up Ukridge's character from several other sources – one school friend in particular, Herbert Westbrook, a clothes-borrower, whom he mentions in *Over Seventy*. My guess is that yet another model was James Cullingworth, the amiable villain in Conan Doyle's *Stark Monro Letters*. Cullingworth has a little, timid wife, Hetty, who adores him, and whom Monro (largely Conan Doyle) feels he wants to pick up and kiss. Hetty is not unlike Ukridge's Millie, who has something of the same effect on James Corcoran (largely Wodehouse). Cullingworth calls Monro 'laddie'. Cullingworth is always, he thinks, on the edge of riches, and always, in fact, on the edge of bankruptcy, with duns and county court summonses threatening. Monro's last words on Cullingworth, who was finally planning to make a vast fortune as an eye-surgeon in South America, were:

'He is a man whom nothing could hold down. I wish him luck, and have a kindly feeling towards him, and yet I distrust him from the bottom of my heart, and shall be pleased to know that the Atlantic rolls between us.'

Ukridge appeared in print before Mike Jackson. *Love among the Chickens* in its first version was on the bookstalls three years before the book *Mike*. In fact, although *The White Feather* came out as a serial in the *Captain* in 1905 (the £60 cheque for it went into Wodehouse's bank in October that year), *Love among the Chickens* appeared before the book of *The White Feather*. *Love among the Chickens* came out as a book, without advance serialization, in August 1906, and had grossed £31 5s. 8d. in royalties for its author by January of next year. *The White Feather* was on the bookstalls in October 1907 (advance royalties £17 10s.). The book *Mike* didn't appear till 1909.

It is as well to be a bit bibliographical about this, to establish that Wodehouse wrote a novel about adults and love before he had written his last school book. Put it the other way round: *Mike*, which is his longest and best school novel, was a return to schooldays, written by Wodehouse the novelist. It is as well, also, that, continuing to be bibliographically technical, we should compare the 1906 version of *Love among the Chickens* with its 1921 successor.

In the dedication at the beginning of the 1921 version, Wodehouse says:

. . . I have practically rewritten the book. There was some pretty bad work in it, and it had 'dated'. As an instance of the way in which the march of modern civilisation had left the 1906 edition behind, I may mention that, on page twenty-one, I was able to make Ukridge speak of selling eggs at five for sixpence.

There wasn't really much original bad work, or much rewriting; only some tidying. And Ukridge himself comes through from 1906 and 1921 with hardly a word altered. He is not the main character in the book, anyway. It is Jeremy Garnet's love among Ukridge's chickens. In the Blampied drawing on the dust jacket of the second *Love among the Chickens*, it is Jeremy Garnet in plus-fours chasing the fowls. Of the four charming black-and-white illustrations by H. M. Brock in the 1906 book, only one showed Ukridge. He was leaning on a gate, between his wife and Garnet, looking at chickens. Ukridge is a much bigger person there than Garnet. But in that book and in those days Ukridge was not specifically a clothes-borrower. In the later stories, when Garnet ('Garny, old horse!') became changed to Corcoran ('Corky, old horse!'), Ukridge and his narrator were about the same size sartorially – which Ukridge made the most of, and Corky regretted.

The revised version of *Love among the Chickens* gave Ukridge more prominence only by playing down Garnet. The epilogue of the 1906 book showed the wedding of Garnet and his Phyllis in playlet form. Ukridge was best man, but Garnet and Phyllis were the couple in the fade-out. Wodehouse cut this epilogue out of the 1921 version. The new fade-out shows Ukridge and his Millie doing a moonlight flit from Combe Regis, their debts unpaid, their chickens a flop and Ukridge already thinking big about his next venture, a duck-farm. This gives Ukridge the fat at the end, though it leaves the story of Jeremy and Phyllis a little undecided.

In 1906 the first five chapters were in third-person-singular narrative. After that Jeremy Garnet took over in the first person. In the 1921 *Love among the Chickens* Jeremy Garnet tells the whole story, starting at Chapter I. All the chapter titles, and the order of the chapters, are the same in both versions. Wodehouse changed the price of eggs to suit the march of modern civilization. And Combe Regis was itself a change from the earlier, franker Lyme Regis. In 1906 the flower was the lubin, and in 1921 the lupin. Mr John Redmond became Sir Edward Carson, and the sentence 'If Maxim Gorky were invited to lunch with the Czar . . .' became 'if Maxim Gorky were invited to lunch with Trotsky . . .' Those that say that Wodehouse always lived in a timeless and fantastic world, hampered only by the price of eggs, should take note how stern reality, and the passing of fifteen years of history, affected this story.

But in style we can catch the maturer Wodehouse putting some recognizable new spin on the old ball. In 1906 Chapter VII ended:

'Charawk,' said the hen satirically from her basket.

In 1921 this read:

'Charawk!' chuckled Aunt Elizabeth from her basket, in the beastly, cynical, satirical way which has made her so disliked by all right-thinking people.

The name 'Aunt Elizabeth' had been given to this unpleasant hen by Ukridge, 'on the strength of an alleged similarity of profile to his wife's nearest relative'. Somewhere between 1906 and 1921 Wodehouse had discovered the comedy value of aunts. On the other hand he was still, in 1921, attracted by sixth-form words. In *Jill the Reckless*, published that year, he used 'vagrom' and 'equivoque', and he did not disturb the 1906 use, in *Love among the Chickens*, of the word 'logomachy' when it came to revising for 1921. These three words would never have appeared in the books of Wodehouse's long summer maturity except perhaps in the mouth of Jeeves.

Having used Ukridge as a supporting character the first time, Wodehouse found that he was full of 'capabilities'. He gave him star treatment, put his name in lights (the literary equivalent being the titles of the short stories in which he appeared), and built a company round him.

The Ukridge of the later stories was an Old Wrykynian, and Corky, Tupper and Looney Coote had all been at school with him. He had been sacked from Wrykyn. He broke bounds and rules one night to go to a Fair. He disguised himself in false beard and whiskers, but left his school cap on top of the whole mess and was easily apprehended. But it is the old-school fellowship that makes Ukridge's limpet–rock, predator–prey relationship with Corky and Tuppy understandable and acceptable; and Corky is able to describe his old school friend with the ruthlessness that (outside a family) only an old school friendship really warrants. Shared incarceration at a boarding school produces some embarrassing and incompatible acquaintanceships; but, whatever the candour they encourage in the exchange of personalities, they trail inescapable loyalties. None saw this more clearly than Wodehouse, and no author has used and exaggerated the fact more deliberately, joyously and successfully than Wodehouse. But, whereas Bertie Wooster and his Aubrey-Upjohn's-and-Eton friends play the Old School Loyalty gambit for farce (albeit as a convenient hinge in the plot), Wrykyn is a shade more serious. Mike

Jackson, Sam Shotter, Ukridge, Tuppy, Looney and Corky are a little closer to Wodehouse's heart and further from his funny-bone. Subliminally, Wrykyn is Wodehouse's own school, Dulwich. When he puts Ukridge at Wrykyn, Ukridge is part of the inner family, and in the long run he will be rescued from his worst idiocies. This gives the reader a rewarding sense of security. He feels able to laugh the louder when Ukridge falls, because he knows Ukridge must be put on his feet again and all will be well, not only with Ukridge (temporarily maybe) but with his own old school conscience. So one's hope for a financially set-fair fade-out for Ukridge is valid. A pity Wodehouse never got round to it.

Ukridge is a thief, a blackmailer, a liar and a sponge. He alternates self-glorification with self-pity, and sometimes has a bout of both in the same paragraph. He is as full of precepts as a preacher in the pulpit and, like a preacher, he swoops from the particular to the general, scattering moral judgements. Ukridge himself is a total immoralist, and he dulls the moral sense in others. He is totally selfish. The most that can be said in his favour is that he has knocked round the world on tramp steamers from Naples to San Francisco, he is good with dogs, Bowles admires him and fawns on him, he is not a snob, and girls sometimes, and for short stretches, like him.

Corky at one point calls Ukridge the 'sternest of bachelors', but his success with girls is curiously believable. Certainly after the first mendacious build-up, the girls tend to get caught and crushed, with Ukridge, in the machinery of truth and justice. But Ukridge never lets a girl down as he lets Corky and Tuppy and his other male friends down – at the drop, Tuppy might complain, of a top-hat. Ukridge never fascinates in order to speculate. When he gets engaged to Myrtle Bayliss, daughter of the Sussex jute-king, it is through love and not for her money. When he tries to beat the Bart to the favours of Mabel of Onslow Square, it is for love and not for money or security. Even when he finds himself talked, by her family, into an engagement with Mabel of Clapham Common, he cannot just walk out of the embarrassing involvement, as any strong-minded, sensible rogue would. He is hobbled by the Code. To quote *Jill the Reckless* again: when Sir Derek Underhill breaks his engagement to Jill, Wally Mason, the Anglo-American hero, says to Freddie Rooke:

'I can't understand you, Freddie. If ever there was a fellow that might have been expected to take the only possible view of Underhill's behaviour in this business, I should have said it was you. You're a public-school man. You've mixed all the time with decent people . . . Yet it seems to have made absolutely no difference in your opinion of this man Underhill that he behaved like an utter cad . . .'

This suggests that Ukridge's attempts to save Mabel Price's fat face, and to get their engagement broken *by her*, may be a last enchantment, a last fleck of a cloud of glory, that Ukridge trails from Wrykyn days.

It is a great tribute to Corky/Wodehouse that he can make such an anti-social menace as Ukridge appealing. There is not a word of sentimentality in the Ukridge stories, but they have a positive charm. They are, in technique of construction and writing, Wodehouse short stories at their springtime best. They are vintage stuff. They are extremely funny and yet you feel that Corky, the narrator, is not a humorist. He is a dry commentator, incisive and objective. It is his subject, Ukridge, and Ukridge's story, that make the laughs. You are scarcely conscious that Ukridge is being brilliantly presented and his story brilliantly told; you are so taken with the man in front of the floodlights that you forget the man behind them.

But keep half an eye on Corky. He is really a very interesting background character. He is modest and amusing about his go-anywhere-write-anything trade of Pleasing Editors, but perfectly sure that this is the work he wants to be in. He is fallible and flatterable (he goes and helps Ukridge and Boko at their electioneering largely because he wants to hear the crowds singing the noble election jingle which he has composed for Boko; he falls completely for Ukridge's Millie and her 'Stanley has been telling me what friends you and he are. He is devoted to you'). But he is able to get tough when annoyed. His description of the Pen and Ink Club dance in 'Ukridge Sees Her Through' has, below its alert descriptions of sounds, smells, gilt chairs and potted palms, a cold anger. Here for the first time Wodehouse rolls his sleeves up against the Phonies of the Pen. Charlton Prout, the sleek, stout secretary of the club, whose main relish is pushing his own books and excluding from membership authors who lack 'vision', gets Corky's dagger between the ribs. He gets Miss Julia Ukridge's own wrath later, as a blunt instrument on the side of the head. Corky, having stage-managed Miss Ukridge's attack on Prout, tiptoes away, his heart bleeding delightfully.

Ukridge is to some extent a walking parody of careers-thinking by the young, careers-talk *to* the young by headmasters, uncles and self-made business tycoons interviewed by the magazines, and careers-fantasies encouraged by the fiction in the other pages of the same magazines. 'Vision, and the big, broad, flexible outlook' comes from headmasters, uncles and tycoons in print. The rich uncle from Australia, the rich aunt in Wimbledon, the lonely millionaire who needs a secretary, the bright business idea that leads to fortune – these are from the fiction pages. The only young man with a steady profession in the Ukridge stories – George Tupper of the Foreign Office – is treated as a bit of a bore. He had written sentimental poetry in the school magazine, and was always starting subscription lists and getting up memorials and presentations. He had 'an earnest, pulpy heart'. Ukridge could get fivers out of him with a sure touch.

Orwell, in his Essay on Wodehouse, has pointed out that the first object of the Wodehouse hero is to find a soft spot for sitting pretty on financially; anything that brings the security of three meals a day is good enough for him. Ukridge seeks quick opulence, to finance eternal leisure for himself. His friends certainly hope he will find it, so that he will keep his hands out of their pockets. Even George Tupper thinks he has found an answer when he suggests him as secretary to his friend Bulstrode. It never seems to occur to anybody that Ukridge might become a common-or-garden daily-breader. Did nobody get at him when he was sacked from Wrykyn and try to put him in a bank? Did Aunt Julia's inheritance loom always, preventing him from learning a trade because he saw the promise of getting her money in the end? If so, why was he so keen, while waiting for her money, to make a fortune for himself?

There are still people who say, sometimes in print, that Wodehouse wrote only about the rich and was, by inference, a snob. It is an absurd criticism, and the answer to it is either short and rude or long and boring. One of the pleasantest things about Ukridge is his complete un-class-consciousness. He is genuinely happy in the company of 'Battling' Billson and the boxing fraternity. He is genuinely knowledgeable about the barmaids in Kennington:

> It appears that Billson has fallen in love with one of the barmaids at the Crown in Kennington. 'Not,' said Ukridge, so that all misapprehension should be avoided, 'the one with the squint. The other one. Flossie. The girl with yellow hair.'

Ukridge can go into criminal partnership with all the servants in his aunt's house while she's away and treat them as equals. Yet he enjoys from Bowles, the ex-butler, fawning treatment that, by the rules of his guild, a butler only gives to one of the true gentry. Bowles doesn't treat Corky like that. He wouldn't treat Tupper like that. But Ukridge might be the fourth son of an earl as far as Bowles is concerned.

~ 'She had wanted to borrow my aunt's brooch,' said Ukridge, 'but I was firm and wouldn't let her have it – partly on principle and partly because I had pawned it the day before.'

~ Unlike the male codfish, which, suddenly finding itself the parent of three million five hundred thousand little codfish, cheerfully resolves to love them all, the British aristocracy is apt to look with a somewhat jaundiced eye on its younger sons.

~ The aunt made a hobby of collecting dry seaweed, which she pressed and pasted in an album. One sometimes thinks that aunts live entirely for pleasure.

~ Like so many vicars, he had a poor opinion of curates.

~ 'Mother's idea of a mate for me has always been a well-to-do millionaire or a Duke with a large private income.'

~ 'Can you dance?' said the girl.
   Lancelot gave a short, amused laugh. He was a man who never let his left hip know what his right hip was doing.

~ 'You're too young to marry,' said Mr McKinnon, a stout bachelor.
   'So was Methuselah,' said James, a stouter.

~ Jeeves doesn't exactly smile on these occasions, because he never does, but the lips twitch slightly at the corners and the eye is benevolent.

Love among the Chickens is not the rounded Ukridge or the rounded Wodehouse. The short stories are the thing. There is some beautiful translation of ideas into words in the 1924 collection *Ukridge*. Corky, thrown on to his ear from the pub in the Ratcliff Highway of the East End, is picked up by Billson and, in the process, 'gets a sort of general impression of bigness and blue serge'. And the barman, later ejected by the avenging Billson, 'did a sort of backward foxtrot across the pavement'. Corky, stranded with Flossie the barmaid's ghastly mother with the terrible hat, suggests that they go to Westminster Abbey: 'I had a fleeting notion, which a moment's reflection exploded before it could bring me much comfort, that women removed their hats in Westminster Abbey.' Corky's reaction to the caricature of Boko Lawlor, put up by his enemies in the Redbridge election, is: 'You could see at a glance that here was one who, if elected, would do his underhand best to cut down the Navy, tax the poor man's food, and strike a series of blows at the very root of the home . . .' Boko himself, towards the end of the electioneering, is speaking 'with a husky confidence' in his success. Finally, in that same story, there is Corky's description of the smell coming up on to the platform at the monster meeting at the Associated Mechanics' Hall – 'a mixed scent of dust, clothes, orange-peel, chalk, wood, plaster, pomade and Associated Mechanics'.

In the seven Ukridge short stories that have appeared since *Ukridge*, Corky only narrates one in its entirety. That's 'Buttercup Day'. For the other six, after a page or two of introduction by Corky in the manner of the Oldest Member or Mr Mulliner, Ukridge takes over in double quotes. Ukridge's language and manner of narration are racy and wonderful, but the note of farce is more strongly stressed than in the earlier stories where Corky is the 'I' character. Ukridge has an ebullient style, of forceful parody, injured self-pity, strongly emotional prejudices and cool justification of egregious immorality. Ukridge, that 'human blot'; that 'foe of the human race'; that 'hell-hound'; that giver of false names 'as an ordinary business precaution'; that man with one pair of trousers who spent the night in jail on a plank bed and was – an indignity even for him – forcibly washed by the authorities; that visionary; that manic-depressive; that moralizing immoralist ('. . . I don't know, Corky, if you have ever done the fine dignified thing, refusing to accept money because it was tainted and there wasn't enough of it, but I have always noticed on these occasions . . .') – Ukridge is one of the great Wodehouse creations.

6 ~ LORD EMSWORTH AND BLANDINGS

———————— ~ ————————

Something Fresh (1915), *A Damsel in Distress* (1919), so nearly a Blandings novel that it should be read in the Blandings sequence, *Leave It to Psmith* (1923), *Summer Lightning* (1929), *Heavy Weather* (1933), *Uncle Fred in the Springtime* (1939), *Full Moon* (1947), *Pigs Have Wings* (1952), *Service with a Smile* (1962), *Galahad at Blandings* (1965) and *A Pelican at Blandings* (1969). Those are the novels. Six short stories set at Blandings occur in *Blandings Castle* (1935), one in *Lord Emsworth and Others* (1937), one in *Nothing Serious* (1950) and one in *Plum Pie* (1966).

The long entry on Homer in my edition of the *Encyclopaedia Britannica* is by the late Professor Gilbert Murray. In 1957 Murray said: 'When I became ninety, many telegrams came to congratulate or perhaps condole with me. The first was from the Prime Minister of Australia. The second from the Prime Minister of England. The third from P. G. Wodehouse. I have a great admiration for Wodehouse and the sequence gratified me.'
    Murray did not bring any references to Wodehouse into his encyclo-paedia article on Homer, but I have heard Oxford dons elaborate a theory that, quite apart from Murray's admiration for both, there is a mystical communion between the two authors so widely separated by the cen-turies. These Senior Common Room scholiasts (the *Oxford English Dictionary* defines a scholiast as an ancient commentator upon a classical writer, so I have the *mot juste*) say that Homer and Wodehouse write, with deliberate artistic purpose, about comparable societies, lordly or near-lordly, past, almost timeless, and yet in certain respects engagingly anachronistic; that each author writes a private language, rich in imagery, allusions, repetitions, formulaic expressions and suppressed quotations; that if the sub-title of *The Iliad* was *The Wrath of Achilles*, the sub-title of any *Omnibus* of Bertie Wooster's writings could well be *The Wrath of Aunt Agatha*. And so on.

Personally I would add to the dons' spot passages a quotation from T. E. (Lawrence of Arabia) Shaw's introduction to his translation of *The Odyssey*. Shaw was writing of the sort of man he deduced, from internal evidence, the author to have been. The italics are mine. The parallels are remarkable:

. . . a bookworm, no longer young, living from home, a mainlander, city-bred, domestic . . . a dog-lover . . . fond of poetry, a great, if uncritical, reader . . . with limited sensuous range, but an exact eyesight which gave him all his pictures . . . tender charity of heart and head for serving-men . . . the associate of menials, making himself their friend and defender by understanding . . . loved the rural scene. No farmer, he has learnt the points of a good olive tree [*for Wodehouse read 'pig' or 'pumpkin' for 'olive tree'*] . . . He has sailed upon and watched the sea . . . seafaring not being his trade [*Wodehouse had been destined for the Navy as a boy*]. Neither land-lubber nor stay-at-home nor ninny . . . He makes a hotch-potch of periods . . . pages steeped in a queer naïvety . . . sprinkled tags of epic across his pages . . . very bookish, this house-bred man . . . verbal felicity . . . recurring epithets . . . the tale was the thing . . .

It is at Blandings Castle that Wodehouse seems to offer his Homeric parallels most noticeably.

In shape and size and messuages, Wodehouse told me, his Blandings Castle owes a good deal to his boyhood memory of Corsham, the stately home of the Methuens near Bath. The young Pelham, spending school holidays with a clergyman uncle near by, was taken to Corsham to skate on the lake, and the image of the great house remained on the retina of his inward eye. And when, in his early thirties, a resident alien in New York, writing away for dear life and for any American editor who would buy anything, Wodehouse decided to try farce about the English aristocracy, he called his stately home Blandings, his châtelain Lord Emsworth and his story *Something New* (*Something Fresh* in England, 1915).

Emsworth is, in fact, a town on the border of Sussex and Hampshire, in a district rich in place-names that have acquired glory in song or legend. Hilaire Belloc's Ha'naker and Duncton Hill are near by, and Wodehouse has taken from the villages of Bosham and Warblington names for Lord Emsworth's heir (Lord Bosham) and one of his many sisters (Lady Ann Warblington). Blandings Castle in fiction is in Shropshire. Obviously Belpher Castle in Hampshire, the setting for *A Damsel in Distress* (1919), is, in the literary fourth dimension, somewhere on the Emsworth–Corsham–Blandings road. To all intents and purposes *A Damsel in Distress* is a Blandings novel. Lord Marshmoreton in it is an echo of Lord Emsworth, Lord Belpher of Lord Bosham, Lady Caroline Byng of Lady Constance Keeble, Reggie Byng of Freddie Threepwood, Keggs the butler of Beach the butler, and Macpherson the gardener of McAllister the gardener. In fact, Lord Marshmoreton's family name appears to be Bosham. His second son, Freddie Bosham, marries a Phyllis Jackson of 'the Jackson jam-making family'. In the second Blandings novel, *Leave It to Psmith*, you have Mike Jackson married to Phyllis, stepdaughter of Joe. Lines crossed here, I think.

When an author in a hurry digs down for some names for characters, he will occasionally draw a duplicate. Wodehouse would get his types together before he knew their names, and churn them up into a plot before he knew where the events would happen. He drew his names out of a hat, but in the case of *A Damsel in Distress* forgot that some of these were old ones that had got put back after the last draw. He had not, at the stage of *A Damsel in Distress*, seen saga possibilities in the Blandings set-up of *Something Fresh*. All he knew was that he was happy and at home in an English castle, with a widower earl in the garden, his tough sister as châtelaine, his fat butler in the pantry sipping port, and assorted secretaries, chorus girls and impostors making a plot.

When Blandings assumed saga proportions, the Castle became simply a roof under which any member of the Emsworth family could stay and invite friends to stay, where errant sons and nieces were incarcerated (the incarcerated sometimes referred to Blandings as a Bastille, sometimes as a Devil's Island) to make them cool off from love affairs, where detectives were summoned to watch pigs or jewels, brain-specialists were summoned to watch defective dukes, and librarians, valets and secretaries were hired and fired. Blandings is a place where things happen, with lots of time on everybody's hands for things to happen in, lots of bedrooms to put up unlimited *dramatis personae*, lots of corridors, shrubberies, terraces, gardens, pig-sties, water-meadows and parkland for exits and entrances; and the hamlet of Market Blandings two or three miles away, with plenty of pubs and inns (The Emsworth Arms, The Wheatsheaf, The Waggoners' Rest, The Beetle and Wedge, The Stitch in Time, The Blue Cow, The Blue Boar, The Blue Dragon and The Jolly Cricketers) from which outlying plotters can plan their approaches to the Castle stage.

Rather too close is the village of Much Matchingham, home of the dreaded Sir Gregory Parsloe-Parsloe, so often unworthily suspected by Lord Emsworth and his brother Galahad of trying to do harm to Blandings pig or pumpkin that, in the printed synopsis at the beginning of *Pigs Have Wings*, Herbert Jenkins said '. . . on previous occasions the unscrupulous baronet has made determined attempts to nobble Lord Emsworth's favourite pig'. Not true. Sir Gregory was always innocent of the strategies which the Blandings brothers imputed to him, and Herbert Jenkins ought to have remembered it. Poor Sir Gregory. His only sins (other than overeating) were that, in his hot pre-title youth, he had, or Galahad thought he had, nobbled Galahad's dog Towser before a rat-killing contest and, as a bloated baronet, he had taken on as his pig-man, at higher wages, George Cyril Wellbeloved, who had been guardian, chef and caterer to Lord Emsworth's balloon-shaped Black Berkshire sow, the bemedalled Empress of Blandings.

Galahad Threepwood has spoken frankly and sharply to Sir Gregory of his past known, and present suspected, skulduggeries. Lord Emsworth has his revenge on his fellow J.P., who has decoyed away, with extra money, his gifted pig-man Wellbeloved. The living of Much Matchingham is in Lord Emsworth's gift, and it was with cunning pleasure that Lord Emsworth gave the Rev. 'Beefy' Bingham the vicarage there, trusting that this ham-handed man of God would be as sharp a thorn in Sir Gregory's flesh as he had been in Lord Emsworth's when he had been infesting the Castle and courting Lord Emsworth's niece, Gertrude.

Lord Emsworth, euphoric, amiable, but bone-headed ninth Earl, has changed little in the sixty publishing years between *Something Fresh* and the last unfinished novel. He no longer seems to collect things and his Museum, much in evidence in the first book, is no longer a show-room of the Castle. He is no longer a patron of Christie's in London. His younger son, Freddie, formerly a pain in the neck to his father, no longer gets into debt or writes poetry to chorus girls. Marriage to the daughter of an American millionaire (Aggie, *née* Donaldson, was, incidentally, a relative of the Blandings head gardener, McAllister) has made a man of Freddie. In *Full Moon* (1947) Freddie shows his new-found manhood by turning and rending a roomful of tough aunts, uncles and millionaires who are trying to treat him like the worm he had been. It is a great defiance. Freddie is a hard-working and keen Vice-President of his father-in-law's dog-biscuit business now. In fact, Lord Emsworth, who had long despised his son as a drone and a wastrel, in a late short story ('Birth of a Salesman') was nettled to find his son was now despising *him* for much the same reasons. Lord Emsworth was able to take steps and show himself a salesman and go-getter in America and on American lines.

Lady Constance Keeble is now Lady Constance Schoonmaker. She is

Lord Emsworth's younger brother, GALAHAD,
once a *beau sabreur* of the Pelican Club.

the sister (there is a host of them) who most frequently rules the
Blandings roost, imports too many literary young men to stay, insists on
choosing her brother Clarence's secretaries for him and wants to retire
Beach the butler. She is Rupert Baxter's champion. She sees nothing but
worth in that gimlet-eyed, lantern-jawed efficiency expert and, if she
can't ring him in again as Lord Emsworth's secretary, she rings him in as
tutor to Lord Emsworth's schoolboy grandson. Lord Emsworth, who, in
the first book, was not wholly anti-Baxter. has always, since *Leave It to
Psmith*, been sure he was potty, a judgement which Baxter reciprocates
on Lord Emsworth. Baxter has suffered much indignity at Blandings – the
cold tongue, raided from the larder, against the cheek in the dark, and
thought to be a corpse; the hail of air-gun pellets against the trousers; the
egg, hurled into outer darkness by the Duke of Dunstable, which hit
Baxter in the face; the flowerpot episode and the yellow pyjamas; the pig
parked in his caravan; the perjured persiflage of Lord Ickenham. But
Baxter feels, deep in his lonely soul, that the Castle is a shambles and
Lord Emsworth needs him as managing director.

Lord Emsworth comes of a long-lived family. His father, revealed in *A Pelican at Blandings* to have been irascible and domineering, was killed hunting at seventy-seven. His uncle Robert had lived to nearly ninety, his cousin Claude to eighty-four, when he broke his neck trying to jump a five-barred gate (presumably on a horse). Lord Emsworth's age for Wodehouse's purposes is pegged at just short of sixty – not too old for Galahad to be able, for his private ends, to impute to him an infatuation with a young girl; old enough to be psychosomatically deaf and forgetful, so that his sister Constance and other characters can shout the plot and the plotters to him in a way most comforting to the unalert reader. But Lord Emsworth is too old ever to be moulded by Baxter or made to enjoy his stiff collars, speech-makings, visits to London and other ghastly duties that his sister imposes on him. Give him his flowers to sniff and his pig loading in her calories; give him Whiffle to read in the evenings and a glass of port; keep his multitudinous sisters and all other relatives (with the exception of Galahad) away from him. That's all he asks. And that's what he gets, happily, at the end of the last full-length Blandings novel. Lord Emsworth is one of the very nicest lords in literature.

If you come to suspect from the insistence of the Duke of Dunstable and the exasperations of sister Constance that Lord Emsworth is pottier than the normal run of the Wodehouse aristocracy of England, you might reflect on how many members of his family have made him trustee for their sons and daughters. Possibly the Blandings Estate looks after all the family, from Galahad downwards, and Lord Emsworth has, simply by primogeniture, not by merit or brain, to be the final arbiter of who gets what inheritance and when. Potty or not himself, Lord Emsworth had married a wife with insanity in her own family. She herself appears to have had delusions of poverty. Her only recorded words are 'Oh dear, oh dear, oh dear', spoken when she had given birth to her second son, and occasioned by her fear that his education would be a great expense. An uncle of hers had thought he was a loaf of bread, and had first announced the fact (or fancy) at Blandings. Lord Bosham, heir to Blandings and the Emsworth title, is pretty potty in his turn. He has had a breach-of-promise case in his day, he has bought a gold brick, he has lent Lord Ickenham his wallet and he talks almost total drivel. With Lord Emsworth, Lord Bosham, the Duke of Dunstable and Lord Ickenham all together at Blandings (*Uncle Fred in the Springtime*), the Castle becomes an inferno of potty peers. But Wodehouse holds by the cheerful view that there is pottiness in all the most aristocratic English families, and he is frank and fearless about mentioning its incidences among the forebears of his favourites. (He also indicates that pottiness occurs in the best American families too: the millionaire Milbanks in *The Coming of Bill* and the millionaire Stokers in *Thank You, Jeeves.*)

The potty Threepwood genes have gone more to the males of the young generation than to the female. Except for Veronica Wedge, that lovely dumb blonde who might have come out of an Evelyn Waugh novel, all the Emsworth nieces are girls of mettle, and they tend to marry the nice young men of their own choice, rather than the vapid peers of their Aunt Constance's. Ronnie Fish may have, in his Uncle Galahad's words, looked like a minor jockey with scarlatina, but he married Sue Brown, the charming chorus-girl daughter of Dolly Henderson, who had charmed Galahad and Lord Emsworth when she had been singing at the Tivoli in pink tights. Sue is one of the best in the longish line of nice Wodehouse chorus girls, and Ronnie is lucky to have won her and to have kept her against all the slings and arrows operated by his disapproving mother. I forget now what typically Wodehouse future Ronnie and Sue face together. Ronnie is going to be a bookmaker, or run a roadhouse or a nightclub, or keep an onion-soup bar, or start a gymnasium, or breed dogs, or farm. He has got his girl. He has got his capital out of Uncle Clarence. He has got his eye on a job somewhat more life-enhancing than working for Lord Tilbury. He has driven off in the two-seater towards the unrecorded happiness-for-two reserved for most of the young, however blah, in the last pages of a Wodehouse novel.

At any stately home the size of Blandings there is an interesting life teeming behind the green baize doors. You should reread *Something Fresh* to see this described from a servant's-eye view. Ashe Marson (a detective-story writer) and Joan Valentine (a journalist) represent the main young-love interest. They are both visiting Blandings, for shady reasons, as servants. Ashe is valet to Mr Peters, a dyspeptic American millionaire, and Joan is taken on as lady's maid to Aline Peters, the millionaire's daughter. It is through Ashe's eyes that we get our first close-up view of Sebastian Beach, the Blandings butler, with his appearance of imminent apoplexy, his dignified inertia, his fat hands, his fruity voice 'like tawny port made audible', his fear of Socialism, his corns, his ingrowing toenails, his swollen joints, his nervous headaches, his blurred vision and weak stomach. Most of these complaints are forgotten in subsequent books, possibly because Beach never again has the opportunity to talk about them to another servant. In *Something Fresh* we first meet Mrs Twemlow, the housekeeper, and we count the heads of Merridew, the under-butler, James and Alfred the footmen, a flock of male guests' gentlemen's gentlemen and lady guests' maids. We hear of the chef, the groom of the chambers, Thorne the head gardener (McAllister doesn't come on till a later book), the chauffeur, the boot-boy, and a whole host of laundry maids, housemaids, parlourmaids, scullerymaids, kitchenmaids and between-maids. And the ordering of their lives is described with as much detail and ten times as much humour as in Vita Sackville-West's *The Edwardians*, George Moore's *Esther Waters* or anywhere in Dornford Yates. In later books we shall take the servants' hall for granted and go only to Beach's pantry for port. In *Something Fresh* is a survey of the Servants' Hall which shows us that Wodehouse knew his stuff about below-stairs grandeur, loved the grandees and sympathized with the whole company, from butler to buttons.

Blandings footmen come and go in later books; the office of attendant to the Empress, pig-man or pig-girl, is apt to change hands dramatically; Beach rounds out into being a force for good in every plot, even if he does have to put a green baize cloth over his bullfinch's cage when young lovers talk, or bribe, him into stealing his master's pig. Beach possesses the finest library of thrillers in Shropshire, having inherited Freddie Threepwood's collection when Freddie went West. Beach is no innocent. In really critical moments (such as when Lord Emsworth decides to grow a beard) Beach will regretfully decide to resign his long-held post. Sometimes, tried just short of resignation, he will drink brandy in his pantry instead of port.

His physical ailments forgotten in the later books, Beach remains a rock, a stately procession of one, a sportsman and a sentimentalist. For the people he likes he will do anything. For Lord Emsworth and his niece Angela, Beach chants 'Pig-hoo-o-o-o-ey!' to the Empress. He brings Galahad a whisky and soda all the way to the Empress's sty. He gets kissed by Sue Brown for all the help he has given her and her Ronnie in their troubled wooing. It's a pity that the autograph manuscript of Galahad's memoirs was consumed by the Empress, because there were mentions of Beach in its chapters. Beach, and Beach's mother in Bournemouth (or was it Eastbourne?), would have been pleased to see the family name honoured in print. It was good, though, that Beach had time to read in the manuscript the story of Gregory Parsloe and the prawns. It is possibly the only time in Wodehouse that we see a butler really laugh. 'HA . . . HOR . . . HOO!' he roared, admittedly believing himself alone and unobserved. (Wodehouse died without telling *us* the story of those prawns, or of Lord Ickenham and Pongo at the Dog Races.)

Is the Gutenberg Bible still in the Blandings Library? A copy, described as probably the last in private hands, was, in 1974, being offered by a dealer at a sum of Swiss francs equivalent to £1 million sterling. Does Galahad still wind clocks when time hangs heavy? Is Blandings now frequently open to the public? There are bedrooms in it so magnificent that they have never been slept in since the first Queen Elizabeth's day. Is Jno. Banks still the Market Blandings hairdresser? At The Emsworth Arms (G. Ovens, Propr.) is the 'large, pale, spotted waiter' still waiting, and is there still the smell of 'cold beef, beer, pickles, cabbage, gravy soup, boiled potatoes and very old cheese' in the coffee-room? Does the boiled turbot still come up as a 'rather obscene-looking mixture of bones and eyeballs and black mackintosh'? And does the inkpot still contain that 'curious sediment that looked like black honey'? Does Blandings still run the old Hispano-Suiza car? And what are the trains to and from Paddington these days? Wodehouse was constantly changing their times, and it is a constant astonishment to me that so many impostors managed to catch them and arrive safely to get down to their plottings at the Castle.

The last chapter of *A Pelican at Blandings* (1969) had been a very happy requiem. The Empress in her bijou residence had turned in for the night. Voules the chauffeur was playing his harmonica somewhere. Beach brought Lord Emsworth and Galahad their dinner (leg of lamb, boiled potatoes and spinach, followed by well-jammed roly-poly pudding) in the library. Lord Emsworth was wearing his old shooting coat with the holes in the elbows, and his feet were sensuously comfortable in bedroom slippers. Through the open window came the scent of stocks and tobacco flower. Constance, the Duke of Dunstable, assorted godsons, impostors and pretty girls had all paired off and gone away. The skeleton novel on which Wodehouse was working in hospital when he died was yet another set at Blandings, and the typed scenario showed that after many chapters of fitful fever Lord Emsworth would be left to blissful solitude and monotony again, without a sister in sight.

Evelyn Waugh in his tribute to Wodehouse on his eightieth birthday wrote: 'For Wodehouse there has been no fall of Man: no "aboriginal calamity" . . . the gardens of Blandings Castle are the original gardens from which we are all exiled.'

7 ~ UNCLE FRED, LORD ICKENHAM

————————— ~ —————————

The story 'Uncle Fred Flits By' in *Young Men in Spats* (1936), *Uncle Fred in the Springtime* (1939), *Uncle Dynamite* (1948), *Cocktail Time* (1958), *Service with a Smile* (1962).

Lord Ickenham leads the dance in a short story and four novels. He is an excellent invention and worth a little study.

Wodehouse in *Performing Flea* refers to this sprightly old earl as 'a sort of elderly Psmith'. 'Don't *talk* so much!' said Freddie Threepwood to Psmith in *Leave It to Psmith*. 'Don't *talk* so much, Uncle Fred!' said Myra Schoonmaker in *Service with a Smile*. Lord Ickenham referred to himself in *Uncle Dynamite* as 'one of the hottest earls that ever donned a coronet'. He emerged, a rounded character, fully fledged and fully armed to deceive, in an excellent short story, and it shows Wodehouse's pleasure in him that, though his next appearance was in a Blandings novel, he had his name in the title. He is a whirring dynamo of misrule. As a boy he was known as 'Barmy' and now, in what should be the autumn of his days, he plays the giddy goat with an irrepressible springtime frivolity.

Frederick Altamont Cornwallis, fifth Earl of Ickenham, is in his middle-sixties, with iron-grey hair, a slim, youthful figure, an American wife (always off-stage) who tries to keep him under control ('American girls try to boss you. It's part of their charm'), and a stately home, with far too many nude statues in it, at Bishop's Ickenham in Hampshire. Luckily for us, Lady Ickenham occasionally let the fifth Earl go to London, for reputable reasons like the Eton and Harrow match, though threatening to skin him with a blunt knife if he didn't return on the dot. And occasionally she herself departed for the South of France or the West Indies to tend an ailing mother; which gave Lord Ickenham his freedom to go A.W.O.L.

It is Lord Ickenham's nephew and heir, Pongo Twistleton-Twistleton, who suffers most acutely from his Uncle Fred's enlargements. Lord Ickenham claims that London brings out all the best in him and is the only place where his soul can expand like a blossoming flower and his generous nature find full expression. Pongo has rooms in Albany – or had until Uncle Fred saw to it that he married Sally Painter. Uncle Fred descends on Pongo and, sooner or later, the trouble starts. The first time, often referred to but never reported in detail, Uncle Fred had lugged Pongo to the Dog Races, and they had been in the hands of the constabulary in ten minutes. Lord Ickenham complained that they were letting a rather neurotic type of man into the Force these days, and that on this occasion a better stamp of magistrate would have been content with a mere reprimand. But, as he had given his name in court as George Robinson, of 14 Nasturtium Road, East Dulwich (the first recorded of his many impersonations), Lady Ickenham presumably never heard about it.

Lady Ickenham believes in a strong centralized government and handles the Ickenham finances. She gives her husband enough for golfballs, tobacco and self-respect. No more. Pongo, loyally or spinelessly, doesn't sneak on his Uncle Fred to his Aunt Jane; but Pongo's sister Valerie, a girl of spirit, is quite prepared to threaten these reprisals when she finds her Uncle Fred interfering in her love-life. Uncle Fred is a keen matchmaker, and, in bringing A and B together, he generally has to bust up their existing unsuitable engagement to C and D respectively. 'Help is a thing I am always glad to be of,' says this splendid old nuisance: his mother had been frightened by a Boy Scout.

Lord Ickenham is an intrepid impersonator. He has claimed that the only people he wouldn't be able to impersonate are a circus dwarf and Gina Lollobrigida. In the story 'Uncle Fred Flits By' he was driven to seek shelter from the rain in a suburban house, and he pretended to be (a) a vet come to clip the parrot's claws (Pongo was to be his deaf and dumb assistant. 'Tap your teeth with a pencil, and try to smell of iodoform!'), (b) a Mr Roddis and (c) a Mr Bulstrode – in that order as the plot developed, in the space of about one hour.

In *Uncle Fred in the Springtime* he is not only himself impersonating Sir Roderick Glossop, but he takes with him to Blandings Polly Pott, a bookmaker's daughter, who has to pretend to be his (Sir Roderick's) daughter, and his nephew Pongo, who has to pretend to be his (Sir Roderick's) secretary. In *Cocktail Time* Lord Ickenham becomes Inspector Jarvis of Scotland Yard. If impersonation fails temporarily, he has a smooth technique with knock-out drops. 'It is madness to come to country houses without one's bottle of Mickey Finns,' he says. He used these tranquillizers with effect at Blandings ('Pongo lit a reverent cigarette; he did not approve of his Uncle Fred, but he could not but admire his work'), and wished he had had them handy in *Uncle Dynamite*. He admits that he sometimes feels like a caged skylark at Ickenham, with Lady I. forbidding his sweetness-and-light-spreading excursions. 'There are no limits, literally none, to what I can accomplish in the springtime,' he says. In the noble sentence from the first story, repeated for reminder and emphasis in the later books, a Crumpet at The Drones says to his guest: 'I don't know if you happen to know what the word "excesses" means, but these are what Pongo's Uncle Fred from the country, when in London, invariably commits.'

He is the best buzzer in all Wodehouse. His joy in impersonation, lying and blackmail, his manic generation of muddle and mayhem as a challenge to his own powers of Houdini-like escape – these enabled Wodehouse to ravel his plots into webs apparently hopelessly tangled and then, in magical dénouement, to shake them out into happy endings, with all the right couples paired off. And, although one must at all times and at all costs avoid accusing Wodehouse of offering us messages, Lord Ickenham in his middle sixties is a high-stepping proof that, for the elderly as for the young, the brow should be worn low and unfurrowed, the hat should be perched on the side of the head and the shirt should not be stuffed.

Also – and perhaps this really was a message – rank is but a penny stamp. I had a feeling that, in *Uncle Fred in the Springtime*, Lord Ickenham's friend 'Mustard' Pott, a real vulgarian in name and nature, was a shade over the odds of credibility, and that, even though he had that charming daughter, happily paired in the end to the boxer-poet Ricky, nephew of a Duke, 'Mustard' would not in fact have been so democratically accepted at The Drones and at Blandings as Wodehouse asked us to believe. Still, if 'Mustard' Pott was a bit of a strain, he was a strain in the right egalitarian direction. But when, in *Cocktail Time*, Lord Ickenham's ex-ship's steward, now butler, friend Albert Peasemarch won the love of Phoebe Wisdom, sister of the pompous Q.C., and thus half-sister of Lady Ickenham herself, I found myself hardening in my suspicions that this was a sop to the American reading public. I was inspecting *Cocktail Time* again just when Behrman's articles on Max Beerbohm were appearing in the *New Yorker*. Behrman, the American, comments on Beerbohm's long-felt unease about servants and servant-hood.

> In all times, of course, domestic service has been a demoralising state of existence. To belong to one class and to live in close contact with another, to 'live hardly' in contemplation of more or less luxury and idleness, to dissimulate all your natural feelings because you are forbidden to have them, and to simulate other feelings because they are expected of you – this has always been an unnatural life, breeding always the same bad qualities . . . We, during the last thirty years, have been smiling over the blessings of universal education, and we are just beginning to realise, with horror, that we ought to have postponed that system until all menial duties could be performed by machinery.

So my thoughts about *Cocktail Time* ran, and still run, like this: that after more than fifty Wodehouse books about the English nobility and gentry, however feeble-witted, with their butlers and valets, however superior, complaints may have been levelled by captious American critics that this kind of English master/man relationship was not only ludicrous but regrettable; that Wodehouse, who did not, thank heaven, ride either the tygers of wrath or the horses of instruction, might conceivably, for *Cocktail Time*, have decided to crack the pattern that his own books had genially set – just to show it could be done – and that therefore the butler courts the châtelaine and wins her, and Lord Ickenham himself, having given the match his encouragement, ends up by going off on a toot with the said butler in London, this being the ultimate proof that the friendship between earl and manservant was a friendship between equals.

My feeling of disquiet about Lord Ickenham's good fellowship with both 'Mustard' Pott and Albert Peasemarch is the result, not of my own snobbery, but of my great admiration for Lord Ickenham as a wit, *farceur*, *flâneur* and *boulevardier*. I don't think Pott or Peasemarch could really have kept Lord Ickenham amused long enough to make such good fellowship even fictionally valid. But, if Wodehouse wanted occasionally to put in a plug for the classless society, Lord Ickenham was a fine vehicle for his plug.

Wodehouse gave Lord Ickenham a wider background reading, and memory of reading, than he gave even to Jeeves. He shows familiarity, in reference and quotation, with all the stock Wodehouse sources, the Bible, Shakespeare, Tennyson, Gilbert, *et al.* But he also shows his converse with Pierre Louÿs's *Le Roi Pausole*, Walter Pater, Damon

Runyon, Hemingway, the Sitwells, Sinclair Lewis, Fenimore Cooper, Newbolt, Evelyn Waugh, Proust and Kafka. And he once dives into the deep end of *Pickwick* with all the aplomb of a Bernard Darwin and in a way which must have made his current hearers wonder what on earth he was talking about.

In *Service with a Smile* he meets Lord Emsworth in Moss Bros. Both had been attending the opening of Parliament and both are now bringing back their suitcases full of hired finery.

'Were you at that thing this morning?' said Lord Emsworth.

'I was indeed,' said Lord Ickenham, 'and looking magnificent. I don't suppose there is a peer in England who presents a posher appearance when wearing the reach-me-downs and comic hat than I do. Just before the procession got under way, I heard Rouge Croix whisper to Bluemantle "Don't look now, but who's that chap over there?", and Bluemantle whispered back, "I haven't the foggiest, but evidently some terrific swell."'

When Peter Fleming wrote fulsomely of Wodehouse's *Louder and Funnier* in the *Spectator*, he received a letter from the Alpes Maritimes:

Dear R.P.F.,

Thanks awfully for your kind review. The local peasants as I pass whisper to one another '*Il me semble que Monsieur Vodehouse est satisfait de lui aujourd'hui.*'

Uncle Fred, Lord Ickenham, was '*satisfait de lui*' all the time. And can one blame him?

8 ~ THE LIGHT NOVELS

———————————— ~ ————————————

A Gentleman of Leisure (1910), *The Prince and Betty* (1912), *The Little Nugget* (1913), *Uneasy Money* (1917), *Piccadilly Jim* (1918), *A Damsel in Distress* (1919), *The Coming of Bill* (1920), *Jill the Reckless* (1921), *Indiscretions of Archie* (1921), *The Girl on the Boat* (1922), *The Adventures of Sally* (1922), *Bill the Conqueror* (1924), *Sam the Sudden* (1925), *The Small Bachelor* (1927), *Money for Nothing* (1928), *Big Money* (1931), *If I Were You* (1931), *Dr Sally* (1932), *Hot Water* (1932), *The Luck of the Bodkins* (1935), *Laughing Gas* (1936), *Summer Moonshine* (1938), *Quick Service* (1940), *Money in the Bank* (1946), *Spring Fever* (1948), *The Old Reliable* (1951), *Barmy in Wonderland* (1952), *French Leave* (1956), *Something Fishy* (1957), *Ice in the Bedroom* (1961), *Frozen Assets* (1964), *Company for Henry* (1967), *Do Butlers Burgle Banks?* (1968), *The Girl in Blue* (1970), *Pearls, Girls and Monty Bodkin* (1972), *Bachelors Anonymous* (1973).

'Light novels' is a category of Wodehouse's output that includes many more than the thirty-six listed above. In fact, short stories, autobiography, plays and essays apart, all Wodehouse's books are light novels. The earliest ones were fairly light, and the subsequent ones became lighter and lighter. In the last forty-five years they were, almost uninterruptedly, farces. This chapter takes a short look at the novels which are not parts of sagas and in which the recurrent characters, if any, are not dominant.

Objection: all Wodehouse's books have recurrent characters. Objection sustained. But the characters differ in names and in local habitations: the fresh young men and brisk maidens, the willowy young men and intellectual maidens, wrongly paired at the beginning, properly paired at the end of the book, the aunts and uncles, the short-tempered American millionaires, the bossy wives and widows, the hen-pecked husbands, the crooks, the butlers, the policemen, the magistrates, the genial alcoholics, the over-efficient secretaries, the private eyes, the poets, the bad artists, the retired colonials, the pimply office boys, the ex-pugilists, the theatrical producers and the impoverished peers. Egregious characters are rare. *Summer Moonshine* contains two, surprising enough to be memorable in an otherwise run-of-the-mill novel. One is the 'plasterer', an American whose job it has been to find absconders from The Law and to plant summonses on them. His hobby in retirement, just for the excitement of the chase, is to be a plasterer still. The other is Princess Dwornitzchek, a really unpleasant stepmother, almost a villainess. But, to illustrate similarity, compare the young heroes of *Summer Moonshine* with those of the next light novel in date, *Quick Service*. Joe Vanringham and Joss Weatherby are practically identical except in name. Compare their elderly employers, Mr Busby and Mr Duff, practically identical except in name.

Compare *Spring Fever* with its next in date, *The Old Reliable*. The names are changed, sometimes not very much. The local habitation is changed – a country house in England and a big house in Hollywood – but otherwise you might say the two books were the same story. They were.

Wodehouse mined his ore in several seams and often the seams criss-crossed. A play became a novel; a novel became a play. Something that was originally sketched out as a play, but not produced, was skilfully filled out with descriptive narrative and sent to the mint as a novel. *Ring for Jeeves* was the novel Wodehouse wrote from the play written by Guy Bolton for which Wodehouse had loaned him Jeeves as a butler character. In the case of *Spring Fever* and *The Old Reliable*, one idea produced two novels and one play. The play was never produced but both novels were.

Wodehouse wrote *Spring Fever* as a novel. It already had the three-act rhythm in its plot. After it had been published Wodehouse heard that the American actor, Edward Everett Horton, was looking for a play with a juicy butler part in it for himself. Horton, Wodehouse and their attendant agents had a transatlantic discussion, and terms were decided. Wodehouse turned *Spring Fever* into a play, but for Horton's American audiences. Characters and settings became American. The local habitation became Hollywood. Spink the butler became Phipps the butler, Lord Shortlands became Smedley Cork. The gorgon, Lady Adela Cobbold, daughter of Lord Shortlands, became the gorgon, Mrs Adela Cork in Hollywood (even the Christian name remained the same there). After Wodehouse had done much tailoring and rewriting of the script for Horton, Horton's other commitments finally made him decide he couldn't put the play on. So now Wodehouse had a play script on his hands, and it was so far from the original novel that he thought he could make it pay further dividends. He made it into a new novel.

Within the meaning of the act, *The Old Reliable* is a new novel. Only a professional ferret would notice the way it rhymes with *Spring Fever*. My advice is simply that, except for purposes of professional analysis, you don't read *Spring Fever* and *The Old Reliable* in that order on the same weekend. That might induce a slight feeling of what the American plasterer in *Summer Moonshine* called 'onwee'.

Nowhere in Wodehouse is there a breath of a political message about Anglo-American friendship, and yet his books have probably had a considerable influence in helping the English and the Americans not to be frightened of each other. The eruptive American millionaire, Pop Stoker, finds to his horror that English policemen can't be bribed; he gets talked down by Jeeves; he loses his elder daughter Pauline in marriage to Lord Chuffnell and his younger, Emerald, to Gussie Fink-Nottle. Pop Stoker is a twenty-minute American egg forcibly softened up by the English way of life in the end. Bill Dawlish (William FitzWilliam Delamare Chambers, Lord Dawlish) decides to go to America to make his fortune:

> 'Hang it,' said Bill to himself in the cab. 'I'll go to America!' The exact words probably which Columbus had used, talking the thing over with his wife.
>
> Bill's knowledge of the great republic across the sea was at this period of his life a little sketchy. He knew that there had been unpleasantness between England and the United States in seventeen-something and again in eighteen-something, but that things had eventually been straightened out by Miss Edna May and her fellow missionaries of *The Belle of New York* Company, since which time there had been no more trouble. Of American cocktails he had a fair working knowledge, and he appreciated ragtime. But of other great American institutions he was completely ignorant.
>
> (*Uneasy Money*, 1917.)

Wodehouse gives you Chichester Clam, the American shipping tycoon, imprisoned in a potting-shed at Lord Worplesdon's English country house in Steeple Bumpleigh (*Joy in the Morning*), and Lord Emsworth in America doing a nice American girl a good turn by selling encyclopaedias for her. He gets treed by a dog in the process ('Birth of a Salesman'). Lord Haveshot goes to Hollywood and marries a nice American girl (*Laughing Gas*). Film star Mike Cardinal comes from Hollywood and marries Lady Teresa (Terry) Cobbold (*Spring Fever*). He is another good Wodehouse 'buzzer' hero. The only thing against him in the Wodehouse Code is that he is too handsome. However, he gets his face bashed crooked in a fracas with a burglar in an English castle, and everybody's happy, Mike included. Americans come to England to learn, and Mike Cardinal has learnt something the hard way, and wouldn't have had it any other way. He gets his Terry, and his impoverished future father-in-law, Lord Shortlands, sells his white-elephant English castle and is all set to go to Hollywood to play butler parts in films. Silly ass Archie Moffam goes to America (*Indiscretions of Archie*) and learns to love baseball. He also learns to love (with less difficulty) Lucille, daughter of an American millionaire. In *If I Were You*, the earl marries the American manicurist, Polly Brown. *Hot Water* adds an Old Etonian French viscount to the Anglo-American salad bowl.

Such are the Wodehousian resolutions of the problem of Americans and English being separated by a common language. Put them in some good farcical fights, mix in some pretty girls, and the New World will redress the bank balances of the Old, and have a fine time doing it. Wodehouse is an advocate for more and prettier American chorus girls marrying into the English peerage, and for more and prettier English girls marrying rich Americans – or even poor ones, if they're pleasant. Peers and pugilists, millionaires and chorus girls, butlers and confidence tricksters – mix them up and they'll soon be looking so silly that nationalisms will have disappeared and the western world will be that much a better place.

There was poetic justice in Wodehouse adding American citizenship to his British in his seventies. He had served both countries well in his books. He had been an honorary American since before the First World War, and he has his constant readers and cultists there as here. Referring to a date that would be 1926 or 1927, George Arakian, writing about the American jazz musician Bix Beiderbecke, says:

Whenever Bix was in New York, he had a standing invitation to play at the Princeton dances. Frank Norris and Squirrel Ashcraft, independently of one another and in almost the same words, made clear . . . that when Bix was around the talk was seldom about music. 'Bix had some unusual things in common with us,' says Ashcraft. 'We discovered that he could quote long passages from P. G. Wodehouse as well as we could, and we could spot the approximate page and the exact character who said any chosen line from his books – he had written forty-eight.'

('The Bix Beiderbecke Story' in *The Art of Jazz*, edited by Martin Williams.)

The Luck of the Bodkins, published in 1935, is largely farce, played out on an Atlantic liner. Most of the play is made by a Hollywood film star, Lotus (Lottie) Blossom, a high-spirited beauty with a pet baby alligator and a penchant for 'larkiness'. (This is the word used by her steward, Albert Peasemarch, later Lord Ickenham's friend in *Cocktail Time*.) Lottie has a fine command of persiflage and repartee. She is involved with two English brothers, Ambrose and Reggie Tennyson. They differ radically in their attitudes to jobs and living on other people's money. Wodehouse's uncritical blessing goes out to both of them.

Reggie's views on jobs were peculiar, but definite. There were some men – he himself was one of them – who, he considered, had no need for a job. A fair knowledge of racing form, a natural gift for bridge and poker, an ability to borrow money with an easy charm which made the operation a positive pleasure to the victims – these endowments, he held, were all that a chap like himself required, and it was with a deep sense of injury that he had allowed his loved ones to jockey him into the loathsome commercial enterprise to which he was now on his way. A little patience on their part, a little of the get-together spirit, a temporary opening of the pursestrings to help him over a bad patch, and he could have carried on in such perfect comfort. For Reggie Tennyson was one of those young men whom the ravens feed.

But, and this was the point, the ravens do not feed the Ambroses of this world. The Ambroses need their steady jobs. Here is a conversation between Reggie and Lottie Blossom about Reggie's brother:

'Ambrose and I can't get married now,' said Lottie.

'Oh, come,' said Reggie. 'He may be broke, having given up his job at the Admiralty, but you've enough for two, what?'

'I've enough for twenty. But what good is that? Ambrose won't live on my money. He wouldn't marry me on a bet now.'

'But, dash it, it's no different to marrying an heiress.'

'He wouldn't marry an heiress.'

'What!' cried Reggie, who would have married a dozen, had the law permitted it. 'Why not?'

'Because he's a darned ivory-domed, pig-headed son of an army mule,' cried Miss Blossom, the hot blood of the Hoboken Murphys boiling in her veins. 'Because he isn't human. Because he is like some actor in a play, doing the noble thing with one eye counting the house and the other on the gallery. No he isn't,' she went on, with one of those swift transitions which made her character so interesting and which on the Superba-Llewellyn lot had so often sent over-wrought directors groping blindly for the canteen to pull themselves together with frosted malted milk, 'He isn't anything of the kind. I admire his high principles. I think they're swell. It's a pity there aren't more men with his wonderful sense of honour and self-respect. I'm not going to have you saying a word against Ambrose. He's the finest man in the world, so if you want to sneer and jeer at him for refusing to live on my money, shoot ahead. Only remember that a cauliflower ear goes with it.'

Lottie, Corky, Nobby, Bobbie: these hell-raising girls are literary descendants of the young Middle School raggers of the early Wodehouse school stories. Festive young squirts, androgynous mischief-makers, they are charming, unscrupulous, quarrelsome, mettlesome, demanding, jealous, wheedling, quick to tears ('oomph! oomph!'), quick to wrath, especially with their loved ones, and always apt to 'start something'. They may be headaches. They are never bores. They are the sort of girls that Uncle Fred particularly admires. In a discussion with Bill Oakshott about his imperious girlfriend, Uncle Fred says: 'I don't suppose Hermione Bostock has ever made so much as an apple-pie bed in her life. I'd give her a miss.'

The bores among the Wodehouse girl friends are the Gertrudes, Honorias, Madelines and Florences. Gertrude is a hockey international, Madeline thinks the stars are God's daisy-chain, Florence is literary and Honoria is the daughter of Sir Roderick Glossop. They are not bores to the reader, but they all represent authority, and that puts them on the Other Side.

Sally's happy-go-lucky girl friend Gladys, in *The Adventures of Sally*, gives Sally a piece of advice which provides us with hope for the married happiness of the burbling bachelors of The Drones Club and their less privileged equivalents.

'Chumps always make the best husbands. When you marry, Sally, grab a chump. Tap his forehead first, and if it rings solid, don't hesitate. All the unhappy marriages come from the husbands having brains. What good are brains to a man? They only unsettle him.'

'Brains only unsettle a husband,' says Leila Yorke in Wodehouse's 1961 novel *Ice in the Bedroom*. Wodehouse wrote it when he was seventy-nine, and it is as fizzy as any in the list. It has a spring sprightliness and an autumn benignity. Wodehouse had, till now, been irreverent, just short of unkindness, to our then colonial empire, the people who went there and, particularly, the people who came back. Here he has given a prize Drone to Kenya, and Kenya's gain would be Mayfair's loss. Another act of benignity in this novel is the finally unreserved glorification of the status of bestseller female bilge-novelist. Leila Yorke here is built very much on the lines of Bertie Wooster's excellent Aunt Dahlia. She smokes cigars, likes plenty of champagne, talks good pithy slang, is kind to the young, makes £15,000 a year and finds her long-lost husband (a failed actor, mother-ridden and suppressed) performing seedily as a waiter at a Pen and Ink Club luncheon. She rescues him, discovers that his mother has at last done the right thing and passed on, and whisks him off to a life of luxury and sunshine that they will both enjoy.

There is a pleasant reversal of this pleasant rags-to-riches theme for another, less important, couple in the book. The aged, white-bearded Mr Cornelius, a house-agent, lives happily in his little corner of Valley Fields, pottering, playing chess, feeding his rabbits and writing a history of the district. (We met Mr Cornelius before in *Sam the Sudden* and *Big Money*.) It is Mr Cornelius who lends Freddie Widgeon the £3,000, but Freddie mustn't tell Mrs Cornelius. Why? Because Mr Cornelius has just inherited a million pounds or so from a distant brother, and if Mrs Cornelius were to get to hear about it, she would take steps:

'Mr Widgeon, have you any conception of what would happen, were my wife to learn that I was a millionaire? Do you think I should be allowed to go on living in Valley Fields, the place I love, and continue to be a house agent, the work I love? Do you suppose I should be permitted to keep my old friends, like Mr Wrenn of San Rafael, with whom I play chess on Saturdays, and feed rabbits in my shirt-sleeves? No, I should be whistled off to a flat in Mayfair, I should have to spend long months in the South of France, a butler would be engaged and I should have to dress for dinner every night. I should have to join a London Club, take a box at the opera, learn to play polo,' said Mr Cornelius, allowing his morbid fancy to run away with him a little. 'The best of women are not proof against sudden wealth. Mrs Cornelius is perfectly happy and contented in the surroundings to which she has always been accustomed – she was a Miss Bulstrode of Happy Haven at the time of our marriage – and I intend that she shall remain happy and contented.'

Valley Fields is Mr Cornelius's own, his native land. Valley Fields, Wodehouse's fond memory of West Dulwich, is south-east of London and the number 3 bus connects it with Piccadilly Circus. Castlewood, Peacehaven and The Nook, the property of Lord Uffenham's retired butler, Keggs, have been adjacent houses there in two previous novels, *Something Fishy* and *Big Money*. (Barry Conway is living at The Nook with his bossy old Nannie in *Big Money*.) It was to Valley Fields that Lord

Ickenham brought his nephew Pongo in the 'Uncle Fred Flits By' story. Here, in other stories, have come other Drones Club members, one at least with false beard to escape his creditors, and not a few Old Wrykynians in some of the early novels of the 1920s.

The great thing about Valley Fields for Wodehouse was that it gave him adjacent small houses, with fences between of a decent height for a small bachelor to lean over and see a small, pretty girl. In each garden there is certainly a tree for putting deckchairs under in the almost perpetual sunshine, and probably a statue of a nude infant with a bit of a tummy on him. If there is a policeman in the offing, he lives at one of the houses and so can be in uniform or mufti as the plot requires. Everything is peaceful. Valley Fields is an island valley of Avilion where a Drone can live on a clerk's salary. The Drone feels like a caged eagle at the office, but in Valley Fields he can sit in the garden in flannels and his Eton Rambler blazer, and he can get to know that pretty girl, who is herself probably in reduced circumstances too. In Valley Fields live the happy lower-middle classes, and burglars only find it a good hunting ground if other burglars have cached 'ice' in a bedroom from a theft at a country house far away. Mr Cornelius won't move from Valley Fields for anybody's money. Keggs has his money invested in property there, but he is a resident alien. He goes on round-the-world cruises. An ex-butler would know that the property values in Valley Fields were sound, but his sophisticated upbringing as a butler would make him hanker to go on long cruises occasionally.

In 'Uncle Fred Flits By', when his uncle takes Pongo to the London suburb most of which used to belong to the Ickenhams, the name is Mitching Hill. But in later references to this story Mitching Hill becomes Valley Fields. I suspect that Wodehouse, needing a London suburb as a setting for action in *Do Butlers Burgle Banks?* (1968) pencilled in Valley Fields and then said to himself 'No, we can't have Valley Fields getting all the action. I'll change it to Wellingford this time. That'll fool the too constant reader.' If so, he forgot to rub out one pencilled 'Valley Fields', in Chapter 4, part four, and it has gone through to the book. Even if it is a mistake, it is still a sort of tribute to the London suburb of Wodehouse's fondest memories. It drifts again, gently and this time without error, into *Bachelors Anonymous*, published when he was over ninety.

~ 'Odd stuff, this,' said Kay, sipping her cognac. 'Probably used for taking stains out of serge suits.'

~ 'Bertie, I think you're a pig!' she said.
'A pig, maybe: but a shrewd, level-headed pig,' I replied.

~ His was not a high code of ethics . . . indeed, in the course of a chequered career he had frequently been guilty of actions which would have caused a three-card-trick man to purse his lips and shake his head.

~ 'As a sleuth you are poor. You couldn't detect a bass drum in a telephone booth.'

~ The Peke followed him. It appeared to have no legs, but to move by faith alone.

~ Years before, and romantic as most boys are, his lordship had sometimes regretted that the Emsworths, though an ancient clan, did not possess a Family Curse. How little he had suspected that he was shortly to become the father of it.

~ 'I say,' he said, 'my father's missing.'
'On how many cylinders?' asked Lord Bromborough. He was a man who liked his joke of a morning.

~ Sir Raymond's attitude towards those about him – his nephew Cosmo, his butler Peasemarch, his partners at bridge, the waiters at the Demosthenes and, in particular, his sister, Phoebe Wisdom, who kept house for him and was reduced by him to a blob of tearful jelly almost daily – was always that of an irritable tribal god who intends to stand no nonsense from his worshippers and is prepared, should the smoked offering fall in any way short of the highest standard, to say it with thunderbolts. To have his top hat knocked off with a Brazil nut would, in Lord Ickenham's opinion, make him a better, deeper, more lovable man.

9 ~ THE SHORT STORIES

————————— ~ —————————

The Man Upstairs (1914), *The Man with Two Left Feet* (1917), *The Clicking of Cuthbert* (1922), *The Heart of a Goof* (1926), *Meet Mr Mulliner* (1927), *Mr Mulliner Speaking* (1929), *Mulliner Nights* (1933), *Mulliner Omnibus* (1935), *Blandings Castle* (1935), *Young Men in Spats* (1936), *Lord Emsworth and Others* (1937), *Eggs, Beans and Crumpets* (1940), *Nothing Serious* (1950), *A Few Quick Ones* (1959), *Plum Pie* (1966).

In the 1920s and 30s there were many illustrated magazines on both sides of the Atlantic paying high for good humorous short stories, five- to eight-thousand-word episodes, complete with sunny plot, a beginning, middle and end, and the young happily paired off in the fade-out. Wodehouse wrote for this profitable market. He became one of the golden boys of the magazines and, not necessarily the same thing, a master of his craft.

The *Strand* was paying Wodehouse a peak 500 guineas a story in the 1930s, the *Saturday Evening Post* $4,000 and the *American Magazine* (for one Mulliner series) $6,000. Twelve short stories could gross Wodehouse the equivalent in dollars and guineas of £20,000 from the magazines before they became a book. Multiply that up to today's values and it's great riches.

His first two short story collections, *The Man Upstairs* and *The Man with Two Left Feet*, are of interest now only to remind us that young Wodehouse, though possibly a born writer, had a long period of hack apprenticeship before he found his form and, jettisoning sentimentality and seriousness, came into his birthright. Wodehouse made no apologies for it. In *Performing Flea* and elsewhere he said that, though he worked hard and kept his income rising year by year, he never felt he had more than a toe-hold on the craft of his profession till the 1920s, by which time he was in his personal forties. He always envied, nostalgically, the young who wrote well virtually from the egg. Perhaps only someone totally established in maturity, and genuinely unsentimental about himself when young, could have allowed 'In Alcala', an early, pulpy item written for the pulps, to survive through and reach Penguin form in *The Man with Two Left Feet*. 'In Alcala' is a strangely untypical Wodehouse story, a collector's item, perhaps, because in it Wodehouse uses seriously a formulaic expression ('showering kisses on her upturned face') that he laughs at as a Rosie M. Banks tripe-type cliché in a dozen contexts in later books.

In one of the Bingo Little stories, Bingo's wife Rosie has gone to Droitwich with her mother. Bingo, left with the baby and no money for cocktails and cigarettes, gets a letter from Rosie enclosing £10, with instructions to open a wee savings account for the baby. Another pram-pushing father, who meets Bingo and son in the park that day, bets Bingo a tenner that his son is uglier than Bingo's, a passing policeman to be judge. Bingo, holding that his Algernon Aubrey looks like a homicidal fried egg, takes the bet with confidence, and loses his baby's tenner with horror. He faces a fearful get-together with Rosie when he goes to Paddington to meet the Droitwich train. What, she will ask, about that wee pass-book?

'I've got to take Mother to the flat,' said Rosie on the platform. 'She's not at all well.'
'No, I noticed she seemed to be looking a bit down among the wines and spirits,' said Bingo, casting a gratified glance at the old object, who was now propping herself up against a passing porter.

Bingo has enormous troubles of his own. His mother-in-law has never raised a finger to harm him in any of the chronicles. She is an elderly invalid, and is now in a bad way after a testing railway journey. But Bingo has time to relish the old object's distress. Nobody sees Bingo's gratified glance except the reader, and the reader is delighted by this gratuitous swipe at old age and invalidism by one who is young and healthy.

If you think that the mature Wodehouse held any subject sacred, point to it in his books. Sex? No, he doesn't hold sex sacred. He simply by-passes it or transmutes it. In his light novels his nice chorus girls easily give the brush-off to theatrical producers who hint at the price of advancement to an acting part. There would presumably be licentious clubmen at The Drones, but Wodehouse's formula purifies them into the Pongo/Bingo/Barmy/Freddie type of opisthognathous romantics. They are constantly falling in love, and are not laggard in pursuing the objects of their desires, if that is the right word. But they pursue strictly with flowers, lunches, lushing up the girl's parents, kid brothers and dogs, and

with object matrimony. There is no suggestion that either clubman or
girl would recognize a double bed except as so much extra sweat to make
an apple-pie of.

With the possible exceptions of Percy Pilbeam, marcelled hair in the
male, English lecturers in America and phoney young *littérateurs* generally, Wodehouse seems to have had no strong dislikes. But he was
funny and irreverent about practically every sacred cow in the British
pasture. Several of the subjects about which he was most irreverent in
print were, we know, personal enthusiasms of his own – cricket, rugger,
boxing, keep-fit exercises, dogs, cats, Tennyson, Shakespeare, the Old
School and, by his own account, golf.

> As a writer of light fiction, I have always till now been handicapped by the fact
> that my disposition was cheerful, my heart intact, and my life unsoured.
> Handicapped, I say, because the public likes to feel that a writer of farcical stories
> is piquantly miserable in his private life, and that, if he turns out anything
> amusing, he does it simply in order to obtain relief from the almost insupportable
> weight of an existence which he has long since realised to be a wash-out. Well,
> today I am just like that.
>
> Two years ago, I admit, I was a shallow *farceur*. My work lacked depth. I wrote
> flippantly simply because I was having a thoroughly good time. Then I took up
> golf, and now I can smile through the tears and laugh, like Figaro [*sic*], that I may
> not weep, and generally hold my head up and feel that I am entitled to respect.
>
> If you find anything in this volume that amuses you, kindly bear in mind that it
> was probably written on my return home after losing three balls in the gorse and
> breaking the head off my favourite driver . . .

Wodehouse established the Oldest Member, himself full of reverence
for the sacred game, to tell some of the most hilariously irreverent stories
about it in all its literature. There is no cricket after *Mike*, except one
story in *Nothing Serious* (1952), where the young man and the lovely girl
are united in thinking that cricket is a ridiculously boring game. But they
cannot marry until the young man manages to get out, with financial
allowances intact, from under the thumb of a rich uncle to whom cricket
and Lord's are a religion. There is only one game of rugger after the
school stories, and that's when Tuppy Glossop insists on playing in a
village match in order to impress a girlfriend. Bertie Wooster, who tells
the story as one to whom the Rugby code is a mystery, makes it an epic of
irreverence.

After *The Coming of Bill*, which is unsentimental but fairly serious,
Wodehouse allowed himself to be firmly irreverent about children. At

the cot age, they look like mixtures of Edward G. Robinson, Boris Karloff and Winston Churchill, and later they are either fiends or sissies. The child who comes out best in all the books is the slum girl on fête-day at Blandings in 'Lord Emsworth and the Girl Friend'. This girl cops McAllister, Lord Emsworth's gardener, on the shin with a stone and helps Lord Emsworth to defy his sister Constance. The child who comes out worst is the small son of golfing parents who gets into bad Christopher Robin habits and, when saying his prayers, counts the house through the little hands on which he has drooped his little gold head. He also asks his father to write poetry for him. His mother (bless her) says 'Does mother's little chackabiddy want his nose pushed sideways? Very well, then!' We are left with the comfortable certainty that the child reformed.

Wodehouse has been irreverent about magistrates, old nannies, policemen, poets, peers, politicians, aunts, alcohol, uncles, adolescent spots, baronets, invalids, old age, publishers ('Don't kill him, Bill. He's my publisher!'), Christmas, butlers, ex-butlers, millionaires, Chekhov and the other Great Russians, the good grey poets, colonial ex-governors, newspaper magnates, popular novelists, amateur dictators (Spode and his Black Shorts) and Hollywood.

He has been irreverent about Royalty and the Church. There are only two passing references to a reigning monarch in the stories, and they are both small gems. Lord Emsworth, worried about his cherished prize pumpkin, has a dream in which he takes the King to see it. When they get to the frame in which it should have been basking in its enormous glory, they find it has shrivelled to the size of a pea, and 'Lord Emsworth woke, sweating, with his sovereign's disappointed screams ringing in his ears'. And the great hatters, Bodmins of Vigo Street, by appointment to His Majesty – that means that 'when the King wants a new topper, he ankles round to Vigo Street and says "Bodmin, we want a new topper."' Though the Prince of Wales wore soft silk shirts with a black tie in France in the evenings, Jeeves would not allow Bertie to wear them in London. Jeeves was conservative, but Jeeves was right.

For sustained innocuous irreverence, without a hint of mockery, towards a subject that popular humorists tend tastelessly to misuse or cravenly to avoid, see Wodehouse on the Church. Perhaps taking his original cue from W. S. Gilbert, but, after that, out on his own, with his own words and music, Wodehouse has given us a succession of splendid men of God, several superb church interiors and many most human predicaments suffered by clergymen in pursuance of their saintly duties. There is an excellent quarrel between a hot-tempered vicar and his bishop (they were at school together and slip easily into schoolboy slang in the heat of argument) about the number of orphreys the vicar is wearing on his chasuble. They are about to come to blows when the curate, Augustine Mulliner, calms them down and makes them shake hands and apologize. The Bishop of Bongo-Bongo is saved by his cat, Webster, from making an ass of himself and marrying an unsuitable widow. A country vicar's daughter, Angelica Briscoe, with whom Barmy Fotheringay Phipps and Pongo Twistleton-Twistleton both fell in love at first sight, turned out to be a competent schemer, well able to put those two city slickers through useful martyrdoms (the School Treat and the Mothers' Outing) and then to ditch them both. The Wodehouse 'message' is that clergymen's daughters know all the responses. Corky Pirbright's uncle in his country cure of souls is plagued by an atheist policeman of the village who makes sneering remarks about Jonah and the Whale. 'The Great Sermon Handicap' provides all the makings of a colossal racecourse gamble for Bertie, his friends and the fiendish Steggles. Stiffy Byng's clumsy fiancé, the Rev. 'Stinker' Pinker, has to steal the village constable's helmet for her. The Rev. 'Beefy' Bingham, full of good intentions and love for Lord Emsworth's niece, gives Lord Emsworth horse-liniment for his twisted ankle; and when Lord Emsworth, after a restless night, has gone to swim in the lake at Blandings, the Rev. 'Beefy' tries to rescue him from 'drowning' with a good punch on the jaw far from land. The vicar in 'Anselm Gets His Chance' would never let Anselm preach on Sunday evenings, until a burglar blacked his (the vicar's) eye on a Saturday night.

Wodehouse's treatment of the Church of England is frequent, knowledgeable, irreverent, friendly and funny. He had sat on many hard pews through many sermons, at school and in the holidays. All his clergymen are 'gentlemen'. One gets sent to the South of France by his doctor, and his replacement is the nephew and heir of a Liverpool shipping millionaire. Some have been rugger players and boxers of repute. Some have ungovernable tempers, others ungovernable daughters or nieces. It was the bishop catching his teenage daughter reading that shocking book, and attacking it in the pulpit, that started the popularity of *Cocktail Time*. All Wodehouse's clergymen are human. Not a single one is shown in the act of being pious or holy, though it is never suggested that they aren't. 'If they find me out, bim will go my chance of becoming a bishop.' That was the headmaster when, recovered from his Buck-U-Uppo, he realized that his forgetful friend and companion, the bishop, had left his shovel hat on the head of the statue of the school benefactor which they had been out painting pink the night before.

Wodehouse's Mr Mulliner, Oldest Member, Eggs, Beans and Crumpets are narrators chosen to tell whatever stories Wodehouse feels suitable for them. Their phraseologies differ, but they tell stories of roughly similar structure. Wodehouse's Oldest Member seems to sit on the terrace at a variety of golf club-houses, in England and in America. But even if he is a type and even if he is virtually interchangeable with Mr Mulliner except for the sorts of stories each tells, he is a comforting old sage, and one settles back to hear his stories with a good deal more pleasure than most of the auditors he nailed for them on the terrace. He himself has not played golf since the rubber-cored ball superseded the old dignified gutty. The course of his Club has a period flavour too, with cottages round its boundaries which can be rented furnished, with housekeeper, at a moment's notice and its members, old and young, almost entirely untrammelled by jobs. The Oldest Member hears their confidences, watches over their love affairs and philosophizes on all aspects of the great game:

'When I played, I never lost my temper. Sometimes, it is true, I may, after missing a shot, have broken my club across my knees; but I did it in a calm and judicial spirit, because the club was obviously no good and I was going to get another one anyway . . .'

Mr Mulliner holds his court in the bar parlour of The Anglers' Rest, drinking hot Scotch and lemon, courteously ordered from, and courteously served by, Miss Postlethwaite, the barmaid. He surveys a wider field than the Oldest Member, but, like the O.M., he dominates his audience and they have to listen. His stories are almost all about his nephews, and he has one in almost every profession – the Church, photography, Hollywood script-writing, detection, poetry, to name a few. Since the locale of his tales can change from Mayfair to Malibu, his audience can check on his statements even less than the Oldest Member's audience can on his. So Mr Mulliner tells 'stretchers'. He was Wodehouse's favourite mouthpiece for the really tall story. He tells his 'stretchers' with determination, grace, ease and solemnity. He has a vocabulary of phrase and situation dredged almost wholesale from popular bilge literature. Some of his characters have lives in stories other than his. Roberta ('Bobbie') Wickham made her first appearance in a Mulliner story, later played lead in 'Mr Potter Takes a Rest Cure' (which Wodehouse related without an intermediate narrator) and later came into Bertie Wooster's orbit, for two short stories and a whole novel. Wodehouse saw saga possibilities in her and let her cause trouble for a succession of young men. Bertie thought he was in love with her and tried to push it along. By the end of *Jeeves in the Offing*, Bobbie seemed destined for the altar with 'Kipper' Herring.

The Young Men in Spats and the Eggs, Beans and Crumpets told their stories mostly in the bar of The Drones. That club deserves a monograph, but will not get it from me. You must look for The Drones in Dover Street when you're next in the district; it is on the east side, and has steps going down to the street. In *Leave It to Psmith* it had Thorpe and Briscoe, coal merchants, opposite it. In *Cocktail Time* it faced The Demosthenes Club. The place where I should put it, from the geographic evidence in the books, is No. 16 Dover Street. It is the club above all that I should like to belong to, and, as Percy Gorringe, a side-whiskered Bloomsburyite from Liverpool, was a member and 'Mustard' Pott acceptable as a guest, I don't see why it need be too exclusive for me. Is there any club so hallowed in English fiction? There 'youth holds carnival' as Wodehouse said in *Leave It to Psmith* in a rather Dornford-Yates-sounding, but prophetic, phrase. And some of those youths, considering their pin-headedness, tell remarkably good stories remarkably well.

Wodehouse gave us other London clubs briefly: The Senior Conservative, to which Lord Emsworth and, in his moneyed days, Psmith belonged; The Senior Buffers, to which Lord Shortlands and Lord Yaxley belonged: The Morpheus, to which Lord Marshmoreton belonged; the old Pelican, where Galahad Threepwood and his friends revelled; The Six Jolly Stretchercases, a club without premises except in the Pump Room at Droitgate Spa; The Senior Bloodstain, where detectives gathered; The Snippers and The Senior Bay-Rum for hairdressers; The Senior Test-Tubes for chemists; The Negative and Solution for photographers; The Junior Lipstick, where Mayfair's girlhood laid bets about one another's forthcoming engagements; and The Junior Ganymede in Curzon Street, where butlers and gentlemen's personal gentlemen met, drank, played bridge and discussed their masters. (Jeeves was taking the chair at one of its recent lunches, and he is doubtless its most eminent member.)

But The Drones is the home from home and water-hole of Bertie Wooster and all Wodehouse's best young men. Wodehouse made The Drones, made its membership and made the language of its dining- and smoking-rooms. If the Spirit of Wodehouse has a single address, it is The Drones Club, Dover Street, London, W1.

10 ~ BERTIE WOOSTER

~

The story 'Extricating Young Gussie' in *The Man with Two Left Feet* (1917); four stories in a collection of eight entitled *My Man Jeeves* (1919); *The Inimitable Jeeves* (1923), a loosely stitched novel of eighteen chapters which make ten separate stories in *The Jeeves Omnibus* (1931); *Carry On, Jeeves* (1925), a collection of ten stories, four of them from *My Man Jeeves*, a fifth which, in *My Man Jeeves*, had been told by and about Reggie Pepper and is here tailored to make a Bertie/Jeeves story, 'Fixing It for Freddie' (in this Aunt Agatha's name is still apparently Miss Wooster: so it should strictly ante-date the lot), one describing Jeeves's arrival from the agency, and a last one narrated by Jeeves himself; *Very Good, Jeeves* (1930), a collection of eleven stories; *The Jeeves Omnibus* collects and re-collects thirty-one stories: Wodehouse distinctly edited and tidied the old material for this new collection. In *A Few Quick Ones* (1959) is 'Jeeves Makes an Omelette', a rewrite of another old Reggie Pepper story in *My Man Jeeves*. There is one short story in *Plum Pie* (1966). The first proper novel is *Thank You, Jeeves* (March 1934); *Right Ho, Jeeves* followed the same year (October 1934); *The Code of the Woosters* (1938); *Joy in the Morning* (1947); and *The Mating Season* (1949). *Ring for Jeeves* (1953) is the only Jeeves novel not told by Bertie; he is mentioned in it, but does not appear. *Jeeves and the Feudal Spirit* (1954), *Jeeves in the Offing* (1960), *Stiff Upper Lip, Jeeves* (1963), *Much Obliged, Jeeves* (1971) and *Aunts Aren't Gentlemen* (1974).

'Providence looks after the chumps of this world; and personally I'm all for it,' said Bertie Wooster in 1925. Providentially he was with us to the end, as delightful a young chump as ever.

In France, some time ago, I read in a local paper one of those horror news-stories that encourage me, when motoring anywhere south of the Loire, to keep to the main roads. In some village in the Mauriac district there had been, in the course of a single weekend and at the time of the full moon, a series of blood-curdling crimes, topped off by the unsuccess-ful burning down of a cottage – unsuccessful, because its two aged.

inhabitants escaped. The *coupable* had not yet been found, but the police were looking for an *innocent* of the village, who had disappeared. They seemed to be confident that this *innocent* would, when located, prove to be the *coupable*.

I like this French use of the word *innocent* – the village idiot. My mind was very full of Bertie Wooster at the time. *Mutatis mutandis*, and with all the crimes deodorized, I saw the Gironde village as a Steeple Bumpleigh, Totleigh, Brinkley or Skeldings, with Bertie Wooster, the lunatic innocent, generating 250 pages of alarm and confusion. He is, to me, one of the most engaging innocents in print. My heart aches for him in his enormous agonies and rejoices with him in his puny exaltations. But Jeeves is right – Bertie is mentally negligible.

And Wodehouse made him his medium in more than a dozen books. They are tales told by an idiot, but Bertie proves to be an unselfconsciously brilliant narrator. This has needed very careful handling. As a character in the books, Bertie's only claim to literary achievement (and he is outspokenly proud of it) is the 'piece' he once contributed to his Aunt Dahlia's magazine, on 'What the Well-dressed Man is Wearing'. But as Wodehouse's medium, Bertie has written all those stories and novels, and this fictional dichotomy does not grate for a moment. As a storyteller Bertie is his own central character, and he has to narrate strictly from the first-personal point of view, often writing scenes in such a way that Bertie-the-character must not realize the purport of what Bertie-the-narrator is narrating, but his readers must. Very difficult, and he does it very smoothly. But still Bertie the writer must project his fictional self as a man capable of being mightily proud of a single incursion into print, in *Milady's Boudoir*.

Wodehouse's other recurrent mouthpieces tell their stories with themselves standing on the side-lines, and with narrator's licence. They may start in double quotes, stating the facts from personal experience. But soon the double quotes disappear, the voice of the specified narrator fades out, and narrator Wodehouse takes over. We are told what a man and a girl say, declaring their love, in a golf-bunker or a two-seater, and we do not ask 'How do you know they said that if you were not there?' Author Wodehouse/Oldest Member is a fly on the wall of the bunker; author Wodehouse/Mulliner is a fly on the windscreen of the two-seater. But Bertie is the core of his own stories, and he has to be there throughout, or fill in with reported speech, delivered to himself. One or two other narrators sustain this technique for a single book (Jeremy

BERTIE WOOSTER, constantly in trouble trying to help his friends
out of trouble.

Garnet for the second edition of *Love among the Chickens* and Reggie
Havershot in *Laughing Gas*). Bertie has done it for ten novels and
fifty-odd short stories.

At his preparatory school, Bertie was known as 'Bungler' Wooster.
This nickname may not have had associations with the Conan Doyle/
Sherlock Holmes stories ('Scotland Yard bunglers') in the minds of
Bertie's masters and friends. It certainly had those associations in
Wodehouse's mind. I seem to keep finding, or I keep seeming to find,
trace elements of Conan Doyle in the Wodehouse formulations. I sense a
distinct similarity, in patterns and rhythms, between the adventures of
Jeeves as recorded by Bertie Wooster and the adventures of Sherlock
Holmes as recorded by Dr Watson: Holmes and Jeeves the great brains,
Watson and Bertie the awed companion-narrators, bungling things if
they try to solve the problems themselves; the problems, waiting to be
tackled almost always in country houses, almost always presented and
discussed at breakfast in London; the departure from London, Holmes
and Watson by train, Jeeves and Bertie by two-seater; the gathering of
the characters at the country house; the gathering of momentum,
Holmes seldom telling Watson what he is up to, Jeeves often work-

ing behind Bertie's back; the dénouement; the company fawning on
Holmes or Jeeves; the return trip to 'the rooms' in town; possibly
Holmes's '. . . and I pocket my fee' paralleled by Bertie Wooster's 'How
much money is there on the dressing-table, Jeeves? . . . Collar it all.
You've earned it!'

On another level you may see Bertie Wooster as a modern Don
Quixote, constantly setting out on adventures to help his friends and
constantly making an endearing ass of himself. Don Quixote has a wiser
vade mecum in Sancho Panza; Bertie has the wiser Jeeves. Bertie, like
Don Quixote, has his brain curdled with romance. Don Quixote's
romance came from books of knight-errantry; Bertie's from Edwardian
fiction and a regular diet of detective novels. Don Quixote's enchanting
books were burnt, but he carried the gist of them always in his mind;
Bertie has an ever-ready memory of the plot-clichés of the Rosie M.
Banks writers of his boyhood. When he tries to disentangle his friends'
problems along Rosie M. Banks's lines, he gets those lines crossed and
the entanglements made worse. He is a prime bungler. A good-natured
romantic, but a bungler. One comes back to the Conan Doyle word.

The important thing, if you study Bertie, is not so much the width of
his reading of bilge literature as the depth to which he absorbs the stuff.
His little mind keeps a gooey sludge of words, phrases and concepts from
what he has read, and it gives him a magpie vocabulary of synonyms and
quotations. It contributes largely to his Code. He is a fantasist. Even,
perhaps specially, in moments of tension and peril, his attention seems to
wander, and he gets beside himself, watching himself, aligning himself
with the heroes of his reading, adopting their attitudes, blurting out their
clichés of speech. Bertie shares his escape-route with Mr Pooter, Walter
Mitty, Billy Liar, Catherine Morland, Emma Bovary and other literary
dreamers. So far Bertie has only encountered Sir Roderick Glossop, the
loony-doctor, socially. Never in the consulting-room. But Sir Roderick
may still be waiting for Bertie fairly confidently as a patient.

In *Right Ho, Jeeves*, Bertie, while nobly, if cautiously and anonymously, pleading Gussie's cause with Madeline Bassett, makes it appear to
Madeline that he is brokenly and shyly pleading his own love for her. It
was an old Wodehouse plot-shape; indeed much older than Wodehouse. For a brief, climactic moment Bertie finds that Madeline has
received his words as a proposal. And his book-bred Code says that no
gentleman can break off his engagement to however disastrous a girl.
You'd expect, if you didn't know Bertie, that in this crisis his brain would

either cease to function or, ice-cold in an emergency, would attend to the matter in hand with single strictness. Not so. Bertie, clenching his fists in agony, is wondering whether his knuckles are, or are not, standing out white under the strain. And when, seconds later, Madeline tells Bertie that she is sorry, the thing's impossible, you'd expect that the relief would clarify Bertie's mind wonderfully and pinpoint his attention on the facts. Again not so. The relief is great, yes. But Bertie the fantasist lets his mind wander and is instantly beside himself again, seeing the event in homely images:

'I am sorry . . .' said Madeline . . .
The word was like one of Jeeves's pick-me-ups. Just as if a glassful of meat sauce, red pepper and the yolk of an egg . . . though, as I say, I am convinced that these are not the sole ingredients . . . had been shot into me, I expanded like some lovely flower blossoming in the sunshine. It was all right, after all. My guardian angel had not been asleep at the switch.

If you say that this is Bertie the narrator, remembering in tranquillity and with a trained literary mind events which allowed no such mental gymnastics at the time, I am not convinced. Bertie's mind drifted *during the crisis* into mazes of metaphor and meat sauce. He was carried off on a stream of semi-consciousness and free association, with time for a parenthesis stating his doubts about the Jeeves pick-me-up recipe. Then he sees himself in the guise of some lovely flower blossoming in the sunshine. He is back to his books.

Bertie hops through the looking-glass and stands beside himself very often and at slight provocation. His memory is so full of the words and music of heroic action that he can find a phrase to fit almost any situation. His narrative and conversation are larded with second-hand alternatives to direct description. By mixing his soiled metaphors and colliding his clichés, he fabricates a burbling language of evocative innocence. Quite often in narration he drops into the Bertie-beside-himself third person singular:

Those who know Bertram Wooster best are aware that he is a man of sudden, strong enthusiasms and that, when in the grip of one of these, he becomes a remorseless machine, tense, absorbed, single-minded. It was so in the matter of this banjolele-playing of mine . . .

And:

'Yes, Jeeves?' I said. And though my voice was suave a close observer in a position to watch my eyes would have noted a steely glint . . .

And:

> When I wore it [the white mess-jacket] at the Casino at Cannes, beautiful women nudged one another and whispered; 'Who is he?'

And:

> He quivered like a mousse. I suppose it must always be rather a thrilling experience for the novice to watch me taking hold . . .

In his last book of all, Bertie is still watching himself in a mirror, hearing himself talk and ready with self-applause when it is earned.

> 'Hullo, old ancestor,' I said, and it was a treat to hear me, so full of ginger and loving kindness was my diction.

Bertie laughing down from lazy eyelids and flicking specks of dust from the irreproachable Mechlin lace at his wrists; Bertie answering an angry questioner 'with a suavity that became me well' (and I wish somebody would tell me what original Wodehouse was echoing when he wrote, as he did a dozen times or more, that succession of words); Bertie inspecting his imagination and finding that it boggled; Bertie saying 'Oh' and meaning it to sting – with Bertie, we are dealing with a young man whose boyhood reading has been wider than a church door, and whose memory of it is deeper than a well. Bertie is a shining example of a magpie mind cherished whole into adult life.

Shakespeare had a magpie mind too. It is only the fine, imaginative, noticing mind, like Shakespeare's and Bertie Wooster's, that dares wander down the garden path without losing its way back. Your lawyer and chartered accountant would feel naked and lost so far from home. If they look wistfully out into the garden, and to the perilous seas and faery lands beyond, they take good care to keep the magic casement shut, lest they start climbing through. Shakespeare equates the lunatic, the lover and the poet – types who can't keep their feet on the ground or their minds on the subject under advisement. Bertie is three parts lunatic. He sometimes loves. In his wild imagery he is not far off from being a poet.

Bertie asked Pauline Stoker to marry him. It was in New York, at the Plaza. Bertie relates the incident only in a flashback, as a necessary starting point for *Thank You, Jeeves*; necessary because it gives an excuse for a good jealousy-teeth-grinding-let's-see-the-colour-of-his-insides menace to Bertie from his old friend Chuffy, who is now, three months later, in love with Pauline. The green-eyed Chuffy questions Bertie keenly about what went on when he and Pauline were engaged. He grills Bertie into revealing that, during the two days' betrothal, he never kissed the adored object even once:

> 'I hope you will be very, very happy [says Bertie to Chuffy]. I can honestly say that I always look on Pauline as one of the nicest girls I was ever engaged to.'
> 'I wish you would stop harping on that engagement.'
> 'Quite.'
> 'I'm trying to forget that you were ever engaged to her.'
> 'Quite, quite.'
> 'When I think that you were once in a position to . . .'
> 'But I wasn't. Never lose sight of the fact that the betrothal only lasted two days, during both of which I was in bed with a nasty cold.'
> 'But when she accepted you, you must have . . .'
> 'No, I didn't. A waiter came into the room with a tray of beef sandwiches and the moment passed.'
> 'Then you never . . .?'
> 'Absolutely never.'
> 'She must have had a great time, being engaged to you. One round of excitement. I wonder what on earth made her accept you?'

That engagement was broken up by Pop Stoker, abetted by Sir Roderick Glossop. But, although Wodehouse frequently juxtaposed sentiment and food, romance and greediness, as incongruities to make comic bathos, for the moment I want to put the lights on that tray of beef sandwiches at the Plaza in New York.

When Bertie recalls those beef sandwiches, is he babbling the free associations of a wondering mind? Or is he half-way to poetry? Shakespeare, as we know, was all for free association. Take Juliet's nurse, her woolly old mind swithering about trying to pinpoint Juliet's age. She remembers, she remembers . . . yes, she'll get it soon. Yes, she had weaned Juliet . . . yes, she had put the wormwood to her dug,

> Sitting in the sun under the dove house wall;
> My Lord and you were then at Mantua.

Forty years ago I wrote in a note against those two lines in my Temple *Romeo and Juliet*: 'cf. Bertie W's beef sandwiches'. Juliet's nurse, under Shakespeare's guidance, remembers the sun and the dove house and the wall. Bertie, earthier, remembers the beef sandwiches.

Bertie admits that he has a tendency to babble in moments of tension. In a burst of sympathy for the cloth-headed newt-fancier Gussie, who, terrified by the arrival of the mood, the moonlight and the expectant Madeline all together, started talking about newts, Bertie remembers how, in the dentist's chair, he had, through sheer nerves, held up the man behind the forceps with a silly story of an Englishman, an Irishman and a Jew. But often in a crisis he repeats sounds without knowing their meaning. He refers to someone in an advanced state of gloom looking like a cat in an adage. When Tuppy Glossop is reaching for Bertie's neck in the garden, to wring it for (as Tuppy believes) having traduced him (Tuppy) to the girl (Angela) whom he (Tuppy) loves, Bertie says:

'I have always regarded you with the utmost esteem. Why, then, if not for the motives I have outlined, should I knock you to Angela? Answer me that. Be very careful.'
'What do you mean, be very careful?'
Well, as a matter of fact, I didn't quite know myself. It was what the magistrate had said to me on the occasion when I stood in the dock as Eustace Plimsoll, of The Laburnums; and as it had impressed me a good deal, at the time, I just brought it in now by way of giving the conversation a tone . . .

If Bertie wrenches logic and language into perilous distortions, it is not entirely through vapidity. It is partly a genuine hankering for the *mot juste*, the vivid phrase, the exact image. At another moment of acute crisis he can pause to express his shock at discovering that Uncle Tom's second name is Portarlington, or to ask Jeeves to check a quotation for him. Referring to Aunt Dahlia and her weekly magazine, *Milady's Boudoir*, he writes: 'Seeing it go down the drain would be for her like watching a loved child sink for the third time in some pond or mere . . .'

That 'or mere' comes with the pride of a magpie which has collected a gold ring *and* a silver paper milk-bottle top; it is the poet hoarding an alternative for rhyming; it is the pin-head who lets his feeble mind wander in word-associations when an aunt is in peril. This one may be a Tennysonian evocation. Bertie's sources may be anything from the Psalms (frequently) to Scott's last message from the Antarctic (once). He hasn't the discrimination to be a snob about his sources. To go to the Old Vic with his cousin Young Thos, at Aunt Agatha's orders, to witness Shakespeare or Chekhov is torture, to him as to Thos. But once a literary phrase has got tamped down in his memory, it becomes a fiery particle of his vocabulary. In Jeeves he has a walking lexicon and dictionary of quotations, which he adds to his simmering brew of tosh and tag-ends, thin on reason but often producing a sweet poetry.

Reason has moons, but moons not hers
    lie mirror'd on her sea,
confounding her astronomers,
    but O! delighting me.

Bertie hardly ever tries to be funny and he is not a bit witty. He will use a piffling phrase for a lofty sentiment or a lofty phrase for a piffling sentiment. He bubbles and burbles, innocent and vulnerable. Fantasist, schizo, duffer, do-gooder, hungry for praise, Bertie has a mind that is a tape-recorder for sounds and rhythms, but has no discipline or control in playing them back. This is the quintessence of the highly disciplined and tightly controlled Wodehouse burble. Bertie is its chief executant. But make no mistake, 'Bertie Wodehouse' language has power, suppleness and great speed of communication. When Hilaire Belloc wrote that Wodehouse was the best writer of English alive, he was paying tribute not only to his control of schizophrenic imagery, but to his discipline in telling a complicated story quickly and clearly. Wodehouse can, in Bertie's artificial language, get from A to B by the shortest route and still litter all sorts of flowers at your feet as you follow it.

Tuppy Glossop was the fellow, if you remember, who, ignoring a lifelong friendship in the course of which he had frequently eaten my bread and salt, betted me one night at the Drones that I wouldn't swing myself across the swimming bath by the ropes and rings, and then, with almost inconceivable treachery, went and looped back the last ring, causing me to drop into the fluid and ruin one of the nattiest suits of dress-clothes in London.

Try altering or cutting a word in that sentence. You can't. Every *mot* is *juste*. When Bertie describes the warning note of an angry nesting swan as being 'like a tyre bursting in a nest of cobras', it shows Bertie, again at a moment of tension, day-dreaming into a poetic image even as his adrenal reflexes (fight or flight) send him skimming up the wall of the summer-house. But it is a glorious image, expressed in words which themselves, of their structure, menace and explode with sibilants.

Bertie Wooster's age stays put at about twenty-four, but you can spot certain changes in his slang styles as the publishing years advance. He stopped saying 'chappie', 'dear boy' and the parenthetical 'don't you know' in the 1920s. He stopped saying 'rattled' (meaning pleased), and 'rotten' as a universal pejorative, in the 1930s. By the middle 1930s he had virtually made his own language, and it became frozen and timeless to the last. A great number of people have tried to parody the 'Bertie.

Wodehouse' style in print. Rather fewer have tried to imitate it without parody. None has succeeded. The best parodies of Bertie's style are by Wodehouse himself when he let a page go to the printer without quite the necessary polish. Then you are probably reading the sixth draft, rather than the tenth. At his polished best the burble that Wodehouse put into Bertie's mouth is beautiful stuff.

It is pretty generally recognised in the circles in which he moves that Bertram Wooster is not a man who lightly throws in the towel and admits defeat. Beneath the thingummies of what-d'you-call-it, his head, wind and weather permitting, is as a rule bloody but unbowed, and if the slings and arrows of outrageous fortune want to crush his proud spirit, they have to pull their socks up and make a special effort.

Nevertheless, I must confess that when, already weakened by having to come down to breakfast, I beheld the spectacle which I have described, I definitely quailed. The heart sank, and, as had happened in the case of Spode, everything went black. Through a murky mist I seemed to be watching a negro butler presenting an inky salver to a Ma Trotter who looked like the end man in a minstrel show.

The floor heaved beneath my feet as if an earthquake had set in with unusual severity. My eye, in fine frenzy rolling, met Aunt Dahlia's, and I saw hers was rolling, too.

Twelve Woosterisms in fifteen lines: the general clash of jargon phrases, the Bertie-beside-himself third person singular of the whole first paragraph, a botched quotation from Henley, and two, less botched, from Shakespeare, the babu interposition of the presumably nautical 'wind and weather permitting' inside the botched Henley, the boxing image, the good old Wodehousian elaboration of the 'everything went black' cliché, the good old Wodehousian 'earthquake had set in with unusual severity' (that's generally 'Judgement Day', not 'earthquake'), the medical use of 'the' heart instead of 'my' heart, the medical 'weakened' to emphasize that Bertie had breakfasted downstairs that day for once, the enforced use of the single eye, forgivable in the first case, because Bertie is quoting Shakespeare, but foolishly cyclopean when transferred to Aunt Dahlia in the second.

Since Wodehouse wrote in his Bertie Wooster voice more, much more, than in any other, it is reasonable to suppose that he put it on more comfortably than any other. Is it also reasonable to suppose that we find more of the Wodehouse personal identity hidden in Bertie than in any other of Wodehouse's puppets? I think so. Wodehouse himself used to say that Lord Emsworth, absent-minded, hen-pecked, all for a quiet life, was perhaps his nearest *alter ego*. But I propose Bertie for the post.

The self-derogatory first-person-singular has been a staple of English language humour over the last seventy-five years. If 'He slipped on a banana skin' is funny, 'I slipped on a banana skin' is conceivably funny and charming. This is not the only technique of whimsy, but it is a very frequent factor in whimsy. 'Whimsy' and 'whimsical' are rude words in literary criticism these days. But three-quarters of a century ago, and through the majority of Owen Seaman's years on *Punch*, the value-judgement in the words was for the most part kind and appreciative. Seaman's *Punch* catered for, and then overfed, the taste for whimsy. The magazine of his day was full of self-derogatory first-person-singular pieces. Admittedly one's suspension of disbelief in *Punch* was made more unwilling by the magazine's weird habit of having, in an issue containing, say, ten 'I' pieces, three signed by initials, three by pseudonyms and four not signed at all. But the fact remains that the 'I' piece has been, for three-quarters of a century of English humorous writers, a favourite stand-by. Its main laws have remained unaltered since Thackeray and Burnand.

Wodehouse, whose *floruit* spanned much of the whimsy era of *Punch*, wrote very little direct 'I' stuff. In *Louder and Funnier* and *Over Seventy* he showed that he could do it expertly. But if you suppose that any good funny writer with a taste for editorial cheques would use a profitable technique for all it was worth to him, you may be surprised that Wodehouse did not cash in more on his opportunities.

Subliminally, I believe, Bertie Wooster was, and increasingly became, Wodehouse's main surrogate outlet for the self-derogatory first-person-singular mood. The name Wooster is significantly close to Wodehouse. Bertie, in portions of his background and many of his attitudes (though not in his Eton and Oxford status), is the young Wodehouse that the older Wodehouse remembered with amusement, candour, modesty and (a sixth-form tag that Wodehouse himself used in one or more of his youthful books) *pothos* and *desiderium*. The identification in ages is between Bertie at an eternal twenty-four and Wodehouse in that *annus mirabilis* of mental age at which most Wodehouse farce is played – fifteen.

A doctor has told me that when a patient is coming out from under anaesthetic, the anaesthetist needs some test of the stages of his re-emergence. So the anaesthetist starts saying to the patient 'How old are you?', 'How old are you?' And (the doctor told me), however advanced the age of the patient, his first mumbling answer is frequently 'Nineteen'. He may say 'Nineteen' two or three times till adequate consciousness returns, and then he gets it right at fifty-five or sixty-five or seventy-five.

Belloc wrote of the unchanging place where all we loved is always near, where we meet our morning face to face and find at last our twentieth year. Nineteen is (according to the doctor) the usual *annus mirabilis.* Fifteen was Wodehouse's, and Wodehouse, significantly, often let Bertie take him back to the green pastures of that irresponsible period, the last moment at which he could see himself unselfconsciously.

Bertie's manner of life, his money, his personal servant, his riding, shooting (once), rackets (once), squash, darts and tennis, his clubs, his idleness, his love for fancy dress balls, his contemptible cunning, risible ruses and puny piques, his overweening optimism and his babu burble of clashing clichés and inattentive images – these are creations of Wodehouse the storyteller. Bertie, the kind, the chivalrous, the greedy, the aunt-ridden, the Code-ridden, the girl-fearing, the pal-helping, the tag-quoting, the slug-abed – he is a poetic, middle-voice throw-back to the dewy, pie-faced schoolboy romantic that Wodehouse saw himself as having been before he struck out into the world for himself. Bertie, in two separate senses, is more of an 'I' character than anyone else in the books. On some spiritual, astral plane, Bertie Wooster and P. G. Wodehouse, their dross shed, may have now met as twin souls.

Bertie is the only one of Wodehouse's heroes or protagonists for whom the mere release from terror and pain is always a sufficiently happy ending. This modest sufficiency is very much in the formula of the technique of 'I' humour. Reggie Havershot, narrator and hero of Wodehouse's light novel, *Laughing Gas,* survives ten chapters of bewilderment, indignity and bullying by an 'aunt' figure. But he is rewarded in the end by winning a jackpot and a Wodehouse heroine in marriage. It is sufficient for the first-personal Bertie that others get the jackpots and girls, and that he be simply released from bewilderment, indignity, bullying by aunts and other circumambient menaces. Bertie, indeed, almost always actually pays for his releases by some kind of atonement-forfeit (Old Etonian spats) or punishment (the great midnight bicycle ride from Brinkley and back). It is acceptable to the reader as a minor, but regular, nemesis for Bertie's earlier hubristic certainty that he can settle his friends' problems, either better than Jeeves can or at all. Wodehouse allows such forces of misrule as Uncle Fred and Aunt Dahlia to go scot-free from the debt of their immoralities. But not first-personal Bertie. Bertie suffers, and, through suffering, he is kept in place. The addition of punishment to the massive terrors and embarrassments that Bertie gets into through his desire to please is artistically supportable, and indeed rewarding, to the reader only because the story is being told by someone cordially underwritten by the author whose name appears on the spine of the book.

Wodehouse autobiography, chopped small, drifts like thistledown into Wooster fiction. The novel *The Mating Season*, published in 1949, contains an interesting collection of the sort of memory-accretions, many of them anachronistic, which give strength to the theory that, consciously or unconsciously, Wodehouse used his own nineteenth-century childhood as a general source of Bertie's twentieth-century youth. Bertie is stuck in a house full of aunts – not his own in the book, but giving him frequent cause to philosophize about aunts. Bertie recalls boyhood dancing-classes, boyhood recitations, boyhood pimples, a boyhood Little-Lord-Fauntleroy suit and a boyhood nannie. He is made to help at a village concert, and he is wise in the ways of village concerts, as Wodehouse doubtless was when he lived with aunts-married-to-clergymen in his school holidays. Village concerts as a regular threat to country life must have been severely hit by the arrival of radio and killed stone-dead by television. But there, in 1949, is Bertie in the midst of one. Nobody sings 'The Yeoman's Wedding Song', but Muriel Kegley-Bassington comes across with 'My Hero' from *The Chocolate Soldier* followed by 'Oh, who will o'er the downs with me' as an encore. Except for the Christopher Robin verses, every turn has an 1890-ish date to it. The vicar's niece, who organizes the concert, is Corky Pirbright, now a Hollywood star. Her brother, Catsmeat, though a member of The Drones, is an actor. There is much talk of the low esteem in which the respectable gentry holds members of the acting profession – an Edwardian, not later-Georgian attitude. Bertie in this book is unusually full of stage jargon, and is deft to compose a lyric for the squire (who loves Corky) to sing at the concert. This surely is the young Wodehouse, whose dabbling in, and success at, writing for the theatre must have caused his own flock of aunts to think he was getting into bad company in his twenties, much more dangerous than the friends he would have made if he had stayed in the Bank.

For the length of *The Mating Season*, and the date still being 1949, Bertie stays at Deverill Hall, a house more or less run by these strict aunts, but where champagne is served without question at dinner; a house full of modern conveniences, but where all sudden announcements from the outside are made by telegram, not by telephone. Bertie meets the butler, Silversmith (Jeeves's uncle), and is reminded of the old-fashioned, sixteen-stone butlers who made him feel insignificant and badly dressed as a young man. But Bertie *is*, for the purposes of the story, a young man. Aged twenty-four in 1949, he would have been born in 1925, a good fifty years too late for him to have been bothered by Little-Lord-Fauntleroy suits, childhood recitations of 'Mary Had a Little Lamb' and 'Ben Battle', and the sort of village concert that this one turned out to be. Wodehouse was giving his own stripling memories to Bertie, in spite of a difference of fifty years in period. In another book Bertie remembers his Little-Lord-Fauntleroy suit again, and this time he also remembers that he wore his hair in ringlets to match. I don't know if the boy Wodehouse was made to wear his hair in ringlets. Nor do I know for sure (though I would make a bet) that Bertie was speaking for his ninety-three-year-old author in *Aunts Aren't Gentlemen* when he said, 'When I was a child, my nurse told me that there was One who was always beside me, spying out all my ways, and that if I refused to eat my spinach I would hear about it on Judgement Day.'

John Hayward in *The Saturday Book* of 1942 made the point that Wodehouse had 'a wide knowledge of English literature and Shakespeare's plays'. He may have had, but the knowledge that he exhibited is essentially schoolboy stuff. Bertie and Jeeves between them bandy quotations from the poets freely. But where these are not from Shakespeare and the classical poets (and an A-level schoolboy of today might have the same stock), they are from such minor Victorian sources that a boy might have learnt them for Repetition at school in the late 90s, but not in the 1920s. And a significant number of Bertie's images (the tiger and his breakfast coolie, the Pathan sneaking up on the *sahib* across the *maidan*) seem to jump right out from illustrations in *Chums* and similar magazines of the 1890s. This again is Wodehouse giving his memories to Bertie. Bertie once or twice looks back to the days of Covent Garden Balls, fights with costermongers and nights spent at the hammams, almost like the original, eighteenth-century William Hickey. Bertie is an ageless young man, spanning the ages.

Bertie started life as a type and he became a character. He remains the Knut, the Piccadilly Johnny and the playboy bachelor. But, because Wodehouse liked him and wrote through his eyes so often, Bertie became

more three-dimensional than any other character in these highly artificial books. In *Performing Flea* Wodehouse says: 'I go off the rails unless I
stay all the time in a sort of artificial world of my own creation. A real
character in one of my books sticks out like a sore thumb.' Bertie comes
alive in the sense that he is predictable. He dictates his own terms for plot
and characterization. While other cardboard characters walk into the
soup and displace hardly a spoonful, Bertie displaces it in credible waves.
We go in there with him and suffer with his suffering. When Freddie
Widgeon, Bingo, Ukridge or a Mulliner go into the soup, we stay on the
rim of the tureen and laugh. With Bertie we share the agony and the
wetness. His mental deficiency is such that our own brains feel powerful.
But we love Bertie and identify ourselves with him, as Wodehouse did to
the limits of his own very rigid modesty and self-esteem.

Bertie looks back to a childhood and boyhood of normal rowdiness.
When, in 'The Love That Purifies', he sees a septuagenarian asleep in the
garden in a deckchair, he tells Jeeves that, in his boyhood, he would
certainly have done something drastic to such a septuagenarian, probably with a pea-shooter. He stole and smoked one of Lord Worplesdon's
cigars at the age of fifteen. He may not have been as fiendish a young
gangster as his cousin Thos when he was Thos's age, but he wasn't a prig,
like Edwin Craye, or a sissy, like Sebastian Moon. He went through
Malvern House, Eton and Oxford at the proper pace. But, somewhere
about the age of twenty-four, Bertie stopped ageing.

The Code of the Woosters is part public school, part novelette. Its two
main commandments are: (1) Thou shalt not let down a pal; and (2)
Thou shalt not scorn a woman's love. Most of the plots of Bertie's stories
hinge on one or the other, or both, of these commandments. Bertie has a
genuinely kind heart, and, though Palmanship forces him to undertake
terrible exploits, he really is made happier when he can do a good turn for
a friend, and especially for two friends, a man and a girl with a lovers' tiff
to be tidied up.

What does Authority mean to someone with a family, social and
educational background such as Bertie's? I think it is based in the
public-school system. In public schools, both of fiction and of fact,
headmasters, housemasters and their lackeys, the prefects, represent
Authority in a highly undemocratic state. The serfs and proles of the
Lower and Middle Schools have no say in who bosses them. Authority is
always elected from above. Prefects are not, in any school that I know of,
chosen by an electorate of juniors saying 'Please govern us.' The

housemaster nominates the prefects, the headmaster nominates the housemaster and the Governing Body nominates the headmaster. Young Johnny's parents pay large sums for young Johnny to live in this hieratic discipline, subdued until the time comes for him, as a prefect, to subdue.

Bertie Wooster's relationship with Jeeves seems to me a public-school arrangement, easy for Bertie, though surprisingly accepted by Jeeves. Bertie sometimes berates Jeeves like a prefect berating a fag, not like a master berating a servant. And as Bertie is always wrong on these occasions, and Jeeves knows it, Bertie is extremely lucky to have a servant who understands his master's Code and forgives it. But in the wider Wodehouse social set-up, though Authority does not specifically employ the public-school indignification of beating grown-up people on the 'billowy portions', it does, in the public-school manner, work to a set of sanctions, checks and balances of great power, but, almost all of them, non-valid in, and beyond the reach of, Common Law. You can't have the law on an aunt when she makes you steal pearl necklaces for her, but you know that, if you don't comply, the cooking of the best chef in England will be wiped from your greedy lips in indefinite punishment. Call it blackmail, but can you tell it to the magistrate? You can't have the law on a ghastly girl when she says she's going to marry you, but you'll put yourself in peril of the law by pinching a policeman's uniform in order to set in motion a series of events which will culminate (if Jeeves is working them out) in your quasi-honourable release from the engagement. When Stiffy Byng makes her fiancé, the sainted Rev. 'Stinker' Pinker, prove his love for her by bringing her policeman Oates's helmet, he can do nothing but wail 'If the Infants' Bible Class should hear of this!' When Florence Craye makes her fiancé, Stilton, grow a moustache, he is powerless except to grind a tooth or two. When an ex-London magistrate, a maniac collector of old silver, puts a rival maniac collector out of the running for the acquisition of a rare antique by, with cunning aforethought, feeding him cold lobster at lunch and so confining him to quarters with writhing indigestion, the second maniac's ever-loving wife knows that the law cannot help. Bertie must go and steal the cow-creamer back for its 'rightful' owner. In Wodehouse's farces everybody is playing cops and robbers in a law-free society.

Bertie, the most innocent of do-gooders temperamentally, has no inborn authority of his own. He never uses his money to buy authority and, apart from money, what is he? He has accepted the position of being a 'Hey-you' to aunts, uncles and quite a lot of girls. But Wodehouse is in

Bertie's corner, and Wodehouse gives Bertie Jeeves. With certain reservations about white mess-jackets, Old Etonian spats and banjoleles, Jeeves is completely and self-effacingly pro-Bertie. All three, Bertie, Jeeves and Wodehouse, are transparently anti-prefect (Aunt Agatha), anti-fag (Edwin) and pro the status of the fifteen-year-old public-school boy.

But watch Bertie when he suddenly does get the moral cosh of authority into his hands. He knows all the prefect's manner of speech. Though he is properly the bossed, the chivvied, the man in the ranks, the man on the receiving end of orders and objurgations, Bertie can snap, with absurd ease, into the jargon of authority. Listen to him come the headmaster over terrible Spode, when he has blessedly remembered the magic word 'Eulalie', and thus has the goods on this pestilential amateur dictator:

'I shall be very sharp on that sort of thing in the future, Spode.'

'Yes, yes, I understand.'

'I have not been at all satisfied with your behaviour since you came to this house. The way you were looking at me during dinner . . . and calling me a miserable worm.'

'I'm sorry I called you a miserable worm, Wooster. I spoke without thinking.'

'Always think, Spode. Well, that is all. You may withdraw.'

Macaulay wrote of the 'arrogant humility' of the younger Pitt. Bertie's humble arrogance is a much more touching thing.

Bertie has still not suffered that 'fate worse then death – *viz*. marriage'. But he has run it fine with eight or nine girls at one time or another. Bertie is no wolf. If Jeeves finds Bertie's bed un-slept-in, he assumes, and correctly, that Bertie has spent the night in jug somewhere, not with any girl. Aunts and friends break in on Bertie's bedroom before breakfast, with never a suspicion that he may have company there. When Bertie, by mistake, climbs into Florence Craye's bedroom window at Brinkley, Florence, to whom he has been engaged once or twice already, assumes that, still yearning, he has come to kiss her while she sleeps. Bertie (who possibly hasn't read Kipling's 'Brushwood Boy') is pained by such advanced modern thought. When Pauline Stoker, to whom Bertie has also once been engaged, is revealed in Bertie's bed, in Bertie's pyjamas, unchaperoned, in Bertie's little seaside cottage at midnight, Bertie is shocked to his foundations. Bertie is pure as driven snow, if not purer. He refers to himself as a 'reputable bachelor who has never had his licence so much as endorsed'.

Pauline Stoker put it well when she said there was a 'woolly-headed duckiness' about Bertie. 'Mentally negligible, but he has a heart of gold,' says Jeeves of the young master. When Bertie is old and grey and full of sleep, he will look back on his romantic youth and probably decide that the greatest compliment he was ever paid was from Pauline's father. Pop Stoker, an incandescent American millionaire, hearing that his daughter had spent the night in Bertie's cottage, captured Bertie in his yacht and proposed to keep him there till he had married the errant girl. Pop Stoker, at any rate, believed Bertie had passions that he could unbridle, and Pop Stoker had a nasty Victorian sense of etiquette to deal with the situation as he guessed it.

Pauline would not have been too bad a wife for Bertie. But, when the smoke has cleared away, we accept Jeeves's judgement that Bertie is one of nature's bachelors. We're glad that Bertie lasted the course in single strictness, with Jeeves to look after him and to bring tea for one to the bedroom in the mornings.

———————— ∼ ————————

∼ He felt like a man who, chasing rainbows, has had one of them suddenly turn and bite him in the leg.

∼ Poets, as a class, are business men. Shakespeare describes the poet's eye as rolling in a fine frenzy from heaven to earth, from earth to heaven, and giving to airy nothing a local habitation and a name, but in practice you will find that one corner of that eye is generally glued on the royalty returns.

∼ He got through the song somehow and limped off amidst roars of silence from the audience.

∼ 'I was in musical comedy. I used to sing in the chorus, till they found out where the noise was coming from. And then I went to Hollywood. You would like Hollywood, you know. Everybody does. Girdled by the everlasting hills, bathed in eternal sunshine. And if you aren't getting divorced yourself, there's always one of your friends who is, and that gives you something to chat about in the long evenings. And it isn't half such a crazy place as they make out. I know two-three people in Hollywood that are part sane.'

∼ The Aberdeen terrier gave me an unpleasant look and said something under his breath in Gaelic.

∼ The magistrate looked like an owl with a dash of weasel blood in him.

∼ With 'Catsmeat' Pirbright's sister Corky the general effect is of an angel who eats lots of yeast.

———————— ∼ ————————

11 ~ JEEVES

———————— ~ ————————

(The only book in which Jeeves appears without Bertie Wooster is *Ring for Jeeves* (1953).)

The Times obituary of Eric Blore, the film-actor, in 1959, ended:

He made a speciality of that most English of all professions . . . the gentleman's gentleman or manservant, the very epitome of Jeeves. Indeed, he and another English actor, Mr Arthur Treacher, may be said to have made a virtual corner in butler parts in Hollywood during the thirties, and no study of an upper-class English or American household was complete without one or other of them. Treacher, tall and thin, was haughty and austere, a man with a permanent smell under his nose. Blore, who was shorter and slightly tubby, was a trifle more eccentric in manner, but equally capable of registering eloquent but unspoken disapproval of any untoward behaviour. But he could yet suggest a taste for a lower life, and it was Blore who introduced into an American film *It's Love I'm After* the eloquent line: 'If I were not such a gentleman's gentleman I could be such a cad's cad.'

It is just tribute to Wodehouse that *The Times* could already use 'Jeeves' like that, without quotation marks and without acknowledgement. To some extent it was due to Wodehouse's glorification of the English manservant that Treacher and Blore could live their prosperous lives in Hollywood. Butlers had always been useful in plays, to come on and explain the set-up, in dialogue with a dusting housemaid or into a telephone while the audience settled down. But Hollywood's cameras could wander around and show direct what a stage butler had to get across in speech. Hollywood used the stately and funny butler because he was a fat part and he paid dividends. Wodehouse had put butlers on the map. Hollywood used them where they stood, and paid Wodehouse scant thanks. Incidentally, I understand that there are today more butlers –

real butlers, and most of them English – in Hollywood homes than there are in the whole of England. Jeeves was, in fact, a valet.

Wodehouse wrote a good deal, for him, about writing about butlers and gentlemen's gentlemen. He told us that his love for the tribe on the other side of the green baize door started when he was a boy and used to be lugged round by aunts and clergymen uncles to call on the great houses. Young Pelham was a bust as a conversationalist in the drawing-rooms over the cucumber sandwiches, so his uncles and aunts often sent him off with the butler to have his tea in the servants' hall. And there young Pelham kidded back and forth with footman and housemaid and everybody was very happy – the boy showing off, the servants encouraging him in a way his uncles and aunts never did.

Doubtless even then Wodehouse was awed by the majesty of the butlers. Ukridge's visual description of Oakshott really stands for all butlers: 'Meeting him in the street and ignoring the foul bowler hat he wore on his walks abroad, you would have put him down as a Bishop in mufti or, at the least, a plenipotentiary at one of the better courts.' The first sentence of 'The Good Angel' in the book of short stories *The Man Upstairs* (1914) is: 'Any man under thirty years of age who tells you he is not afraid of an English butler lies.' Lord Ickenham, for all his insistence that earls had a right, and almost a duty, to be haughty, was equally at home in castle and cottage. But, though he was at least sixty, his affection for his butler, Coggs, was tempered by awe. Bertie Wooster himself, who normally treats servants as to the manor born, was overawed by Silversmith, butler at Deverill Hall in *The Mating Season*. This was one of those flickers of Wodehouse–Wooster autobiography.

In an unrepublished *Strand* story, in 1914, 'Creatures of Impulse', Wodehouse told of a perfect servant, Jevons (the name Jeeves may have been taking shape even then), who, on an impulse, put ice down the neck of his Baronet master at the dinner table. The Bart sacked him. But then, later, the Bart got an air-gun in his hands in the country and, on an impulse, shot a gardener in the trouser-seat with it. He couldn't think what had come over him, but he realized he had wronged Jevons and he summoned him back by telegram. Obviously bits of this story went into the making of 'The Crime Wave at Blandings'. Wodehouse gives us good butlers and bad butlers. Julia Ukridge's butler Oakshott was called 'inky-souled' by no less a rogue than Ukridge himself. It is pleasant to see Oakshott taking off his coat to cuddle a housemaid on his knee in his pantry. It is pleasant to see Oakshott, in a moment of panic, dive into a

JEEVES, the perfect, now archetypal,
'gentleman's personal gentleman'.

wardrobe when he thought the police were after him. Another butler
preached Socialism in Hyde Park. Another played the fiddle. Beach of
Blandings kept a bullfinch and stole pigs. And what about the bank-
burgling butler? These are good grace-notes.

You will find fine Wodehouse butlers in fifty books, Attwater, Barlow,
Barter, Bayliss, Baxter, Beach, Benson, Blizzard, Bowles (ex-butler),
Bulstrode, Chibnall, Coggs, Ferris, Gascoyne, Keggs, Oakshott, Pollen,
Ridgway, Silversmith, Slingsby, Spenser, Sturgis, Swordfish, Vosper
and Watson being the names that spring to the mind. Swordfish (the
name that Sir Roderick Glossop took when pretending to be the butler at
Brinkley in *Jeeves in the Offing*) was indeed a name that sprang to the
mind of that scheming young menace Bobbie Wickham. But there is
virtually only one gentleman's personal gentleman in the books, and
that's Jeeves. You will find a few other valets or what passed for valets,
including Archie Mulliner's Meadowes and that other Meadowes,
Jeeves's predecessor in Bertie's service (he sneaked Bertie's socks), and
Jeeves' substitute in *Thank You, Jeeves*, who got tight, trolled hymns and
went after Bertie with the meat knife. But Jeeves is supreme.

'There is none like you, none, Jeeves,' says Bertie, thereby showing a knowledge of Tennyson's *Maud*, but a number of gaps in his reading. The *débrouillard* manservant was a staple of Greek and Roman comedy. Chesterton described Sam Weller as 'something new – a clever comic servant whose knowledge of the world is more than that of his master, but who is not a rascal'. Barrie's Crichton follows Weller. The stately, orotund manservant, often called Jeames, was in and out of *Punch* as early as the 1860s. John Buchan's Sir Archie Roylance had an encyclopaedic manservant who 'patently educated' him.

In Cynthia Asquith's memoir of Barrie is a description of Barrie's own butler, Thurston, who read Latin and Greek while polishing the silver and would correct Barrie's literary guests when they got their quotations wrong. Frank Thurston became Barrie's manservant in 1922, at a time when Jeeves was already coming out serially in print. If you read Chapter 4 of Cynthia Asquith's *Portrait of Barrie*, you'll see how the factual Thurston resembled the fictional Jeeves:

Dictionaries and various learned tomes cluttered up the pantry . . . I discovered him poring over a Spanish book. 'Is that a difficult language, Thurston?' I asked. 'No, My Lady, it presents little difficulty if one has a fair knowledge of Latin and French.' . . . He could supply any forgotten date or quotation . . . Barrie would counsel guests that, if they must take a 'thriller' to bed, they had better 'hide it in between a Pliny and the latest theory of Ethics', or they might feel abashed when Thurston came to draw their curtains in the morning . . . 'You are inimical to your apparel, Sir,' said Thurston to Barrie, who used to burn his clothes with sparks from his pipe . . . 'I still haven't found out,' Barrie said one day, 'what it is that Thurston doesn't know, but I don't give up hope.' . . . From Italy he wrote to me, 'The beauty of Venice is almost appalling, and so was Thurston's knowledge of it as we entered it' . . . Thurston, uncommunicative, inscrutable, puma-footed . . . no one ever heard him enter or leave a room . . . was so unusual, indeed, so mysterious a being that he might almost have been written by his master . . . A man who inspired not only instantaneous respect, but – for his heart was as good as his head – growing affection. In the last letter Barrie wrote (it was to Thurston) Barrie said 'I want you besides the monetary bequest to pick for yourself a hundred of my books. Few persons who have entered that loved flat have done more honour to books.'

This is a remarkable consonance with Jeeves. Denis Mackail, a good friend and great admirer of Wodehouse, and author of a fine *Life* of Barrie, said there was no need to think there is any link, in any dimension, between Thurston and Jeeves. Wodehouse didn't know

Barrie well and never went to the Adelphi flat. It is probable that Cynthia Asquith, when she came to write about Thurston, had herself come to equate him with Jeeves and unconsciously to use some of the Wodehouse brushwork for her portrait of Thurston.

Bring on the Girls suggests a factual origin for Jeeves, but it post-dates Jeeves's arrival and naming by at least ten years and must be ignored. More likely as germ-carriers for the idea of Jeeves are two fictional manservants in the books of Conan Doyle (once more), Ambrose, the cravat-tying, coffee-making valet to the Regency buck, Sir Charles Tregellis in *Rodney Stone*, and Austin, Professor Challenger's servant in *The Poison Belt* (1913).

'I'm expecting the end of the world today, Austin.'
'Yes sir, what time, sir?'
'I can't say. Before evening.'
'Very good, sir.' The taciturn Austin saluted and withdrew.

Compare with this the Bertie/Jeeves dialogue in the first story of all, 'Extricating Young Gussie':

'Jeeves,' I said, 'we start for America on Saturday.'
'Very good, sir. Which suit will you wear?'

There is a difference between a gentleman's personal gentleman and a butler, but it is only that the former is thin and the latter fat, and they have different spheres of duties. Wodehouse would have claimed no originality for Jeeves as a broad type. What Wodehouse could have claimed as his own patent with Jeeves was his successful use of him as a recurrent, funny and credible agent in plot-making.

The Wodehouse farce plots are highly complicated, and Wodehouse took immense trouble in handling them ingeniously. Other good authors, having achieved plots one stage less involved, would feel perfectly justified in their artistic consciences to allow their dénouements to start through a coincidence or act of God. Wodehouse, in the Jeeves stories, used Jeeves as an extra dimension, a godlike prime mover, a master brain who is found to have engineered the apparent coincidence or coincidences. When Bingo Little was sorely harassed by his wife Rosie's old school chum, it would still have been a good story if the picnic basket had been put in the wrong car in error, and if Bertie's car had run out of petrol in the wilds at tea-time by chance. That would have sufficed to cause the flaming row between Rosie and her chum and to have restored sanity to the way of life of the Little household. But Jeeves had engineered it all. There was no error, no chance.

Jeeves in most stories is the rim of the wheel and the hub, the plotter and the plot. Bertie sometimes insists on handling problems his own way. Jeeves, in his background planning, can not only allow for Bertie's mistakes; he can estimate their extent in advance and make them a positive part of the great web he is himself spinning. And he is so confident of his success that he will often take his reward before his success has actually happened and before his reward has been offered.

'Jeeves, you may give away those plus-fours of mine you dislike so.'
'Thank you, sir, I gave them to the under-gardener yesterday.'

Jeeves has a genuine fondness for Bertie, and enjoys helping him and his friends. He likes them to appeal to him and is not annoyed to be summoned by telegram back from the middle of his summer seaside holiday to rescue them from their idiocies. He takes their side calmly. He remains perfectly polite and seems quite impartial to the current opposition. He simply out-generals it. If Bertie, through asininity, sets up an unexpected diversion, Jeeves doesn't let that cramp his style. He envelops it and out-generals Bertie too. He usually makes Bertie pay a forfeit. But, godlike in this too, Jeeves chastens and still loves, loves and still chastens. He accepts Bertie's sacrifice (in the case of the banjolele, a burnt offering), and the score is settled.

Bertie does not bear his grudges against Jeeves for long. Jeeves does not bear grudges against Bertie at all. There is nothing maudlin about their association either. Bertie can be demanding and even rude. Jeeves can be cold and non-cooperative. Bertie sacked Jeeves twice in a single story and would be silly enough to do it again if there were a major clash of wills. Jeeves has resigned twice and he would do it again at the drop of a bowler hat if Bertie continued in some absurd course. Jeeves means it when he resigns. Even he could not plot the happy end of Bertie's banjolele. It was a menace and Jeeves would not be in the same cottage with it. So he resigned and was immediately snapped up by Lord Chuffnell. As it happened, Chuffy, thanks largely to Jeeves's machinations, was able to woo and win Pauline Stoker, which meant that Jeeves did not propose to stay on as his servant. In Jeeves's experience, when a wife comes in at the front door, a valet goes out at the back. As it happened, Bertie's cottage went up in flames and the banjolele was burnt. The *casus belli* between master and man was removed and, on Bertie's assurance that banjolele-playing was a thing of the past for him, Jeeves gladly consented to team up with him again. Honour was preserved on all fronts, though Bertie had had to forfeit a good deal of face (with bootblack on it most of the time) as punishment for his diversionary activities in the middle chapters.

When, in Kipling's *First Jungle Book*, Mowgli is flattered by the *bandar-log* and whisked off by them terrifyingly to the Cold Lairs, Baloo and Bagheera, his fond mentors, have their work cut out to rescue him. But Mowgli had disobeyed their instructions in having anything to do with the *bandar-log* in the first place, and Mowgli has to be punished when the night's alarms and excursions are over. Baloo and Bagheera give him a beating. The principle of Bertie's punishment (not by any means always inflicted by Jeeves) is the same as the principle of Mowgli's, and of Greek tragedy, and of the Old Testament. Hubris not only gets its nemesis. It requires it, especially with such a childlike character as Bertie. Otherwise, childlike, he would go on swanking. Childlike, he would not have the sense to understand the small print on the social contract. He would not renounce his silliness without punishment. And, for the readers, he would not start the next story with the required clean-slate innocence. The slate would carry an unsettled score. We wouldn't mind about that with Ukridge, Aunt Dahlia or Uncle Fred. We would mind with Bertie.

Why Jeeves, with that brain and that confidence in his own brain, should remain a gentleman's personal gentleman is fairly mysterious. He is a keen and shrewd gambler. He could make a fortune in the City and have all the time he wanted for fishing, shrimping, sea-travel and reading. You can't suspect Jeeves of snobbish motives in staying in service with the nobility and gentry; nor of timidity in not wanting to better himself. I am sure he has read Karl Marx and has been exposed to all the dialectic that might persuade lesser valets to work only for the Red Dawn, or to try to collar the means of production and thus become a master rather than a serf. Jeeves just isn't a lesser valet. He lets the foolish Bertie pull rank on him and call him an ass. A lesser valet of spirit wouldn't allow that. Jeeves takes it in the spirit (public school) in which it is dished out. Which is rather superb. But Jeeves is a rather superb person. Bertie calls him an ass occasionally. Bertie snubs him and tells him to put a sock in his reminiscences and poetic analogies. Bertie tells him his brain is softening. Bertie treats him, in fact, not like a social inferior, but like an equal. And Jeeves calmly goes on treating Bertie like an employer first and like a mentally negligible favourite child second. It is a delicate balance to maintain. Jeeves maintains it. Jeeves gets his way and Bertie pays his forfeits. The forfeit is always necessary for Bertie's atonement, but often it is also part of the way Jeeves gets.

Before we study and theorize about Jeeves's reading and education (he plays bridge and can type and do shorthand), we should perhaps gather what little else of his history has been revealed. Jeeves says he 'dabbled in' the First World War to a certain extent. It seems generally accepted that he feeds largely on fish, and that fish supplies phosphorus to the giant brain. Himself, he has said that he eats 'little or no' fish, but Bertie keeps forgetting this. (A prep-school headmaster whom I knew, a Wodehouse addict, in the summer terms took groups of his top-form boys to sit for public-school scholarships and, a tribute to Jeeves, it was fish for breakfast at the hotels each morning for all his young hopefuls. That was an order.) Alcohol has a sedative not a stimulating effect on Jeeves. He says once that he smokes only gaspers, though he has been seen enjoying a cigar and, when Bertie asked him, in *Thank You, Jeeves*, if he had such a thing as a cigarette on his person, Jeeves offered him a choice of Turkish and Virginian. Bertie describes Jeeves as 'tallish, with one of those dark, shrewd faces' and reiterates that his head sticks out at the back. When he wears a hat, it is a size-eight bowler. He probably wears it for shrimping at Bognor.

Jeeves's mother had thought him intelligent as a child, and in adult years he reads Spinoza, Nietzsche and Professor Mainwaring. Also Dostoyevsky and the Great Russians. I have made a cursory count of the sources from which he has ready quotations, and can establish Lucretius, Pliny the Younger, Whittier, Fitzgerald, Pater, Shelley, Kipling, Keats, Scott, Wordsworth, Emerson, Marcus Aurelius, Shakespeare, Browning, Rosie M. Banks, Moore, Virgil, Horace, Dickens, Tennyson, Milton, Henley, the Bible, Stevenson, Gray, Burns, Byron and whoever it was who wrote 'The Wreck of the Hesperus'. Wodehouse has clearly siphoned off into Jeeves all his tags of sixth-form reading, and Jeeves speaks copperplate *Times* Augustan to Bertie's *Sporting Life* vernacular.

'The scheme I would suggest cannot fail of success, but it has what may seem to you a drawback, sir, in that it requires certain financial outlay.'
'He means,' I translated to Corky, 'that he has got a pippin of an idea, but it's going to cost a bit.'

Bertie's friends, Reggie Foljambe and Alistair Bingham-Reeves, have tried to lure Jeeves away for gold. So has Sir Watkyn Bassett. Lord Chuffnell would have liked him to stay on. But Jeeves is bribe-proof so long as Bertie behaves, doesn't play the banjolele and doesn't marry. He runs his 'big Mayfair consulting practice' from Berkeley Mansions and Bertie is quite used to finding people consulting the oracle direct, without coming to him first. 'Jeeves isn't the only onion in the hash,' says Bertie, piqued. But in his calmer moments Bertie knows that that is just what Jeeves is. Jeeves's motto is 'Resource and Tact', and he knows that employers need managing. He managed Bertie for sixty happy years.

~ There is only one real cure for grey hair. It was invented by a Frenchman. He called it the guillotine.

~ He talks French with both hands.

~ As fine a young fellow as he had ever met and one who – a rarity in Russell Clutterbucks's experience – though handicapped by being a Frenchman, did not louse things up by talking French all the time.

~ 'As the car drove in at the gate, we struck a bumpy patch, and I could hear the milk of human kindness sloshing about inside him.'

~ Major Plank relapsed into a sandbagged silence.

~ 'I have always had the ability to touch the human heart-strings,' said Gally complacently. 'Why, in my early days, when I was at the top of my form, I have sometimes made bookies cry.'

~ 'I don't know, Corky, if you have ever done the fine, dignified thing, refusing to accept money because it was tainted and there wasn't enough of it,' said Ukridge.

~ 'Prison's all right for a visit, I always say, but I wouldn't live there if you gave me the place.'

~ 'I don't know whether I am standing on my head or my heels.'
   'Sift the evidence. At which end of you is the ceiling?'

~ 'What a curse these social distinctions are. They ought to be abolished. I remember saying that to Karl Marx once, and he thought there might be an idea for a book in it.'

Appendix 1 ~ THE BERLIN BROADCASTS

———————— ~ ————————

As I have written earlier, it took Wodehouse many years to accept fully that hardly anybody in England had heard his broadcast talks, and nobody had read them, so hardly anybody knew how totally innocuous they had been. It must indeed have been a comparatively meagre audience that heard them even in America, and, again, nobody read them. Werner Plack had offered the talks to both the big American radio networks, A.B.C. and C.B.S., which had offices and correspondents in Berlin, big listenerships in America and programmes which could have carried the Wodehouse talks. But the networks said, 'No, thank you.' So the Wodehouse talks went out on programmes in English on a German shortwave channel, for want of a much bigger audience they might have had in America. But bear in mind that it was not till thirteen years after the broadcasts that anybody could read them in print.

With Iain Sproat's permission, I have taken from his book *Wodehouse at War* (Ticknor & Fields, New York, 1981) the following texts. They are from copies found in the German Foreign Office wartime papers, and they must be as close to verbatim 'as broadcast' as makes no matter. The introductions to the first, second and fourth talks were spoken by Werner Plack. The mis-spelling of Bertie's surname as Worcester is most likely a contribution by a German typist who didn't know the books as Plack did, and was hearing the talks through earphones. It is interesting to note that these texts spells Liége with its *accent aigu* over the first 'e'. This is correct. When the talks were published (at last), the place was mis-spelt Liège.

Wodehouse considered adding the texts of the talks to the hardback *Performing Flea*, published in 1953. But he finally decided against it. It was not till *Encounter* ran the talks in two issues in 1954 that we could read a 98 per cent version of what Wodehouse had spoken into the microphone in Berlin in 1941 (by that time Wodehouse had done some innocent professional editing on the originals). The first Penguin edition of *Performing Flea* did not carry the talks. The second did, with the texts as in *Encounter*, Liège and all.

Note that in Wodehouse's own introduction to his fourth talk, he ascribed his early release – four months or so before his sixtieth birthday – to the efforts of his friends. He meant his American friends. He had some in Berlin at the time, but he meant particularly Senator Barbour of New Jersey and Guy Bolton and others. They had sent an appeal to the German Consul-General in Washington, Dr Hans Thomsen, that special care be given to Wodehouse's health in internment, and suggesting that he might, with advantage to all, be freed and sent back to America. Wodehouse later wished they hadn't made the appeal; it led him to the microphone, and into great trouble.

In the original *Performing Flea* (Herbert Jenkins, 1953) and the Penguin edition of it, a letter is quoted, to Wodehouse from John Leeming, an author whom Wodehouse did not know and who had been for two and a half years a prisoner of war in Italy. He said that he had been personal assistant to the late Air Marshal Boyd of the R.A.F., and that they had been prisoners together. He and the Air Marshal, said Leeming, had read Wodehouse's broadcasts when they were in the Italian P.O.W. camp, and the Air Marshal had expressed great surprise that the Germans had let Wodehouse say all that he had said. 'There is some stuff about being packed in cattle trucks and a thing about Loos jail that you would think would send a Hun crazy. Wodehouse has probably been shot by now.'

I do not think it occurred to Wodehouse and Townend, who prepared *Performing Flea* together, to ask, as I do, how the Berlin broadcasts were available in readable form in a prison camp in Italy by, at the latest, 1943, which is when Italy dropped out of the war and its Allied prisoners – those who had not been taken north by the Germans – were restored to freedom.

~ *The First Broadcast* ~

This is the German Shortwave Station. Here in our studio in Berlin tonight is Mr. P. G. Wodehouse, the well-known father [sic] of the inimitable Jeeves, of Bertie Worcester [sic], Lord Emsworth, Mr. Mulliner, and other delightful persons. Mr. Wodehouse has been in Germany for almost a year since German troops occupied his residence in Northern France. During that time he has finished a new novel which, I understand, is on its way to the United States for publication, and started with another one. We felt that his American readers might be interested to hear from Mr.

RODERICK SPODE set himself up as an amateur dictator,
head of the Black Shorts.

Wodehouse, so we have invited him to this microphone to tell you in his own words how it all happened.
Mr. Wodehouse:

It is just possible that my listeners may seem to detect in this little talk of mine a slight goofiness, a certain disposition to ramble in my remarks. If so, the matter, as Bertie Wooster would say, is susceptible of a ready explanation. I have just emerged into the outer world after forty-nine weeks of Civil Internment in a German internment camp and the effects have not entirely worn off. I have not yet quite recovered that perfect mental balance for which in the past I was so admired by one and all.

It's coming back, mind you. Look me up a couple of weeks from now, and you'll be surprised. But just at the moment I feel slightly screwy and inclined to pause at intervals in order to cut out paper dolls and stick straws in my hair – or such of my hair as I still have.

This, no doubt, is always the effect of prolonged internment, and since July the twenty-first, 1940, I have been spending my time in a series of Ilags. An Ilag must not be confused with an Offlag or a Stalag. An Offlag is where captured officers go. A stalag is reserved for the rank and file. The Civil Internee gets the Ilag – and how he loves it!

Since I went into business for myself as an internee, I have been in no fewer than four Ilags – some more Ilaggy than others, others less Ilaggy than some. First, they put us in a prison, then in a barracks, then in a fortress. Then they took a look at me and the rest of the boys on parade one day, and got the right idea at last. They sent us off to the local lunatic asylum at Tost in Upper Silesia, and there I have been for the last forty-two weeks.

It has been in many ways quite an agreeable experience. There is a good deal to be said for internment. It keeps you out of the saloons and gives you time to catch up with your reading. You also get a lot of sleep. The chief drawback is that it means your being away from home a good deal. It is not pleasant to think that by the time I see my Pekinese again, she will have completely forgotten me and will bite me to the bone – her invariable practice with strangers. And I feel that when I rejoin my wife, I had better take along a letter of introduction, just to be on the safe side.

Young men, starting out in life, have often asked me 'How can I become an Internee?' Well, there are several methods. My own was to buy a villa in Le Touquet on the coast of France and stay there till the Germans came along. This is probably the best and simplest system. You buy the villa and the Germans do the rest.

At the time of their arrival, I would have been just as pleased if they had not rolled up. But they did not see it that way, and on May the twenty-second along they came, – some on motor cycles, some on foot, but all evidently prepared to spend a long week-end.

The whole thing was very peaceful and orderly. Le Touquet has the advantage of being a sort of backwater, off the line of march. Your tendency, if you are an army making for the coast, is to carry on along the main road to Boulogne, and not to take the first turning to the left when you reach Étaples. So the proceedings were not marred by any vulgar brawling. All that happened, as far as I was concerned, was that I was strolling on the lawn with my wife one morning, when she lowered her voice and said "Don't look now, but there comes the German army". And there they were, a fine body of men, rather prettily dressed in green, carrying machine guns.

One's reactions on suddenly finding oneself surrounded by the armed strength of a hostile power are rather interesting. There is a sense of strain. The first time you see a German soldier over your garden fence, your impulse is to jump ten feet straight up into the air, and you do so. About a week later, you find that you are only jumping five feet. And then, after you have been living with him in a small village for two months, you inevitably begin to fraternize and to wish that you had learned German at school instead of Latin and Greek. As all the German I know is 'Es ist schönes Wetter', I was a spent force, and we used to take out the rest of the interview in beaming at one another.

I had a great opportunity of brushing up my beaming during those two months. My villa stands in the centre of a circle of houses, each of which was occupied by German officers, who would come around at intervals to take a look at things, and the garden next door was full of Labour Corps boys. It was with these that one really got together. There was scarcely an evening when two or three of them did not drop in for a bath at my house and a beaming party on the porch afterwards.

And so, day by day, all through June and July, our quiet, happy life continued, with not a jarring incident to mar the serenity. Well, yes, perhaps one or two. One day, an official-looking gentleman with none of the Labour Corps geniality came along and said he wanted my car. Also my radio. And in addition my bicycle. That was what got under the skin. I could do without the car, and I had never much liked the radio, but I loved that bicycle. I looked him right in the eye and said 'Es ist schönes Wetter' – and I said it nastily. I meant it to sting. And what did he say? He didn't say anything. What could we have said? P.S. He got the bicycle.

But these were small things, scarcely causing a ripple on the placid stream of life in the occupied areas. A perfect atmosphere of peace and goodwill continued to prevail. Except for the fact that I was not allowed out of my garden after nine at night, my movements were not restricted. Quite soon I had become sufficiently nonchalant to resume the writing of the novel which the arrival of the soldiery had interrupted. And then the order went out that all British subjects had got to report each morning at twelve o'clock at the Kommandantur down in Paris Plage.

As Paris Plage was three miles away, and they had pinched my bicycle, this was a nuisance. But I should have had nothing to complain of, if the thing had stopped there. But unfortunately it didn't. One lovely Sunday morning, as I was rounding into the straight and heading for the door of the Kommandantur, I saw one of our little group coming along with a suitcase in his hand.

This didn't look so good. I was conscious of a nameless fear. Wodehouse, old sport, I said to myself, this begins to look like a sticky day. And a few moments later my apprehensions were fulfilled. Arriving at the Kommandantur, I found everything in a state of bustle and excitement. I said 'Es ist schönes Wetter' once or twice, but nobody took any notice. And presently the interpreter stepped forward and announced that we were all going to be interned.

It was a pretty nasty shock, coming without warning out of a blue sky like that, and it is not too much to say that for an instant the old maestro shook like a badly set blancmange. Many years ago, at a party which had started to get a bit rough, somebody once hit me on the bridge of the nose with an order of planked steak. As I had felt then, so did I feel now. That same sensation of standing in a rocking and disintegrating world.

I didn't realize at the time how much luckier I was than a great many other victims of the drag-net. All over France during that Sunday, British citizens were being picked up and taken away without being given time to pack, and for a week those in Boulogne had been living in what they stood up in at the Petite Vitesse railroad station. For some reason, Le Touquet was given a substantial break. We were allowed to go home and put a few things together, and as my home was three miles away, I was actually sent there in a car.

The soldier who escorted me was unfortunately not one of those leisurely souls who believe in taking time over one's packing. My idea had been to have a cold bath and a change and a bite to eat, and then to light a pipe and sit down and muse for a while, making notes of what to take with me and what could be left behind. His seemed to be that five minutes was ample. Eventually we compromised on ten.

I would like my biographers to make careful note of the fact that the first thing that occurred to me was that here at last was my chance to buckle down and read the complete works of William Shakespeare. It was a thing I had been meaning to do any time these last forty years, but somehow, as soon as I had got – say, Hamlet and Macbeth under my belt and was preparing to read the stuffing out of Henry the Sixth, parts one, two and three, something like the Murglow Manor Mystery would catch my eye and I would weaken.

I didn't know what interment implied – it might be for years or it might be for ever – or it might be a mere matter of weeks – but the whole situation seemed to point to the complete works of William Shakespeare, so in they went. I am happy to say that I am now crammed with Shakespeare to the brim, so, whatever else internment has done for me, I am at any rate that much ahead of the game.

It was a pang to leave my novel behind, I had only five more chapters of it to do. But space, as Jeeves would have pointed out, was of the

essence, and it had to go, and is now somewhere in France. I am hoping
to run into it again one of these days, for it was a nice little novel and we
had some great times together.

I wonder what my listeners would have packed in my place – always
remembering that there was a German soldier standing behind me all the
time, shouting "Schnell" or words to that effect. I had to think quick.
Eventually what I crammed in were tobacco, pencils, scribbling blocks,
chocolate, biscuits, a pair of trousers, a pair of shoes, some shirts and a
sock or two. My wife wanted to add a pound of butter, but I fought her
off. There are practically no limits to what a pound of butter can do in
warm weather in a small suitcase. If I was going to read the complete
works of William Shakespeare, I preferred them unbuttered.

In the end, the only thing of importance I left behind was my passport,
which was the thing I ought to have packed first. The young internee is
always being asked for his passport, and if he hasn't got it, the authorities
tend to look squiggle-eyes and to ask nasty questions. I had never fully
realized what class distinctions were till I became an internee without a
passport, thus achieving a social position somewhere in between a minor
gangster and a wharf rat.

Having closed the suitcase and said goodbye to my wife and the junior
dog, and foiled the attempt of the senior dog to muscle into the car and
accompany me into captivity, I returned to the Kommandantur. And
presently, with the rest of the gang, numbering twelve in all, I drove in a
motor omnibus for an unknown destination.

That is one of the drawbacks to travelling, when you are an internee.
Your destination always is unknown. It is unsettling, when you start out,
not to be sure whether you are going half way across Europe or just to the
next town. Actually, we were headed for Loos, a suburb of Lille, a
distance of about a hundred miles. What with stopping at various points
along the road to pick up other foundation members, it took us eight
hours.

An internee's enjoyment of such a journey depends very largely on the
mental attitude of the sergeant in charge. Ours turned out to be a genial
soul, who gave us cigarettes and let us get off and buy red wine at all stops,
infusing the whole thing [with] a pleasant atmosphere of the school treat.
This was increased by the fact that we all knew each other pretty
intimately and had hobnobbed on other occasions. Three of us were from
the golf club – Arthur Grant, the Pro., Jeff, the starter, and Max, the
caddie master. Algy, of Algy's bar in the Rue St Jean, was there, and

Alfred, of Alfred's bar in the Rue de Paris. And the rest, like Charlie Webb and Bill Illidge, who ran garages, were all well-known Paris Plage figures. The thing was, therefore, practically a feast of reason and a flow of soul.

Nevertheless as the evening shadows began to fall and the effects of the red wine to wear off, we were conscious of a certain sinking feeling. We felt very far from our snug homes and not at all sure that we liked the shape of things to come.

As to what exactly *was* the shape of things to come, nobody seemed to know. But the general sentiment that prevailed was one of uneasiness. We feared the worst.

Nor were we greatly encouraged, when, having passed through Lille, we turned down a side lane and came through pleasant fields and under spreading trees to a forbidding-looking building which was only too obviously the local hoose-gow or calaboose. A nasty-looking man in the uniform of the French provincial police flung wide the gates and we rolled through.

Next week, – the Rover Boys in Loos Prison.

That was Mr. Wodehouse in the first broadcast of a series of weekly talks which he will give from this station.

~ The Second Broadcast ~

This is the German Shortwave Station. Here in our studio in Berlin tonight is Mr. P. G. Wodehouse, the well-known father [sic] of Jeeves, of Bertie Wooster, Lord Emsworth, Mr. Mulliner, and other delightful persons. Mr. Wodehouse has been in Germany for almost a year since German troops occupied his residence in Northern France. During that time he has finished a new novel which, I understand, is on its way to the United States for publication and started with another one. We felt that his American readers might be interested to hear Mr. Wodehouse continuing his story.

P. G. Wodehouse:

I broke off my Odyssey of the internees of Le Touquet last week, if you remember, with our little band of pilgrims entering Loos Prison. Owing to having led a blameless life since infancy, I had never seen the interior of a calaboose before, and directly I set eyes on the official in the front office, I regretted that I was doing so now. There are moments, as we pass through life, when we gaze into a stranger's face and say to ourselves 'I have met a friend'. This was not one of those occasions. There is probably nobody in the world less elfin than a French prison official, and the one now twirling a Grover Whalen moustache at me looked like something out of a film about Devil's Island.

Still, an author never quite gives up hope, and I think there was just a faint idea at the back of my mind that mine host, on hearing my name, would start to his feet with a cry of 'Quoi? Monsieur Vodeouse? Embrassez-moi, maitre!' and offer me his bed for the night, adding that he had long been one of my warmest admirers and would I give his little daughter my autograph.

Nothing like that happened. He just twirled the moustache again, entered my name in a large book, – or, rather, he put down 'Widhorse', the silly son of a bachelor, – and motioned to the bashi-bazouks to lead me to my cell. Or, as it turned out, the communal cell of myself, Algy of Algy's Bar and Mr Cartmell, our courteous and popular piano-tuner. For in those piping times of war – I don't know how it is on ordinary occasions – Loos Prison was bedding out its guests three to the room.

It was now getting on for ten o'clock at night, and it was this, I discovered later, that saved us a lot of unpleasantness. Round about the hour of ten, the French prison official tends to slacken up a bit. He likes to get into something loose and relax over a good book, and this makes him go through the motions of housing a batch of prisoners quickly and perfunctorily. When I got out into the exercise yard next morning, and met some of the men who had been in the place for a week, I found that they, on arrival, had been stood with their faces to the wall, stripped to their B.V.D.s, deprived of all their belongings and generally made to feel like so many imprisoned pieces of cheese. All they did to us was take away our knives and money and leave us.

Cells in French prisons are built for privacy. Where in the gaols of America there are bars, here you have only a wall with an iron-studded door in it. You go in, and this door is slammed and locked behind you, and you find yourself in a snug little apartment measuring about twelve feet by eight. At the far end is a window and under it a bed. Against the opposite wall to the bed there stands a small table and – chained to it – a chair of the type designed for the use of Singer's Midgets. In the corner by the door is a faucet with a basin beneath it, and beyond this what Chic Sale would call a 'family one-holer'. The only pictures on the walls, which are of whitewashed stone, are those drawn from time to time by French convicts – boldly executed pencil sketches very much in the vein which you would expect from French convicts.

Cartmell being the senior member of our trio, we gave him the bed, and Algy and I turned in on the floor. It was the first time I had tried dossing on a thin mattress on a granite floor, but we Wodehouses are tough stuff, and it was not long before the tired eyelids closed in sleep. My last waking thought, I remember, was that, while this was a hell of a thing to have happened to a respectable old gentleman in his declining years, it was all pretty darned interesting and that I could hardly wait to see what the morrow would bring forth.

What the morrow brought forth, at seven sharp, was a rattling of keys and the opening of a small panel in the door, through which were thrust three tin mugs containing a thin and lukewarm soup and three loaves of bread, a dark sepia in colour. This, one gathered, was breakfast, and the problem arose of how to play our part in the festivities. The soup was all right. One could manage that. You just took a swallow, and then another swallow – to see if it had really tasted as bad as it had seemed to the first time, and before you knew where you were, it had gone. But how, not having knives, we were to deal with the bread presented a greater test of our ingenuity. Biting bits off it was not a practical proposition for my companions, whose teeth were not of the best: and it was no good hammering it on the edge of the table, because it simply splintered the woodwork. But there is always a way of getting around life's little difficulties, if you give your mind to it. I became bread-biter to the community, and I think I gave satisfaction. At any rate, I got the stuff apart.

At eight-thirty, the key rattled again, and we were let out for air, recreation and exercise. That is to say, we were taken into an enclosure with high brick walls, partially open to the sky, and allowed to stand there for half an hour.

There was nothing much we could do except stand, for the enclosure – constructed, apparently, by an architect who had seen the Black Hole of Calcutta and admired it – was about twelve yards long, six yards wide at the broad end, tapering off to two yards wide at the narrow end, and we had to share it with the occupants of other cells. No chance, I mean, of getting up an informal football game or a track-meet or anything like that.

Having stood for thirty minutes, we returned to our cells, greatly refreshed, and remained there for the next twenty-three and a half hours. At twelve, we got some soup, and at five some more soup. Different kinds of soup, of course. Into the twelve o'clock ration a cabbage had been dipped – hastily, by a cook who didn't like getting his hands wet, and in the other there was a bean, actually floating about, visible to the naked eye.

Next day, the key rattled in the lock at seven, and we got soup, and at eight-thirty our scamper in the great open spaces, followed by soup at twelve and more soup at five. The day after than, the key rattled in the lock at seven, and we . . . But you get the idea. What you would call a healthy, regular life, giving a man plenty of leisure for reading the Complete Works of William Shakespeare – as, if you remember, I had resolved to do.

Apart from Shakespeare, who is unquestionably a writer who takes you away from it all, what made existence tolerable was the window. I had always understood that prison cells had small windows of ground glass, placed high up near the ceiling, but ours was a spacious affair of about five feet by four, and you could open it wide and even, by standing on the bed, get a glimpse from it of a vegetable garden and fields beyond. And the air that came through it was invaluable in keeping our cell smell within reasonable bounds.

The cell smell is a great feature of all French prisons. Ours in Number Forty-Four at Loos was one of those fine, broad-shouldered, up-and-coming young smells which stand on both feet and look the world in the eye. We became very fond and proud of it, championing it hotly against other prisoners who claimed that theirs had more authority and bouquet, and when the first German officer to enter our little sanctum rocked back on his heels and staggered out backwards, we took it as almost a personal compliment. It was like hearing a tribute paid to an old friend.

Nevertheless, in spite of the interest of hobnobbing with our smell, we found time hang a little heavy on our hands. I was all right. I had my Complete Works of William Shakespeare. But Algy had no drinks to mix, and Cartmell no pianos to tune. And a piano-tuner suddenly deprived of pianos is like a tiger whose medical adviser has put it on a vegetarian diet. Cartmell used to talk to us of pianos he had tuned in the past, and sometimes he would speak easily and well of pianos he hoped to tune in the future, but it was not the same. You could see that what the man wanted was a piano *now*. Either that, or something to take his mind off the thing.

It was on the fourth morning, accordingly, that we addressed a petition to the German Kommandant, pointing out that, as we were civil internees, not convicts, there was surely no need for all this Ballad of

Reading Gaol stuff, and asking if it would not be possible to inject a little more variety into our lives.

This appeal to Caesar worked like magic. Apparently the Kommandant had not had a notion that we were being treated as we were – the French had thought it up all by themselves – and he exploded like a bomb. We could hear distant reverberations of his wrath echoing along the corridors, and presently there came the old, familiar rattle of keys, and pallid warders opened the doors and informed us that from now on we were at liberty to roam about the prison at will.

Everything is relative – as somebody once said – probably Shakespeare in his Complete Works – and I cannot remember when I have felt such a glorious sense of freedom as when I strolled out of my cell, leaving the door open behind me, and started to saunter up and down outside.

And, even if it shows a vindictive spirit, I must confess that the pleasure was increased by the sight of the horror and anguish on the faces of the prison personnel. If there is one man who is a stickler for tradition and etiquette, for what is done and what is not done, it is the French prison warder, and here were tradition and etiquette being chucked straight into the ash-can, and nothing to be done about it. I suppose their feelings were rather what those of a golf professional would be, if he had to submit to seeing people dancing on his putting greens in high-heeled shoes.

In the end, we got quite sorry for the poor chaps, and relented to the extent of allowing them to lock us in for the night. It was pathetic to see how they brightened up at this concession. It paved the way to an understanding, and before we left the place we had come to be on quite friendly terms. One of them actually unbent to the extent of showing us the condemned cell – much as the host at a country house takes his guest round the stables.

Our great topic of conversation, as we strolled about the corridors, was, of course, where we were going from here, and when. For we could not believe that Loos Prison was anything but a temporary resting place. And we were right. A week after we had arrived, we were told to line up in the corridor, and presently the Kommandant appeared and informed us that, after our papers had been examined, we were to pack and be ready to leave.

Men of sixty and over, he added, would be released and sent home, so these lucky stiffs went and stood to one side in a row, looking like a beauty chorus. On the strength of being fifty-eight and three-quarters, I attempted to join them, but was headed back. Fifty-eight and three-quarters was good, I was given to understand, but not good enough.

I did not brood about this much, however, for it has just occurred to me that, having left my passport behind, I might quite easily have to stay on after the others had gone wherever they were going. Fortunately, I had twelve stout fellows from Le Touquet to testify to my identity and respectability, and they all lined up beside me and did their stuff. The Kommandant was plainly staggered by this cloud of witnesses, and in the end I just got under the wire.

This was on the Saturday evening, and far into the night the place buzzed with speculation. I don't know who first started the rumour that we were going to the barracks at Liége, but he turned out to be quite right. That was where we were headed for, and at eleven o'clock next morning we were given our mid-day soup and hustled out and dumped into vans and driven to the station.

One would have supposed from the atmosphere of breathless bustle that the train was scheduled to pull out at about eleven-thirty, but this was not the case. Our Kommandant was a careful man. I think he must once have missed an important train, and it preyed on his mind. At any rate, he got us there at eleven-forty a.m. and the journey actually started at eight o'clock in the evening. I can picture the interview between him and the sergeant when the latter returned. 'Did those boys make the train?' . . . 'Yes, sir, – by eight hours and twenty minutes' . . . 'Whew! Close thing. Mustn't run it so fine another time.'

As a matter of fact, all through my period of internment I noticed this tendency on the part of the Germans to start our little expeditions off with a whoop and a rush and then sort of lose interest. It reminded me of Hollywood. When you are engaged to work at Hollywood, you get a cable saying that it is absolutely vital that you be there by ten o'clock on the morning of June the first. Ten-five will be too late, and as for getting there on June the second, that means ruin to the industry. So you rush about and leap into aeroplanes, and at ten o'clock on June the first you are at the studio, being told that you cannot see your employer now, as he has gone to Palm Springs. Nothing happens after this till October the twentieth, when you are given an assignment and told that every moment is precious.

It is the same with the Germans in this matter of making trains. They like to leave a margin.

Summing up my experience as a gaol-bird, I would say that a prison is all right for a visit, but I wouldn't live there, if you gave me the place. On my part, at any rate, there was no moaning at the bar when I left Loos. I was glad to go. The last I saw of the old Alma Mater was the warder closing the door of the van and standing back with the French equivalent of 'Right away'.

He said 'Au revoir' to me – which I thought a little tactless.

That was Mr. Wodehouse in the second broadcast of a series of weekly talks which he will give from this station.

~ The Third Broadcast ~

The last instalment of my serial narrative entitled 'How To Be An Internee And Like It' ended, you may remember, with our band of pilgrims catching the train from Lille by the skin of our teeth, – that is to say, with a bare eight hours and twenty minutes to spare. The next thing that happened was the journey to Liége.

One drawback to being an internee is that, when you move from spot to spot, you have to do it in company with eight hundred other men. This precludes anything in the nature of travel de luxe. We made the twenty-four hour trip in a train consisting of those 'Quarante Hommes, Huit Chevaux' things – in other words, cattle trucks. I had sometimes seen them on sidings on French railroads in times of peace, and had wondered what it would be like to be one of the Quarante Hommes. I now found out, and the answer is that it is pretty darned awful. Eight horses might manage to make themselves fairly comfortable in one of these cross-country loose-boxes, but forty men are cramped. Every time I stretched my legs, I kicked a human soul. This would not have mattered so much, but every time the human souls stretched *their* legs, they kicked *me*. The only pleasant recollection I have of that journey is the time when we were let out for ten minutes on the banks of the Meuse.

Arriving at Liége, and climbing the hill to the barracks, we found an atmosphere of unpreparedness. Germany at that time was like the old woman who lived in a shoe. She had so many adopted children that she didn't know what to do with them. As regards our little lot, I had a feeling that she did not really want us, but didn't like to throw us away.

The arrangements for our reception at Liége seemed incomplete. It was as if one had got to a party much too early. Here, for instance, were eight hundred men who were going to live mostly on soup – and though the authorities knew where to lay their hands on some soup all right, nothing had been provided to put it in.

And eight hundred internees can't just go to the cauldron and lap. For one thing, they would burn their tongues, and for another the quick swallowers would get more than their fair share. The situation was one that called for quick thinking, and it was due to our own resourcefulness that the problem was solved. At the back of the barrack yard there was an enormous rubbish heap, into which Belgian soldiers through the ages had been dumping old mess tins, old cans, cups with bits chipped off them, bottles, kettles and containers for motor oil. We dug these out, gave them a wash and brush up, and there we were. I had the good fortune to secure one of the motor oil containers. It added to the taste of the soup just that little something that the others hadn't got.

Liége bore the same resemblance to a regular prison camp, like the one we were eventually to settle down in at Tost, which a rough scenario does to a finished novel. There was a sort of rudimentary organization – that is to say, we were divided into dormitories, each with a Room Warden – but when I think of Tost, with its Camp Captain, Camp Adjutants, Camp Committees and so on, Liége seems very primitive. It was also extraordinarily dirty, as are most places which have recently been occupied by Belgian soldiers. A Belgian soldier doesn't consider home is home, unless he can write his name in the alluvial deposits on the floor.

We spent a week at Liége, and, looking back, I can hardly believe that our stay there lasted only a mere seven days. This is probably due to the fact that there was practically nothing to do but stand around. We shared the barracks with a number of French military prisoners, and as we were not allowed to mix with them, we had to confine ourselves to a smallish section of the barrack yard. There was not room to do anything much except stand, so we stood. I totted up one day the amount of standing I had done between reveille and lights out – including parades and queuing up for meals – and it amounted to nearly six hours. The only time we were not standing was when we were lying on our beds in the afternoon. For we had beds at Liége, which was about the only improvement on the dear old prison we had left.

Parades took place at eight in the morning and eight in the evening, and as far as they were concerned I did not object to having to stand each time for fifty minutes or so, for they provided solid entertainment for the thoughtful mind. You might think that fifty minutes was a long time for eight hundred men to get themselves counted, but you would have understood, if you had seen us in action. I don't know why it was, but we could never get the knack of parading. We meant well, but we just didn't seem able to click.

The proceedings would start with the Sergeant telling us to form fives. This order having been passed along the line by the linguists who understood German, we would nod intelligently and form fours, then threes, then sixes. And when eventually, just in time to save the Sergeant from having a nervous breakdown, we managed to get into fives, was this the end? No, sir. It was not an end, but a beginning. What happened then was that Old Bill in Row Forty-Two would catch sight of Old George in Row Twenty-Three and shuffle across to have a chat with him, a cigarette hanging from his lower lip.

Time marches on. Presently, Old Bill, having heard all Old George has to say about the European situation, decides to shuffle back – only to find that his place has been filled up, like a hole by the tide. This puzzles him for a moment, but he soon sees what to do. He forms up as the seventh man of a row, just behind Old Percy, who has been chatting with Old Fred and has just come back and lined up as Number Six.

A Corporal with sheep-dog blood in him now comes into the picture. He cuts Bill and Percy out of the flock and chivvies them around for a while, and after a good deal of shouting the ranks are apparently in order once more.

But is *this* the end? Again no. The Sergeant, the Corporal, and a French soldier interpreter now walk the length of the ranks, counting. They then step aside and go into a sort of football huddle. A long delay. Something is wrong. The word goes round that we are one short, and the missing man is believed to be Old Joe. We discuss this with growing interest. Has Old Joe escaped? Maybe the jailer's daughter smuggled him in a file in a meat pie.

No. Here comes Old Joe, sauntering along with a pipe in his mouth and eyeing us in an indulgent sort of way, as who should say 'Hullo, boys. Playing soldiers, eh? May *I* join in?' He is thoroughly cursed – in German by the Sergeant, in French by the interpreter and in English by us – and takes his place in the parade.

As practically the whole of the personnel has left the ranks to cluster round and listen to the Sergeant talking to Old Joe, it is now necessary to count us again. This is done, and there is another conference. This time, in some mysterious way, we have become six short, and a discouraged feeling grows among us. It looks as if we were losing ground.

A Priest now steps forward. He is a kind of liaison officer between us and the Germans. He asks 'Have the six men who came from Ghent registered at the bureau?' But Lord Peter Wimsey is not going to solve the mystery as easily as that. Apparently they have, and there follows another huddle. Then all Room Wardens are invited to join the conference, and it is announced that we are to return to our dormitories, where the Room Wardens will check up their men and assemble them.

My dormitory – Fifty-Two B – goes to the length of getting a large sheet of cardboard and writing on it in chalk the words 'Zwansig Manner, Stimmt' – which our linguist assures us means 'Twenty Men, All Present', and when the whistle blows again for the renewal of the parade, I hold this in front of me like a London sandwich-man. It doesn't get a smile from Teacher, which is disappointing, but this is perhaps not to be wondered at, for he is very busy trying to count us again in our peculiar formation. For Old Bill has once more strolled off to Old George and has got into an argument with him about whether yesterday's coffee tasted more strongly of gasoline than today's. Bill thinks Yes – George isn't so sure.

They are chased back by the Corporal, now baying like a bloodhound, and there is another conference. We are now five short. The situation seems to be at a deadlock, with no hope of ever finding a formula, when some bright person – Monsieur Poirot, perhaps – says, 'How about the men in the hospital?' These prove to be five in number, and we are dismissed. We have spent a pleasant and instructive fifty minutes, and learned much about our fellow men.

Much the same thing happens when we line up at seven a.m. for breakfast, and at eleven-thirty and seven p.m. for lunch and supper – except that here we are in a movement, and so can express ourselves better. For if we are a little weak on keeping the ranks when standing still, we go all haywire when walking, and not many steps are required to turn us into something like a mob charging out of a burning building.

Meals are served from large cauldrons outside the cookhouse door at the far end of the barrack yard, and the Corporal, not with very much hope in his voice, for he has already seen us in action, tells us to form fours. We do so, and for a while it looks as if the thing were really going to be a success this time. Then it suddenly occurs to Old Bill, Old George, Old Joe and Old Percy, together with perhaps a hundred and twenty of their fellow internees, that by leaving their places at the tail of the procession and running round and joining the front row, they will get theirs quicker. They immediately proceed to do this, and are at once followed by about eighty other rapid thinkers, who have divined their thought-processes and have come to the conclusion that the idea is a good one. Twenty minutes later, a white-haired Corporal with deep furrows in his forehead has restored the formation into fours, and we start again.

On a good morning – I mean a morning when Old Bill and his associates were in their best form – it would take three-quarters of an hour for the last in line to reach the cookhouse, and one used to wonder what it would be like on a rainy day.

Fortunately, the rainy day never came. The weather was still fine when, a week from our arrival, we were loaded into vans and driven to the station, our destination being the Citadel of Huy, about twenty-five miles away – another Belgian army center.

If somebody were to ask me whose quarters I would prefer to take over – those of French convicts or Belgian soldiers, I would find it hard to say. French convicts draw pictures on the walls of their cells which bring the blush of shame to the cheek of modesty, but they are fairly tidy in their habits – whereas Belgian soldiers, as I have mentioned before, make lots of work for their successors. Without wishing to be indelicate, I may say that, until you have helped to clean out a Belgian soldiers' latrine, you ain't seen nuttin'.

It was my stay at Liége, and subsequently at the Citadel of Huy, that gave me that wholesome loathing for Belgians which is the hall-mark of the discriminating man. If I never see anything Belgian again in this world, it will be all right with me.

~ *The Fourth Broadcast* ~

Here in our studio in Berlin tonight is Mr. P. G. Wodehouse the well-known father [sic] of Jeeves, of Bertie Wooster, Lord Emsworth, Mr. Mulliner, and other delightful persons. We felt that his American readers might be interested to hear Mr. Wodehouse continuing his story.

Here is Mr. Wodehouse.

Before beginning my talk tonight – the fourth of a series of five dealing with the five phases of my internment – I should like to say another few words on another subject.

The Press and Public of England seem to have jumped to the

conclusion that I have been in some way bribed or intimidated into making these broadcasts. This is not the case.

I did not 'make a bargain', as they put it, and buy my release by agreeing to speak over the radio. I was released because I am sixty years old – or shall be in October. The fact that I was free a few months before that date was due to the efforts of my friends. As I pointed out in my second talk, if I had been sixty when I was interned, I should have been released at the end of the first week.

My reason for broadcasting was a simple one. In the course of my period of internment I received hundreds of letters of sympathy from American readers of my books, who were strangers to me, and I was naturally anxious to let them know how I had got on.

Under existing conditions, it was impossible to answer these letters, – and I did not want to be so ungrateful and ungracious as to seem to be ignoring them, and the radio suggested itself as a solution.

I will now go on to my experiences in the Citadel of Huy – the last of the places where we were lodged before we finally settled at Tost, in Upper Silesia.

In putting [together] these talks on How To Be An Internee Without Previous Training, I find myself confronted by the difficulty of deciding what aspects of my daily life, when in custody, will have entertainment value for listeners.

When the war is over and I have my grandchildren as an audience, this problem, of course, will not arise. The unfortunate little blighters will get the whole thing, night after night, without cuts. But now I feel that a certain process of selection is necessary. A good deal that seems to an internee thrilling and important is so only to himself. Would it interest you, for instance, to hear that it took us four hours to do the twenty-five mile journey from Liége to Huy, and that there were moments during the walk up the mountain-side when the old boy thought he was going to expire? No, I thought not.

It is for this reason that I propose to pass fairly lightly over my five weeks' stay at Huy. Don't let that name confuse you, by the way. It is spelled H-u-y, and in any other country but Belgium would be pronounced Hoo-ey. So remember that, when I say Huy, I don't mean 'we' – I mean Huy.

The Citadel of Huy is one of those show places they charge you two francs to go into in times of peace. I believe it was actually built in the time of the Napoleonic wars, but its atmosphere is purely mediaeval. It

looks down on the River Meuse from the summit of a mountain – the sort
of mountain Gutzon Borglum would love to carve pictures on – and it is
one of those places where, once you're in, you're in. Its walls are fourteen
feet thick, and the corridors are lighted by bays, in which are narrow slits
of windows. It is through these, if you are a married man with a wife
living in Belgium, that you shout to her when she comes to visit you. She
stands on the slope below, as high up as she can get, and shouts to *you*.
Neither can see the other, and the whole thing is like something out of
Il Trovatore.

The only place in the building from which it is possible to get a view of
somebody down below is the window of what afterwards became the
canteen room. Men would rush in there and fling themselves through the
window and lie face down on the broad sill. It was startling till one got
used to it, and one never quite lost the fear that they would lose their
heads and jump. But this lying on sills was forbidden later, as were most
things at Huy, where the slogan seemed to be 'Go and see what the
internees are doing, and tell them they mustn't'. I remember an extra
parade being called, so that we might be informed that stealing was
forbidden. This hit us very hard.

These extra parades were a great feature of life at Huy, for our
Kommandant seemed to have a passion for them.

Mind you, I can find excuses for him. If I had been in his place, I would
have ordered extra parades myself. His headquarters were down in the
town, and there was no road connecting the Citadel with the outer
world – just a steep, winding path. So that, when he came to visit us, he
had to walk. He was a fat, short-legged man in the middle sixties, and
walking up steep, winding paths does something to fat, short-legged men
who are not as young as they were. Duty called him now and then to
march up the hill and to march down again, but nothing was going to
make him like it.

I picture him starting out, full of loving kindness – all sweetness and
light, as it were – and gradually becoming more and more soured as he
plodded along. So that when he eventually came to journey's end with a
crick in the back and the old dogs feeling as if they were about to burst
like shrapnel, and saw us loafing around at our ease, the sight was too
much for him and he just reached for his whistle and blew it for an extra
parade.

Extra parades were also called two or three times a day by the Sergeant,
when there was any announcement to be made. At Tost we had a

noticeboard, on which camp orders were posted each day, but this ingenious system had not occurred to anyone at Huy. The only way they could think of there of establishing communication between the front office and the internees was to call a parade. Three whistles would blow, and we would assemble in the yard, and after a long interval devoted to getting into some sort of formation we would be informed that there was a parcel for Omer – or that we must shave daily – or that we must not smoke on parade – or that we must not keep our hands in our pockets on parade – or that we might buy playing cards – (and next day that we might *not* buy playing cards) – or that boys must not cluster round the guard-room trying to scrounge food from the soldiers – or that there was a parcel for Omer.

I remember once, in the days when I used to write musical comedies, a chorus girl complaining to me with some bitterness that if a carpenter had to drive a nail into a flat, the management would be sure to call a chorus rehearsal to watch him do it, and I could now understand just how she had felt. I don't know anything that brings the grimness of life home to one more than hearing three whistles blow just as you are in the middle of a bath – and leaping into your clothes without drying – and lining up in the yard and waiting twenty minutes at attention – and then being informed that there is a parcel for Omer.

It was not that we had anything against Omer. We all liked him – and never better than when he had just had a parcel, but what embittered us was that there was never a parcel for anyone else. He happened to have been interned right on the spot where all his friends and admirers lived, while the rest of us were far from home and had not yet been able to get in touch with our wives. It was that that made these first weeks of internment such a nightmare. Not receiving parcels was merely a side-issue. It would have been nice to have had some, but we could do without them. But we did wish that we could have got some information as to how our wives were getting on. It was only later at Tost, that we began to receive letters and to be able to write them.

The few letters which did trickle in to Huy from time to time were regarded by the authorities with strong suspicion. After a parade had been called, for us to watch them given out, their recipients would be allowed a couple of minutes to read them – then they would have to hand them back to the Corporal, who tore them up. And when Omer got one of his parcels, its contents would all be opened before he was permitted to take them away – from the first can of sardines to the last bit of chocolate.

I believe this was due entirely to the men who, at the end of the last war, wrote books telling how clever they had been at escaping from German prison camps by means of codes sent by letter and compasses and so on enclosed in potted meat. They meant no harm, but they certainly made it tough for us.

'Tough' is the adjective I would use to describe the whole of those five weeks at Huy. The first novelty of internment had worn off, and we had become acutely alive to the fact that we were in the soup and likely to stay there for a considerable time. Also, tobacco was beginning to run short, and our stomachs had not yet adjusted themselves to a system of rationing, which, while quite good for a prison camp, was far from being what we had been accustomed to at home. We were hearty feeders who had suddenly been put on a diet, and our stomachs sat up on their hind legs and made quite a fuss about it.

Rations consisted of bread, near-coffee, jam or grease, and soup. Sometimes, instead of bread, we would get fifty small crackers apiece. When this happened, a group of men would usually club together, each contributing fifteen crackers, which would be mashed up and mixed with jam and taken to the cookhouse to be baked into a cake. It was always a problem whether it was worth sacrificing fifteen crackers to this end. The cake was always wonderful, but one's portion just slid down one's throat and was gone. Whereas one could chew a cracker.

People began to experiment with foods. One man found a bush in the corner of the yard with berries on it, and ate those – a sound move, as it turned out, for they happened by a fluke not to be poisonous. Another man used to save some of his soup at mid-day, add jam and eat the result cold in the evening. I myself got rather fond of wooden matches. You chew your match between the front teeth, then champ it up into a pulp and swallow. Shakespeare's Sonnets also make good eating, especially if you have a little cheese to go with them. And when the canteen started, we could generally get cheese.

Not much of it, of course. The way the canteen worked was that two men were allowed to go to the town with a guard and bring back as much as they could carry in a haversack apiece – the stuff being split eight hundred ways. It generally worked out at a piece of cheese about two inches long and two wide per man.

When the tobacco gave out, most of us smoked tea or straw. Tea-smokers were unpopular with the rest of their dormitory, owing to the smell caused by their activities – a sort of sweet, sickly smell which wraps itself round the atmosphere and clings for hours. Tea-smoking has also the disadvantage that it leads to a mild form of fits. It was quite usual to see men, puffing away, suddenly pitch over sideways and have to be revived with first aid.

Another drawback to Huy was that it appeared to have been expecting us even less than Liége had done. You may remember my telling you last week that our arrival seemed to come upon Liége as a complete surprise, and that there was nothing provided in the way of vessels to sip our soup out of. What Huy was short on was bedding.

An internee does not demand much in the way of bedding – give him a wisp or two of straw and he is satisfied – but at Huy it looked for a while as if there would not even be straw. However, they eventually dug us out enough to form a thin covering on the floors, but that was as far as they were able to go. Of blankets there were enough for twenty men. I was not one of the twenty. I don't know why it is, but I never am one of the twenty men who get anything. For the first three weeks, all I had over me at night was a raincoat, and one of these days I am hoping to meet Admiral Byrd and compare notes with him.

Though I probably shan't let him get a word in edgeways. He will start off on some anecdote about the winter evenings at the South Pole, and I shall clip in and say, 'Juss a minute, Byrd, jussaminute. Let me describe to you my sensations at Huy from Aug. Three, nineteen-forty, till the day my dressing-gown arrived. Don't talk to me about the South Pole – it's like someone telling Noah about a drizzle.'

Well, now you see what I meant when I said just now that what seems important to an internee merely makes the general public yawn and switch off the radio. From the rockbound coast of Maine to the Everglades of Florida, I don't suppose there is a single soul who gives a hoot that, when I was at Huy, ice formed on my upper slopes and my little pink toes dropped off one by one with frost-bite. But, boy, wait till I meet my grandchildren!

However, as somebody once observed, it is always darkest before the dawn. And, as Methusaleh said to the reporter who was interviewing him for the local sheet and had asked what it felt like to live to nine hundred – 'The first five hundred years are hard, but after that it's pie'. It was the same with us. The first seven weeks of our internment had been hard, but the pie was waiting just around the corner. There was, in short, a good time coming. On September the eighth, exactly five weeks from the day of our arrival, we were paraded and this time informed – not that

Omer had received a parcel, but that we were to pack our belongings and proceed once more to an unknown destination.

This proved to be the village of Tost in Upper Silesia.

~ *The Fifth Broadcast* ~

I broke off last week with our eight hundred internees setting out for the village of Tost in Upper Silesia. I don't know how well acquainted my listeners are with central European geography, so I will mention that Upper Silesia is right at the end of Germany, and that Tost is right at the end of Upper Silesia – in fact, another yard or two from where we eventually fetched up, and we should have been in Poland.

We made the journey this time, not in cattle trucks but in a train divided into small compartments, eight men to the compartment, and it took us three days and three nights, during which time we did not stir from our cosy little cubbyhole. On leaving Huy, we had been given half a loaf of bread apiece and half a sausage, and after we had been thirty-two hours on the train we got another half loaf and some soup. It was at night time that the trip became rather unpleasant. One had the choice between trying to sleep sitting upright, and leaning forward with one's elbows on one's knees, in which case one bumped one's head against that of the man opposite. I had never realized the full meaning of the expression 'hardheaded Yorkshireman' till my frontal bone kept colliding with that of Charlie Webb, who was born and raised in that county.

As a result of this, and not being able to wash for three days, I was not at my most dapper when we arrived at Tost Lunatic Asylum, which had been converted into a camp for our reception. But in spite of looking like something the carrion crow had brought in, I was far from being downhearted. I could see at a glance that this was going to be a great improvement on our previous resting places.

One thing that tended to raise the spirits was the discovery that Scabies had been left behind. This was the affectionate name we had given to one of our fellow-internees at Huy. He was a public menace and had given me many an uneasy moment during the five weeks in which we had been in close contact. His trouble was that he had not only got lice but had contracted a particularly contagious form of skin disease, and in his lexicon there was no such word as 'isolation'. He was a friendly, gregarious soul, who used to slink about like an alley cat, rubbing himself up against people. One time, I found him helping to peel the potatoes. Nice chap – it was a relief to find that he was no longer in our midst.

That was one thing that cheered me up on arrival at Tost. Another was that it looked as if at last we were going to have elbow-room. An Associated Press man, who came down to interview me later, wrote in his piece that Tost Lunatic Asylum was no Blandings Castle. Well, it wasn't, of course, but still it was roomy. If you had had a cat, and had wished to swing it, you could have done so quite easily in our new surroundings.

The Upper Silesian loony-bin consisted of three buildings – one an enormous edifice of red brick, capable of housing about thirteen hundred; the other two smaller, but still quite spacious. We lived and slept in the first-named, and took our meals in one of the others, where the hospital was also situated. The third building, known as the White House, stood at the bottom of the park, beyond the barbed wire, and for the first month or two was used only as a sort of clearing-station for new arrivals. Later, it was thrown open and became the center of Tost life and thought – being the place where our musicians practised and gave their concerts, where church services were held on Sundays, and where – after I had been given a padded cell to myself for working purposes – I eventually wrote a novel.

The park was a genuine park, full of trees, and somebody who measured it found that it was exactly three hundred yards in circumference. After five weeks at Huy, it looked like the Yellowstone. A high wall ran along one side of it, but on the other you got a fine view of some picturesque old barbed wire and a farm yard. There was a path running across its center which, when our sailors had provided a ball by taking a nut and winding string round it, we used in the summer as a cricket pitch.

The thing about Tost that particularly attracted me, that day of our arrival, was that it was evidently a going concern. Through the barbed wire, as we paraded in front of the White House, we could see human forms strolling about, and their presence meant that we had not got to start building our little nest from the bottom up, as had been the case at Liége and Huy. For the first time, we were in a real camp, and not a makeshift.

This was brought home to us still more clearly by the fact that the reception committee included several English-speaking interpreters. And when, after we had had our baggage examined and had been given a bath, a gentleman presented himself who said that he was the Camp Adjutant, we knew that this was the real thing.

It may be of interest to my listeners to hear how a genuine civil internment camp is run. You start off with a Kommandant, some Captains and Oberleutnants and a couple of hundred soldiers, and you put them in barracks outside the barbed wire. Pay no attention to these, for they do not enter into the internee's life, and you never see anything of them except for the few who come to relieve the sentries. The really important thing is the inner camp – that is to say, the part where, instead of being outside, looking in, you are inside, looking out.

This is presided over by a Lagerführer and four Corporals, one to each floor, who are known as Company Commanders – in our case, Pluto, Rosebud, Ginger and Donald Duck. Their job is to get you up in the morning, to see that the counting of the internees on parade is completed before the Lagerführer arrives to inspect, and to pop up unexpectedly at intervals and catch you smoking in the corridor during prohibited hours.

Co-operating with these is the little group of Internee Officers – the Camp Captain, the two Camp Adjutants, the Floor Wardens and the Room Wardens. The Room Wardens ward the rooms, the Floor Wardens ward the floors, the Adjutants bustle about, trying to look busy, and the Camp Captain keeps in touch with the Lagerführer, going to see him in his office every Friday morning with hard-luck stories gleaned from the rabble, – that is to say, me and the rest of the boys. If, for instance, the coffee is cold two days in succession, the proletariat tells the Camp Captain, who tells the Lagerführer, who tells the Kommandant.

There is also another inner camp official whom I forgot to mention – the Sonderführer. I suppose the best way to describe him is to say that he is a Führer who sonders.

The great advantage of a real internment camp, like Tost, is that the internee is left to himself all through the day. I was speaking last week of the extra parades at Huy. In all my forty-two weeks at Tost, we had only three extra parades. The authorities seemed to take the view that all they wanted to know was that we were all present in the morning and also at night, so we were counted at seven-thirty a.m. and again an hour before lights-out. Except for that, we were left to ourselves.

Nor was there anything excessive in the way of discipline and formalities. We were expected to salute officers, when we met them – which we seldom did, and there was a camp order that ran 'When internees are standing in groups, the first to see an officer must shout "Achtung"', – a pleasant variant on the old game of Beaver. 'Whereat', the order continues, 'all face officer at attention, with hands on seam of trousers' – the internees' trousers, of course, – 'and look at him, assuming an erect bearing'. The only catch about this was that it gave too much scope to our humorists. A man can have a lot of quiet fun by shouting 'Achtung' and watching his friends reach for the seams of their trousers and assume an erect bearing, when there is not an officer within miles.

Life in an internment camp resembles life outside, in that it is what you make it. Nothing can take away the unpleasant feeling of being a prisoner, but you can make an effort and prevent it getting you down. And that is what we did, and what I imagine all the other British prisoners in Germany did. We at Tost were greatly helped by the fact that we had with us the sailors from the Orama, who would have cheered anyone up, and the internees from Holland.

Many of these were language teachers and musicians, and we had a great organiser in Professor Doyle-Davidson of Breda University. This meant that we were no longer restricted for intellectual entertainment to standing about in groups or playing that old Army game known alternatively as 'House' or 'Ousey-Ousey' – where you pay ten Pfennigs for a paper with numbers on it and the banker draws numbers out of a hat, and the first man to fill up his paper scoops the pool.

Lectures and concerts were arranged, and we also had revues and a straight comedy – which would have been an even bigger success than it was, but for the fact of the ingenue getting two days in the cooler right in the middle of the run.

It was also possible for us to learn French, German, Italian, Spanish, first-aid and shorthand, and also to find out all there was to find out about French and English literature. In fact, we were not so much internees as a student body. Towards the end of my stay, we had our own paper – a bright little sheet called The Tost Times, published twice a month.

One great improvement at Tost from my viewpoint, was that men of fifty and over were not liable for fatigues – in other words, the dirty work. At Liége and Huy, there had been no age limit. We had all pitched in together, reverend elders and beardless boys alike – cleaning out latrines with one hand and peeling potatoes with the other, so to speak. At Tost, the old dodderers like myself lived the life of Riley. For us, the arduous side of life was limited to making our beds, brushing the floor under and around them, and washing our linen. When there was man's work to be done, like hauling coal or shovelling snow, we just sat and looked on, swapping reminiscences of the Victorian Age, while the younger set snapped into it.

There were certain fatigues, like acting as a server at meals and working in the cookhouse, which were warmly competed for. For these, you got double rations. But the only reward of the ordinary chore, like hauling coal, was the joy of labor. I suppose a really altruistic young man after he had put in an hour or two hauling coal, would have been all pepped up by the thought that he had been promoting the happiness of the greatest number, but I never heard one of our toilers talk along these lines. It was more usual to hear them say, speaking with a good deal of feeling, that, next time their turn came along, they were ruddy well going to sprain an ankle and report sick.

It is a curious experience being completely shut off from the outer world, as one is in an internment camp. One lives principally on potatoes and rumors. One of my friends used to keep a notebook, in which he would jot down all the rumors that spread through the corridors, and they made amusing reading after the lapse of a few weeks. To military prisoners, I believe, camp rumors are known for some reason as 'Blue Pigeons'. We used to call them bedtime stories, and most dormitories would keep a corridor hound, whose duty it was to go through the corridors before lights-out, collecting the latest hot news.

These bedtime stories never turned out to be true, but a rumor a day kept depression away, so they served their purpose. Certainly, whether owing to bedtime stories or simply to the feeling, which I myself had, that, if one was in, one was in and it was no use making heavy weather about it, the morale of the men at Tost was wonderful. I never met a more cheerful crowd, and I loved them like brothers.

With this talk, I bring to an end the story of my adventures as British Civilian Prisoner Number 796, and before concluding I should like once more to thank all the kind people in America who wrote me letters while I was in camp. Nobody who has not been in a prison camp can realize what letters, especially letters like those I received, mean to an internee.

~ Bill was a splendidly virile young man, and if you had had a mad bull you wished dealt with, you could have placed it in no better hands.

~ Captain Bradbury's right eyebrow had now become so closely entangled with his left that there seemed no hope of ever extricating it without the aid of powerful machinery.

~ Like all patrons of coffee-stalls, they were talking about the Royal Family.

~ Freddie had mooned about with an air of crushed gloom that would have caused comment in Siberia.

~ Bobbie's outer crust was indeed of a nature to cause those beholding it to rock back on their heels with a startled whistle. But while equipped with eyes like twin stars, hair ruddier than the cherry, oomph, espièglerie and all the fixings, B. Wickham had all the disposition and general outlook on life of a ticking bomb.

~ 'You suddenly bobbed up, Bertie, like a corpse rising to the surface of a sheet of water.'

~ The Scottie-dog Bartholemew gave me an unpleasantly superior look, as if asking me if I were saved.

~ 'Mustard' Pott walked slowly, with bowed head, for he was counting ten-pound notes.

~ Pongo bared his teeth in a bitter smile.

Appendix 2 ~ D. LITT. (Oxon.)

————————— ~ —————————

In June 1939 Wodehouse, whose father had not been able to afford to send him to Oxford forty years earlier, received from Oxford an Honorary Doctorate of Letters. The Vice-Chancellor, George Gordon, President of Magdalen and Wodehouse's host that day and night, was a great admirer of his works and had proposed him for this honour. In fact it was Gordon who had briefed the Public Orator, Doctor Cyril Bailey, in what to say about him. Doctor Bailey's expert Horatian verses were printed in full in *The Times* next day. Only excerpts were given from the Latin prose praises of the other honorands.

PELHAM GRENVILLE WODEHOUSE

Ecce auctor magicus, quo non expertior alter
delectare animos hominum risusque movere.
Namque novas scaenae personas intulit et res
ridiculas cuique adiunxit. Cui non bene notus
dives opum iuvenis, comisque animique benigni,
nec quod vult fecisse capax, nisi fidus Achates
ipse doli fabricator adest vestisque decentis
arbiter? Aut comes ille loquax et ventre rotundo
cui patruusque neposque agnatorum et domus omnis
miranda in vita – sic narrat – fata obierunt?
Nobilis est etiam Clarens, fundique paterni
et suis eximiae dominus, Psmintheusque 'relicta
cui fac cuncta', Augustus item qui novit amores
ranicularum, aliusque alio sub sidere natus.
Non vitia autem hominum naso suspendit adunco
sed tenera pietate notat, peccataque ridet.
Hoc quoque, lingua etsi repleat plebeia chartas,
non incomposito patitur pede currere verba,
concinnus, lepidus, puri sermonis amator.

*Quid multa? Quem novere omnes, testimonio non eget. Praesento vobis festivum caput
– Petroniumne dicam an Terentium nostrum? – Pelham Grenville Wodehouse,
Societatis Regiae Litterarum sodalem, ut admittatur honoris causa ad gradum Doctoris
in Litteris.*

The Vice-Chancellor addressed Wodehouse in further Latin:

*Vir lepidissime, facetissime, venustissime, iocosissime, ridibundissime, te cum turba tua
Leporum, Facetiarum, Venustatum, Iocorum, Risuum, ego auctoritate mea et totius
Universitatis admitto ad gradum Doctoris in Litteris honoris causa.*

The verses might be translated into English as:

Here is a writer with a magic touch . . . nobody more skilful to lift our spirits and
make us laugh. He has given us a cast of new characters, all ridiculous in different
ways. The rich young man, affable and kind-hearted but never getting anything
right without the help of his Admirable Crichton, himself a great tactician as
well as stern judge of his master's clothes; that portly and unstoppable raconteur
of the strange things that happened to his uncles, nephews and a whole
household of other relatives; Clarence, the Earl, master of the family estates and
of an outstanding pig; Psmith – the word went round 'Leave it to Psmith!';
Augustus, who knew all about the love-life of newts; and dozens more. But this
writer does not wrinkle his nose disapprovingly at his simpletons and sinners. He
marks their lapses with great sympathy and is always happily on their side. And
keep your eye on his language: although there is much use of slang in his pages, he
never lets a lazy sentence stand. He polishes phrases and perfects rhythms. He
uses the common language with uncommon style.

I could go on and on. But as we all know his works, there is no need of any
testimonial from me. I present to you a merry-maker in print – the Petronius,
shall we say, or the Terence of our day. Pelham Grenville Wodehouse, Fellow of
the Royal Society of Literature, to be admitted as an Honorary Doctor of Letters.

Appendix 3 ~ THE FRENCH FOR WODEHOUSE

—————————— ~ ——————————

I mentioned earlier, when discussing the Knut-language which gave something of their conversational style to Psmith and the early Bertie Wooster, that Wodehouse's Lord Tidmouth, in the play *Good Morning, Bill*, produced six separate slang variations for 'Good-bye'. They ranged, in the course of the play, from 'Teuf-teuf' to 'Tinkerty-tonk'. Wodehouse's books have been translated into hosts of modern languages. But how? What foreign language do you know? Well, do you, in that language, know six separate ways, comparable with 'Teuf-teuf' and 'Tinkerty-tonk', in which a blah young English peer with butter-coloured hair and a receding chin could say 'Good-bye'? And that's only the beginning of the difficulties. The mish-mash of elusive allusion of Wodehouse's buzzers and burblers, the hotch-potch of slangs, the quotations, direct or veiled, the wild imagery . . .

French is the only language in which I might begin to judge a Wodehouse translation. When I was in France, I bought *Jeeves, au secours* (Amiot-Dumont, Paris). '*Ce livre parut en langue anglaise sous le titre*: JOY IN THE MORNING.' The translators are Denyse and Benoit de Fonscolombe.

Joy in the Morning is my favourite Bertie/Jeeves novel. *Bref*, as the French say, and in Bertie's own words, it is 'the super-sticky affair of Nobby Hopwood, Stilton Cheesewright, Florence Craye, my Uncle Percy, J. Chichester Clam, Edwin the Boy Scout and old Boko Fittleworth . . . or, as my biographers will probably call it, the Steeple Bumpleigh Horror'. (. . . *cet embrouillamini ou . . . pour prendre la définition qu'adopteront probablement mes biographes . . . l'horrible drame de Steeple Bumpleigh auquel furent mêlés Nobby Hopwood, Stilton Cheese-wright, Florence Craye, mon oncle Percy, J. Chichester Calm* [sic], *Edwin le Boy Scout et ce vieux Boko Fittleworth.*)

EDWIN CRAYE,
only son of Lord Worplesdon.
A dedicated Boy Scout, full of Good Deeds.

I knew that my depth-analysis of the translation wouldn't be easy, as soon as I discovered that two of Bertie's ways of saying 'Good-bye' ('toodle-oo' and 'pip-pip' – neither of which was used by Lord Tidmouth) become in French *bye-bye*. And 'Shropshire' becomes *Skropshire*. This word only appears in the book once, so the French rendering may be a misprint. But I must take it as it comes . . . e.g. *chez Droves* for 'at The Drones' and variously *Catsmeat Ploter-Pirbright*, *Potter Pirbright-tête-de-mou* and *Potter Pirbright dit Tête de mou* for 'Catsmeat Potter-Pirbright'. (*Mou* is the French for butcher's lights.).

Let's take slang and imagery first. You might like to paste the following in your *Michelin Guide* as vocabulary for your next travels in France:

A bucko mate of a tramp steamer	*un bosco de caboteur*
A nice bit of box-fruit, what!	*une belle mélasse*
That will bring home the bacon	*ça rabibochera tout*
A joke salt-shaker	*une salière surprise*
Rollicking	*désopilant*
To render unfit for human con-sumption	*mettre à mal*
To tear limb from limb	*déchiqueter*
To give the little snurge six of the best with a bludgeon	*flanquer au maudit galopin une volée de martinet*

~ Stilton Cheesewright is a man with a pink face and a head that looks as if it has been blown up with a bicycle pump.

~ 'If my Aunt Julia in Hollywood had confined herself to snootering directors, harrying camera-men, and chasing supervisors up trees, nothing would have been said. But there is one thing the artist soul must not do at the Colossal-Superfine, and that is swat the Main Boss with a jewelled hand over the ear-hole.'

~ He writhed like an electric fan.

~ There was something sort of bleak about her tone, rather as if she had swallowed an east wind.

~ Honoria Glossop is one of those robust, dynamic girls with the muscles of a welter-weight and a laugh like a squadron of cavalry charging over a tin bridge.

~ It was one of those still evenings you get in summer, when you can hear a snail clear its throat a mile away.

~ The Empress resembled a captive balloon with ears and tail, and was as nearly circular as a pig can be without bursting.

~ Prudence made a tired gesture, like a Christian martyr who has got a bit fed up with lions.

~ Unseen, in the background, Fate was quietly slipping the lead into the boxing-glove.

To mince yourself to hash	*se faire hacher la viande*
Some rout or revel	*quelques parties ou quelques bamboches*
Stinko	*parti*
My dear old soul (Jeeves)	*mon petit vieux*
The beasel (Florence Craye)	*la pécore*
A girl liberally endowed with oomph (Nobby Hopwood)	*une fille amplement pourvue de chien*
To pull someone's leg	*monter un bateau à quelqu'un*
Cookoo (mad)	*toqué*
A flop	*un loupé*
Oofy	*pourvu de galette*
Rannygazoo	*la corrida*
A bloke	*un zèbre*
Acts of kindness (as enjoined to Boy Scouts, daily)	*des B.A. (bonnes actions)*
Nobby and Boko have hitched up, have they?	*ça biche Nobby et Boko?*
Everything is gas and gaiters	*ça gaze à bloc*
To write stinkers (letters)	*écrire des engueulots*
A blunt instrument	*un instrument massif*
Loony to the eyebrows	*complètement dingo*
To go to the mat and start chewing pieces out of each other	*être en bisbille et commencer à se dire des 'vacheries'*
A sterling chap	*un crac*
To dot him one	*lui en coller un dans la figure*
A bottle from the oldest bin	*une bouteille de derrière les fagots*
A bearded bozo (King Edward The Confessor)	*un bonze barbu*
A wet blanket	*un vrai parapluie*
To snitch	*souffler*
To thrash that pie-faced young warthog Fittleworth within an inch of his life	*rosser, à deux doigts d'en crever, cette face de tarte, cette jeune verrue de Fittleworth*
His eyes popped out of his head and waved about on their stalks	*ses yeux étaient hors de la tête et erraient de-ci, de-là au bout de leur tige, le nerf optique sans doute*
He moved, he stirred, he seemed to feel the rush of life along his	*il remuait, s'agitait comme si la vie dans sa puissance toujours*

keel   *jeune, lui chatouillait la colonne vertébrale*

He realises that dirty work is afoot at the crossroads and that something swift is being slipped across him — *il se rend compte qu'une vilaine besogne est en train de s'accomplir et qu'une peau de banane va lui être incessamment lâchée dans les pattes*

To zoom off immediately (for fear of Aunt Agatha) — *faire un départ à l'anglaise sur le champ*

The bean (head) — *le chef*

The napper (head) — *la cafetière*

The onion (head) — *la caboche*

The old bounder — *le vieux rustre*

You bloodstained (Bertie) — *espèce d'ignoble individu*

You horrible young boll-weevil (Edwin) — *espèce d'horrible graine de charançon*

You fat-headed young faulty reasoner (Edwin) — *espèce de nigaud de raisonneur à l'envers*

You outstanding louse (Bertie) — *espèce de vermine*

You degraded little copper's nark (Edwin) — *infecte petit rabatteur de police*

You blasted object (Bertie) — *espèce de détritus*

To hammer the stuffing out of someone — *étriper quelqu'un*

To spot oompus boompus — *mettre le doigt sur les manigances*

He loved like a thousand of bricks — *il était amoureux comme pas un*

Love's young dream had stubbed its toe — *le rêve de jeunesse et d'amour avait les ailes coupées*

I shall probably play on the old crumb (Lord Worplesdon) as on a stringed instrument — *je jouerai probablement sur les fibres de cette vieille noix comme sur un instrument à cordes*

We Woosters can read between the lines — *nous, Wooster, savons lire entre les lignes*

The menace was null and void — *la menace était nulle et non avenue.*

He ground a tooth or two — *il grinça des dents*

Her ladyship (Aunt Agatha) — *Madame la Baronne*

Butler — *maître d'hôtel*

Butler — *valet de chambre*

Quotations are a test for the Fonscolombes.

'Odd's boddikins, Jeeves,' I said, 'I am in rare fettle this a.m. Talk about exulting in my youth! I feel up and doing, with a heart for any fate, as Tennyson says.'

'Longfellow, sir.'

'Or, if you prefer it, Longfellow. I am in no mood to split hairs.'

– Jeeves, je suis dans une forme rare ce matin. D'une jeunesse triomphante, pourrait-on dire. Je me sens d'attaque; nul arrêt du destin ne saurait étonner mon courage comme dit Tennyson.

– Longfellow, Monsieur.

– Bon, bon, Longfellow, si vous aimez mieux. Je ne suis pas d'humeur à couper les cheveaux en quatre.

'It reminded me of those lines in the poem – "See how the little how-does-it-go tum tumty tiddly push." Perhaps you remember the passage?'

'"Alas, regardless of their fate, the little victims play," sir.'

– Il m'a rappelé ce vers du poème 'Vois jouer les pauvrets, pom, pom, pom, dix, onze, douze'. Peut-être vous rappelez-vous le passage?

– Vois jouer les pauvrets sans souci de leur sort, Monsieur.

'I don't know if you remember the passage? "Ti-tum-ti-tum ti-tumty tum, ti-tumty tumty mist (I think it's mist), and Eugene Aram walked between, with gyves upon his wrist."'

– Je ne sais pas si vous vous rappelez le passage: 'pom, pom, pom, pom, dans la pénombre (je crois que c'est 'pénombre'), Eugene Aram fut emmené, les fers aux pieds, quel drame sombre!'

Even though the French translators put the gyves on Eugene Aram's feet in preference to his wrist, it is nice to see them making up a little poetry of their own.

They are clever in translating a small felicity of orthography, too.

'Did you say "Wee Nooke", Jeeves?'

'Yes sir.'

'Spelled, I'll warrant, with an "e"?'

'Yes sir.'

I breathed heavily through the nostrils.

'Well, listen to me, Jeeves. The thing's off. You understand? Off. Spelled with an o and two f's. I'm dashed if I'm going to be made a – what's the word?

'Sir?'

'Catspaw. Though why catspaw? I mean, what have cats got to do with it?'

'The expression derives . . .'

– *Comment dites-vous?* '*Nostre Nid?*'
– *Oui, Monsieur.*
–*Ecrit, je la parie, avec un 's'.*
– *Oui, Monsieur.*
Je soufflai bruyamment.
– *Arrêtons là, Jeeves. C'est fini, compris? Fini, f, i, fi, n, i, ni. Je veux bien être pendu si je me fais avoir comme le . . . quoi . . . ?*
– *Monsieur?*
– *Comme le chat . . . et pourquoi le chat? Je veux dire qu'est-ce que les chats ont à voir là dedans?*
– *L'expression vient . . .*

And the discreet dots:

I have just one thing to say to you, Wooster. Get out!

Je n'ai qu'un mot à te dire, Wooster, f . . . le camp.

On two points (in addition to the wrists–feet switch for Eugene Aram) I am at a loss to know why the translators have changed things. You remember that occasion when Lord W., much to Bertie's surprise, calls for champagne in his study at 10 a.m. and makes Bertie celebrate with him? In Wodehouse's version Lord Worplesdon is brought two *half*-bottles in succession, and the two of them share them to the dregs. In the French it is two *whole* bottles. The thrifty Wodehouse would never waste two bottles of champagne on two people without staging one of his excellent tipsy scenes to follow. And, anyway, Lord W. is going to get royally plastered that very night on dance champagne (the French ignores that important pejorative 'dance', incidentally) at the East Wibley Fancy Dress Ball. And, next morning, when Lord Worplesdon, still dressed as Sinbad the Sailor with red whiskers, comes fuming to Boko's cottage, Boko and Nobby, trying to cool him down with some breakfast, offer him sardines several times. In the French it is always fried eggs that they offer. Here the English and the French are both right. Wodehouse in France (1947) originally wrote 'eggs', not 'sardines'. His publisher had to remind him that eggs were very tightly rationed then in England. So he changed it to 'sardines'. In France eggs (for an English breakfast) sounded right, sardines wrong.

There are times when the translators simply don't do justice to the English, other times when they admit themselves baffled and leave chunks out, other times when they seem to get it palpably wrong, and other times again when, perhaps to make up for their baffled omissions elsewhere, they pad with *jeux d'esprit* of their own. We'll take examples in that order.

Scrambled syntax. I think the Fonscolombes miss tricks in

'You were mere acquaintances?'
'Mere to the core.'

which becomes,

– *Vous n'étiez que de simples connaissances?*
– *Aussi vrai qu'il fait jour.*

And:

. . . I said, with an intellectual flick of the umbrella

which becomes

. . . *dis-je, avec un petit mouvement du parapluie qui sentait son intellectuel.*

And:

. . . buttering a nonchalant slice of toast

which becomes,

. . . *tartinant nonchalamment un morceau de toast.*

When Bertie, remembering Jeeves's first encounter with his friend Boko Fittleworth, a very successful but very badly dressed author, says that Jeeves had winced and retired to the kitchen, 'doubtless to pull himself together with cooking sherry', the French simply says '*avec un petit verre*'. They omit the 'cooking' significance. And they spoil, for me at any rate, my favourite of all Wodehouse images. Bertie had come on that great oaf, Stilton Cheesewright, nervously buying an engagement ring for Lady Florence Craye in a Bond Street jeweller's. Bertie very properly prods Stilton in the behind with his umbrella.

He spun round with a sort of guilty bound, like an adagio dancer surprised while watering the cat's milk.

The French says,

. . . *Il se retourna d'un bond avec l'air coupable d'une danseuse classique surprise à tirer la queue d'un chat.*

Why a feminine dancer? And why pulling *a* cat's tail, not watering *the* cat's milk? One raises the eyebrows and purses the lips.

Nobby. 'You've known Boko so long.'
Bertie. 'Virtually from the egg.'

becomes,

> – *Vous connaissez Boko depuis si longtemps!*
> – *Pratiquement, du jour où les flancs de sa mère l'ont porté.*

And:

'Oh, hullo, Bertie,' Edwin said, grinning all over his loathsome face.
'Hullo, you frightful squirt,' I responded civilly. 'What are you doing here?'

This becomes, a little bleakly,

> – *Bonjour, Bertie! dit-il en grimaçant de tout son visage.*
> – *Qu'est-ce que tu fais ici?*

And:

'Well, dash it, already I am practically Uncle Percy's ewe lamb. This will make me still ewer.'

becomes,

> – *Eh bien, diable, je suis déjà pratiquement le favori d'oncle Percy, ça me stabilisera dans la place.*

Two passages where the Fonscolombes retire baffled:

It was many years since this Cheesewright and I had started what I believe is known as the plucking the gowans fine, and there had been a time when we had plucked them rather assiduously. But his attitude at the recent get-together had made it plain that the close season for gowans had now set in, and, as I say, it rather saddened me.

They do not attempt those lines at all. And:

. . . He said peevishly that I was just the sort of chap whose car would break down when every moment was precious, adding that it was a lucky thing that it hadn't been me they sent to bring the news from Aix to Ghent, because, if it had been, Ghent would have got it first in the Sunday papers.

becomes only,

> – . . . *Il remarqua avec mauvaise humeur que j'étais exactement le genre de type dont le tacot tombait toujours en panne au moment précis où on avait besoin de lui.*

Boko has nothing to add in the French. The Browning allusion disappears.

In one passage, the Fonscolombes not only give up on a sentence, but, in trying to rehash the sense, get it quite wrong. Bertie had undertaken to plead Boko's cause (as a possible husband for ward Nobby) with Lord Worplesdon. But Boko, in trying to impress Lord W. with the geniality of his nature, had asked him to lunch and sprung his joke goods on him – the surprise salt-shaker which emitted a spider, amongst others. So Bertie's pleading has to be postponed. Meanwhile Boko has had the awful idea of making Bertie act as a burglar at midnight at Bumpleigh Hall (Lord W. is terrified of burglars), so that Boko can chase him off, save the old home and thus get fawned on by its owner (Lord W.). The idea, which Boko and Nobby have discussed, but haven't yet sprung on Bertie, is that Bertie shall (to make it look a professional job) paste brown paper with treacle on the scullery window, break the window and run away . . . Boko then, with exact timing, raising the alarm. So this dialogue between Nobby and Boko takes place in Bertie's presence:

Boko.		'We're all right. Don't you worry.'
Nobby.	'But if Bertie can't plead . . .'
Boko.		'Ah, but you're forgetting how versatile he is. What you are overlooking is the scullery-window-breaking side of his nature. That is what is going to see us through.'

This becomes, in French:

– *Tout va bien. Ne vous en faites pas.*
– *Mais, si Bertie ne peut pas plaider* . . .
– *Oh! Vous oubliez comme il est changeant. Vous perdez de vue sa terreur de voleurs, ce véritable complexe de crainte de cambriolage.*

Somehow the French couple (sister and brother) have made Bertie the one who is afraid of burglars. Absolutely wrong.

They're wrong about the Cabinet Ministers too. Here Bertie *is* pleading Boko's cause to his Uncle Percy, and trying to get into Uncle Percy's fat head that Boko makes a packet of money from his writing and won't be a drain on Uncle Percy's pocket if he marries young Nobby.

'It would be an ideal match. You and he may not always have seen eye to eye in such matters as spiders in salt-cellars, but you can't get away from it that he is one of the hottest of England's young *littérateurs*. He earns more per annum than a Cabinet Minister.'

'He ought to be ashamed of himself if he didn't. Have you ever met a Cabinet Minister? I know dozens, and not one of them that wouldn't be grossly overpaid at thirty shillings a week.'

– *Ce serait un mariage idéal. Vous et lui n'avez peut-être pas la même façon de voir les choses, comme par exemple les araignées dans les salières, mais vous ne pouvez nier le fait qu'il est un des jeunes écrivains les plus dorés d'Angleterre. Il gagne plus qu'un ministre.*

– *Il devrait avoir honte s'il n'en était pas ainsi. As-tu jamais rencontré un ministre? J'en connais des douzaines et pas un qui gagne assez pour se payer une croûte décente.*

The French says, roughly, that Cabinet Ministers *do* get paid thirty shillings a week.

Here, I feel sure, the Fonscolombes have thought that 'You betcher' is a term of endearment:

'He has long chafed at the rottenness of motion pictures, and is relying on me to raise the standard,' said Boko.

'You will, angel,' said Nobby.

'You betcher,' said Boko, swilling coffee.

In French:

– *Il est furieux de l'inanité de leur production là-bas (Hollywood) et il compte sur moi pour en hausser un peu le niveau.*

– *Et vous réussirez, mon ange, susurra Nobby.*

– *Poupée de mon cœur, gargouilla Boko, lampant son café.*

In the following passage a concealed quotation (Young's 'Night Thoughts') seems to have put the wrong idea into the translators' heads. Lord Worplesdon, tired and tight, had been sitting out from the East Wibley Fancy Dress Ball in Boko's enormous car. Boko, thinking that the old chap had gone home on his bicycle, drove himself with Lord W. in the back, fast asleep. (And he left him there, locked in the garage when he got home to Bumpleigh Hall.) But 'tired Nature's sweet restorer' in Wodehouse's typewriter certainly meant sleep, not drink.

Driving away at the conclusion of the recent festivities, Boko must inadvertently have taken Uncle Percy with him. He had sped homewards with a song on his lips, and all unknown to him, overlooked while getting a spot of tired Nature's sweet restorer in the back of the car, the old relative had come along for the ride.

A l'issue des récentes festivités, Boko avait dû ramener oncle Percy dans sa voiture, sans s'en rendre compte. Une chanson sur les lèvres il avait dû foncer sur la route du retour et oublier complètement celui qui l'accompagnait, grâce aux lampées du généreux cordial qu'il avait toujours dans sa voiture pour donner éventuellement un coup de pouce à la Nature.

In the following passage 'the raw spirit' certainly means drink, not courage and innocence. (Boko's plan had been for Bertie to go charging into Uncle Percy's study at 10 a.m. and to start ticking him off and calling him names. Boko was then to appear and defend Uncle Percy. And Boko had typed out a sheet of offensive things that Bertie had to say to Uncle Percy at this early-morning interview):

Typewritten, with single spaces, I suppose the stuff ran to about six hundred words, and of all those six hundred words I don't think there were more than half a dozen which I could have brought myself to say to a man of Uncle Percy's calibre, unless primed to the back teeth with the raw spirit. And Boko, you will recall, was expecting me to deliver my harangue at ten o'clock in the morning.

Tapé à la machine à interligne simple, le texte devait faire, je pense, à peu près six cents mots, et sur ces six cents mots, je ne crois pas qu'il y en ait eu plus d'une demi-douzaine que j'aurais pu me forcer à dire à un homme du calibre d'oncle Percy, à moins d'être farci jusqu'aux dents de courage et d'innocence. Et Boko, vous vous le rappellez, attendait que je débite ma harangue sur le coup de dix heures, ce matin-là.

Now we find the French putting in embellishments.

'. . . No, no, I would have said . . . not Bertie, who was not only at school with me but is at this very moment bursting with my meat.'
This was a nasty one. I wasn't actually bursting with Boko's meat, of course, because there hadn't been such a frightful lot of it, but I saw what he meant. For an instant, when he put it like that, I nearly weakened.

– . . . A d'autres, aurais-je dit. Pas Bertie, qui non seulement a été en classe avec moi, mais qui en ce moment même est encore tout gorgé de ma viande.
Voilà qui était déplaisant. En réalité, je n'étais pas gorgé de sa viande, c'est évident, mais il était exact que j'avais fait une bonne entaille au beefsteak, ce soir en dinant chez lui, pour ne pas mentionner les pommes de terre frites et deux autres légumes.
Un instant quand il exposa ces choses, je faillis faiblir.

What's all that about chips and two other veg?
Here are three longer passages that I would like to see set at the next Foreign Office exam for those offering French . . . in fact everybody. The Fonscolombes' renderings are given as *terminus a quo* for improvements.
Edwin the Boy Scout was trying to do one of his much-feared acts of kindness in cleaning up Bertie's cottage, Wee Nooke. He had shoved

gunpowder up the chimney to clean it, and then poured paraffin (mistaking it for water) on the flames. The cottage was burning merrily, and 'for about two shakes of a duck's tail' Bertie 'stood watching it with quiet relish'.

. . . Then, putting a bit of a damper on the festivities, there came floating into my mind a rather disturbing thought . . . to wit, that the last I had seen of young Edwin, he had been seeping back into the kitchen. Presumably, therefore, he was still on the premises, and the conclusion to which one was forced was that, unless somebody took proper steps through the proper channels, he was likely ere long to be rendered unfit for human consumption. This was followed by a second and still more disturbing thought that the only person in a position to do the necessary spot of firemen-save-my-child-ing was good old Wooster.

I mused. I suppose you would call me a fairly intrepid man, taken by and large, but I'm bound to admit I wasn't any too keen on the thing. Apart from anything else, my whole attitude towards the stripling who was faced with the prospect of being grilled on both sides had undergone another quick change.

Puis, pour étouffer un peu la vivacité de ce plaisir, vint s'insinuer dans mon esprit une pensée assez troublante: la dernière fois que j'avais vu le jeune Edwin, il s'était retiré en direction de la cuisine. Vraisemblablement par conséquent, il était encore sur place et la conclusion à laquelle on se trouvait amené était la suivante: à moins qu'on n'intervint promptement pour prendre les mesures nécessaires, il était probable qu'avant longtemps il serait mis à mal. Cette pensée fut suivie d'une autre encore plus troublante: la seule personne à même de jouer les sauveteurs, rôle indispensable, était le bon vieux Wooster.

Je méditai. Je suppose que, vu de loin et grosso modo, on me tient pour un brave, mais je dois admettre que je ne me sentais pas trop décidé. Entre autres choses, il s'était opéré dans mes dispositions à l'égard du jeune veau qui risquait de se faire rissoler un second changement rapide.

Edwin emerged, missing only his eyebrows, and went off to get the fire-brigade. Enter Uncle Percy, and Bertie, leaning on the gate watching the flames, says 'Hullo'. But he was not feeling at ease. Uncle Percy's son had started the fire, but Bertie was not feeling at ease.

. . . The spine, and I do not attempt to conceal the fact, had become soluble in the last degree.

You may wonder at this, arguing that as I was not responsible for the disaster which had come upon us, I had nothing to fear. But a longish experience has taught me that on these occasions innocence pays no dividends. Pure as the driven snow though he may be, or even purer, it is the man on the spot who gets the brick-bats.

Mes os se liquéfiaient littéralement.

Vous pouvez vous en étonner; car n'étant pas responsable de la catastrophe qui nous frappait, je n'avais rien à craindre. Mais une assez longue expérience m'avait appris qu'en ces occasions-là l'innocence ne rapporte pas. Celui qu'on trouve sur les lieux du désastre a beau être blanc comme neige ou même d'avantage, c'est lui qui paie les pots cassés.

And:

'Jeeves,' I said, getting right down to it in the old Wooster way, 'here's a nice state of things!'

'Sir?'

'Hell's foundations have been quivering.'

'Indeed, sir?'

'The curse has come upon me. As I warned you it would if I ever visited Steeple Bumpleigh. You have long been familiar with my views on this leper colony. Have I not repeatedly said that, what though the spicy breezes blow soft o'er Steeple Bumpleigh, the undersigned deemed it wisest to give it the complete miss in baulk?'

— Jeeves, dis-je, allant droit au fait, en vrai Wooster, nous voilà frais!

— Pardon, Monsieur.

— L'Enfer en a frémi jusque dans ses abîmes sans fond.

— Vraiment, Monsieur?

— La malédiction du Seigneur s'est abattue sur moi. Je vous avais bien dit que c'est ce qui arriverait si je mettais jamais les pieds à Steeple Bumpleigh. Vous connaissez depuis longtemps mes idées sur cet asile de lépreux. Ne vous avais-je pas répété cent fois que même si les souffles parfumés de la béatitude flottaient en permanence sur Steeple Bumpleigh, le plus sage, à mon avis, serait d'éviter ces lieux?

In the hotel where I was staying in France was a Belgian whose English was perfect barring a slight trace of accent. He told me his French was better, so I gave him *Jeeves, au secours* and said: 'Have a look at this and tell me whether it gives the Wodehouse impression in French. And if so, well or very well?' Without opening it, he said: 'I will read it. But there are no equivalents in French for the Wodehouse *layers* of slang. There is no upper-middle class in France comparable to the English public-school type, and French student slang is regional and changes much too quickly. Anyway, French is a Latin language. In German and Dutch you'd possibly find that Wodehouse translates smoothly. But French hasn't got the same *sort* of idioms as English.'

He spent half an hour with the English text, and then half an hour with the French. Then he said: 'No, it hasn't got the Wodehouse spark. And *Skropshire* is a misprint.'

For a quick test of the Belgian's guess that Wodehouse might go into

~ I trod on the starter and we began the journey, Jeeves standing on the pavement, seeing us off like an archbishop blessing pilgrims, his air that of one who would shortly be following by train with the heavy luggage.

~ Young Thos, poising the bucket for an instant, discharged its contents. And old Mr Anstruther received the entire consignment. In one second, without any previous training or upbringing, he had become the wettest man in Worcestershire.

~ Nanny or elder sister . . . you can't ever really lose your awe of someone who used to scrub your face with a soapy flannel.

~ She was feeling like a mother who, in addition to having to notify him that there is no candy, has been compelled to strike a loved child on the base of the skull with a stocking full of sand.

~ The floor was crowded with all that was best and noblest in the county; so that a half-brick, hurled at any given moment, must infallibly have spilt blue blood.

~ Bottleton East is crammed from end to end with costermongers dealing in tomatoes, potatoes, Brussels sprouts and fruits in their season, and it is a very negligent audience there that forgets to attend a place of entertainment with full pockets.

~ He had a voice that sounded as though he ate spinach with sand in it.

~ He, too, seemed disinclined for chit-chat. We stood for some moments like a couple of Trappist monks who have run into each other by chance at the dog races.

German more easily, and in a comparable idiom, I compared the first paragraph of *Leave It to Psmith* with its German translation (*Psmith Macht Alles*, translator Heinrich Fraenkel, published by Kiepenheuer and Witsch). The English reads:

At the open window of the great library of Blandings Castle, drooping like a wet sock, as was his habit when he had nothing to prop his spine against, the Earl of Emsworth, that amiable and boneheaded peer, stood gazing out over his domain.

The German for the *whole* of that sentence reads:

Am offenen Verandafenster in Schloss Blandings stand Lord Emsworth und blickte auf seine weiten Domänen.

Would you say that Herr Fraenkel had wrung the last drop of meaning out of the English? Missing so much and so much is my opinion.

The opening sentences of Wodehouse's early novel *The Prince and Betty* are:

A pretty girl in a blue dress came out of the house, and began to walk slowly across the terrace to where Elsa Keith sat with Martin Rossiter in the shade of a big sycamore. Elsa and Martin had become engaged some four days before, and were generally to be found at this time sitting together in some shaded spot.

The Esperanto version of this (translator G. Badash) is:

Bela junulino en blua vesto eliris el la domo, kaj ekmarŝis malrapide trans la teraso al la loko, kie sidis Elsa Keith kun Martin Rossiter sub la ombro de la granda acerplatano. Elsa kaj Martin fianĉiĝis antaŭ kelkaj tagoj, kaj, ĝenerale oni trovis ilin, je tiu horo, kune sidantaj en iu ombroplena loko.

I don't see how this could be bettered.

~ He tottered blindly towards the bar like a camel making for an oasis after a hard day at the office.

~ Mr Pott disappeared feet foremost, like a used gladiator being cleared away from the arena.

~ The door opened and Gussie's head emerged cautiously, like that of a snail taking a look round after a thunderstorm.

~ 'I daresay you know these Folk Dance people, Corky. They tie bells to their trousers and dance old rustic dances showing that it takes all sorts to make a world.'

~ My Aunt Dahlia has a carrying voice . . . If all other sources of income failed, she could make a good living calling the cattle home across the Sands of Dee.

~ 'I turned him down like a bedspread.'

~ 'The least thing upsets him on the links. He misses short putts because of the uproar of the butterflies in the adjoining meadows.'

~ He's one of those men whose legs you have to count to make sure they aren't mules.

~ 'All I said was "I know you started to learn to play bridge this morning, Reggie, but what time this morning?", but he didn't like it.'

———————— ~ ————————

~ She gave me the sort of look she would have given a leper she wasn't fond of.

~ 'Frederick won't be staying here long, will he?' Lord Emsworth asked, with a father's pathetic eagerness.

~ A golfer needs a wife. It is essential that he has a sympathetic listener always handy to whom he can relate the details of the day's play.

~ The odd noise that he was making I could diagnose, not as the love call which she appeared to think it, but as the stern and censorious gruffle of a man who, finding his loved one on alien premises in heliotrope pyjamas, is stricken to the core, cut to the quick and as sore as a gumboil.

~ 'Well, look at Jael, the wife of Heber. Dug spikes into the guest's coco-nut while he was asleep, and then went swanking about the place like a Girl Guide. No wonder they say "Oh, woman, woman!"'
    'Who?'
    'The chaps who do.'

~ She looked like a vicar's daughter who plays hockey and ticks off the villagers when they want to marry their deceased wives' sisters.

~ Aunt Dahlia uttered a cry like a wail of a master of hounds seeing a fox shot.

~ The unpleasant, acrid smell of burnt poetry.

ABOUT WODEHOUSE: A SELECTION OF GOOD READING MATTER

———————— ~ ————————

Cazalet-Keir, Thelma, ed., *Homage to P. G. Wodehouse*, Barrie & Jenkins, London, 1973. Prepared for his ninetieth birthday. A collection of twelve essays by admirers, and a poem by John Betjeman.

Connolly, Joseph, *P. G. Wodehouse*, Thames and Hudson, London, 1987. A short, jaunty, lavishly illustrated Life, plus bibliography and Collectors' Guide, with details of dustjackets and how to make sure it's a first edition.

Donaldson, Frances, *P. G. Wodehouse: The Authorized Biography*, Weidenfeld & Nicolson, London, 1982. Much new primary source material. A friend of the family, a professional writer and biographer, the author gives close-up evaluations of the man and his writings. Bibliography, with English and American titles, dates and publishers; also plays and musicals. Texts of the broadcasts from Berlin in 1941 and photographs, some from wartime Germany.

Edwards, Owen Dudley, *P. G. Wodehouse*. Martin Brian & O'Keefe, London, 1977. A lecturer at Edinburgh University, widely read in the popular literature of the last hundred years, he quotes from the Wodehouse texts extensively and expertly. Scholarly appendices, including a verbatim examination of the changes that Wodehouse made in *Leave It to Psmith* between its serialization in an American magazine and its publication as a book. Instructive.

Flannery, Harry W., *Assignment to Berlin*, Michael Joseph, London, 1942. Flannery was the Columbia Broadcasting System's Berlin correspondent from December 1940 to November 1941, and Werner Plack of the German Foreign Office seems to have given him an exclusive on Wodehouse's release from internment and arrival in Berlin in 1941. He interviewed Wodehouse for C.B.S., and says he saw Ethel arrive at the Adlon from France, with Wonder the Peke and a trunkload of evening dresses. He puts some unlikely remarks into Wodehouse's mouth in conversation. He wrote that 'the Wodehouse plot' was 'one of the best Nazi publicity stunts of the war'. Not kind to the Wodehouses or Plack. But Flannery was an eyewitness and he published only a year later. After the war Wodehouse tried to sue him for what he had written.

French, R. B. D., *P. G. Wodehouse*, Oliver and Boyd, Edinburgh, 1966. An early, short and scholarly assessment of the books, with bare bibliography, up to that date.

Garrison, Daniel, *Who's Who in Wodehouse*, Peter Lang, New York, 1987. Identity parade, by an American Classics Professor, of more than a thousand characters from the Wodehouse books, novels and short stories. From 'Alice or Toots, Lady Abbott, sister of Sam Bulpitt in SM37, wife of Sir Buckstone and mother of Jane. A large, blonde, calm woman, formerly a New York chorus girl' to 'I. J. Zizzbaum, Beverly Hills dentist who attends Reggie Havershot's wisdom tooth in LG36'.

Green, Benny, *P. G. Wodehouse: A Literary Biography*, Pavilion/Michael Joseph, London, 1981. Good running commentary on the books, with apt and frequent quotations. Expert knowledge of stage, screen and songs. His 'Novelist in a Padded Cell' chapter covers the internment, the broadcasts from Berlin and the Wodehouse Papers when they were finally released.

Hall, Robert A., Jr. *The Comic Style of P. G. Wodehouse*, Archon Books, Hamden, Connecticut, 1974. A brave, learned, academic, grammarian's thesis on 'How does he do it?' and 'Why is he so funny?'

Heineman, James A., with Donald Bensen, *The Catalogue of the Wodehouse Centenary Exhibition at the Pierpont Morgan Library, New York*, Oxford University Press, Oxford, 1981. A hundred jumbo pages of specially commissioned essays, line drawings by Peter van Straaten, scores of photographs of exhibits (90 per cent of them from the Heineman collection) and another hundred pages of meticulous Anglo-American bibliography by Eileen McIlvaine, including foreign translations, plays, films, lyrics, etc. (A much more detailed Wodehouse bibliography, also masterminded by Eileen McIlvaine, is in preparation by St Paul's Bibliographies, Winchester.)

Jaggard, Geoffrey, *Wooster's World*, Macdonald, London, 1967, and *Blandings the Blest*, 1968. Polished thumbnails and amusing researches into the byways of the Wodehouse characters and places: e.g. a list of all known members of The Drones. Two jovial lexicons, but published when Wodehouse was about ten books short of his final total.

Jasen, David, *A Bibliography and Reader's Guide to the First Editions of P. G. Wodehouse*, 2nd edn. Greenhill Books, London, 1986. Excellent readyreference, elaborately indexed, to the characters, places, Anglo-American titles and dates.

— *P. G. Wodehouse: A Portrait of a Master*, revised edn, Continuum, New York, 1981. Well researched, especially on Wodehouse's life in the theatre, and good appendices of bibliography of the novels, short stories and plays (with actors, lyrics, lengths of run and name of theatre). Thirty-two pages of illustrations.

— *The Theatre of P. G. Wodehouse*, Batsford, London, 1979. Slim volume with many illustrations, and programme notes of all the plays in which Wodehouse had a hand.

Morris, J. C., *Thank You, Wodehouse*, Weidenfeld & Nicolson, London, 1981. An Oxford law don and other Senior Common Room pundits set themselves some tangential scholarship questions: Bertie Wooster's cars, money, fiancées, uncles and drinking habits; Jeeves's sex-life; was Ronnie Fish legitimate?; where is Market Blandings?; how many Oldest Members were there? If you think you know the texts backwards, some of these mock-solemn extrapolations will surprise you.

Muggeridge, Malcolm, *The Infernal Grove*, especially Chapter 4 of this second volume of Muggeridge's autobiography, *The Chronicles of Wasted Time*, Fontana, London, 1975. Muggeridge was in Paris at the Liberation in autumn 1944 and, as an officer in M.I.6, was detailed to 'keep an eye on' the Wodehouses, whom the Germans had left housed in the elegant Bristol Hotel. He came to be very fond of them and made it his duty to protect them from 'the buffooneries of war'. Essential reading for the whole question of the Berlin broadcasts. A shorter version of this story was Muggeridge's contribution to the Festschrift *Homage to P. G. Wodehouse* (see Thelma Cazalet-Keir above).

Murphy, Norman, *In Search of Blandings: The Facts behind the Wodehouse Fiction*, Secker & Warburg, London, 1986; Penguin, London, 1987. Murphy's Law is that much of what Wodehouse wrote in his fiction had a traceable time and place in his own life. He concentrates on Blandings (which he identifies as Sudeley Castle). He has studied maps, county chronicles, wills, birth certificates, *Bradshaw's Railway Guides* and Wodehouse's own texts. He claims to have found the remains of the Empress's sty in the grounds of a house in Norfolk that the Wodehouses rented. And much else.

Orwell, George, *Collected Essays*, Secker & Warburg, London, 1961. His 'In Defence of P. G. Wodehouse' appeared in the *Windmill Magazine* in 1945, when Wodehouse's name was still odorous with the filth William (later Sir William) Connor had thrown at him on the B.B.C. in 1941. Orwell seems not to have read much Wodehouse since his schooldays and the school stories, and he finds class messages even in these.

Sproat, Iain, *Wodehouse at War*, Ticknor & Fields, New York, 1981. Sproat, then an M.P. (Cons.), was the first person outside the self-protecting Whitehall 'Security' people to see the Wodehouse Papers, accumulated from the 1944 interrogations in Paris of this putative 'renegade'. The papers were kept under wraps till six years after Wodehouse's knighthood and death. The book includes the German Foreign Office's own verbatim monitorings of the five talks Wodehouse had given to neutral America in 1941 on the German radio. Who was that man who came out of the internment camp with Wodehouse, and why was his name (apparently) enough to scare the authorities into ordering the whole file of papers to be kept away from the public for thirty-plus years?

Wind, Herbert Warren, *The World of P. G. Wodehouse*, Praeger Publishers, New York, 1972; Hutchinson, London 1981. In preparing a 'Profile' on Wodehouse for the *New Yorker*, Wind, whose main subjects in that magazine are golf and tennis, came to know 'the old boy' and to like him. Short text, very smooth. Many illustrations.

INDEX

———————— ~ ————————

FOR THE BEST IN PAPERBACKS, LOOK FOR THE 🐧

In every corner of the world, on every subject under the sun, Penguin represents quality and variety – the very best in publishing today.

For complete information about books available from Penguin – including Pelicans, Puffins, Peregrines and Penguin Classics – and how to order them, write to us at the appropriate address below. Please note that for copyright reasons the selection of books varies from country to country.

In the United Kingdom: Please write to *Dept E.P., Penguin Books Ltd, Harmondsworth, Middlesex, UB7 0DA*

In the United States: Please write to *Dept BA, Penguin, 299 Murray Hill Parkway, East Rutherford, New Jersey 07073*

In Canada: Please write to *Penguin Books Canada Ltd, 2801 John Street, Markham, Ontario L3R 1B4*

In Australia: Please write to the *Marketing Department, Penguin Books Australia Ltd, P.O. Box 257, Ringwood, Victoria 3134*

In New Zealand: Please write to the *Marketing Department, Penguin Books (NZ) Ltd, Private Bag, Takapuna, Auckland 9*

In India: Please write to *Penguin Overseas Ltd, 706 Eros Apartments, 56 Nehru Place, New Delhi, 110019*

In Holland: Please write to *Penguin Books Nederland B.V., Postbus 195, NL–1380AD Weesp, Netherlands*

In Germany: Please write to *Penguin Books Ltd, Friedrichstrasse 10–12, D–6000 Frankfurt Main 1, Federal Republic of Germany*

In Spain: Please write to *Longman Penguin España, Calle San Nicolas 15, E–28013 Madrid, Spain*

In France: Please write to *Penguin Books Ltd, 39 Rue de Montmorency, F-75003, Paris, France*

In Japan: Please write to *Longman Penguin Japan Co Ltd, Yamaguchi Building, 2–12–9 Kanda Jimbocho, Chiyoda-Ku, Tokyo 101, Japan*

P. G. Wodehouse in Penguins

'Mr Wodehouse's idyllic world can never stale. He will continue to release future generations from captivity that may be more irksome than our own. He has made a world for us to live in and delight in' – Evelyn Waugh in a B.B.C. broadcast

The following are some of the titles by P. G. Wodehouse published in Penguins:

Aunts Aren't Gentlemen

Carry on, Jeeves

The Code of the Woosters

Doctor Sally

Heavy Weather

The Heart of a Goof

The Indiscretions of Archie

The Inimitable Jeeves

Jeeves in the Offing

Little Nugget

The Luck of the Bodkins

The Mating Season

Piccadilly Jim

Quick Service

Right Ho, Jeeves

Sam the Sudden

Spring Fever

Stiff Upper Lip, Jeeves!

Summer Moonshine

Uncle Fred in the Springtime

Very Good, Jeeves!

A CHOICE OF PENGUINS

An African Winter   Preston King   With an Introduction by Richard Leakey

This powerful and impassioned book offers a unique assessment of the interlocking factors which result in the famines of Africa and argues that there *are* solutions and we *can* learn from the mistakes of the past.

Jean Rhys: Letters 1931–66
Edited by Francis Wyndham and Diana Melly

'Eloquent and invaluable . . . her life emerges, and with it a portrait of an unexpectedly indomitable figure' – Marina Warner in the *Sunday Times*

Among the Russians   Colin Thubron

One man's solitary journey by car across Russia provides an enthralling and revealing account of the habits and idiosyncrasies of a fascinating people. 'He sees things with the freshness of an innocent and the erudition of a scholar' – *Daily Telegraph*

The Amateur Naturalist   Gerald Durrell with Lee Durrell

'Delight . . . on every page . . . packed with authoritative writing, learning without pomposity . . . it represents a real bargain' – *The Times Educational Supplement*. 'What treats are in store for the average British household' – *Books and Bookmen*

The Democratic Economy   Geoff Hodgson

Today, the political arena is divided as seldom before. In this exciting and original study, Geoff Hodgson carefully examines the claims of the rival doctrines and exposes some crucial flaws.

They Went to Portugal   Rose Macaulay

An exotic and entertaining account of travellers to Portugal from the pirate-crusaders, through poets, aesthetes and ambassadors, to the new wave of romantic travellers. A wonderful mixture of literature, history and adventure, by one of our most stylish and seductive writers.

A CHOICE OF PENGUINS

The Book Quiz Book   Joseph Connolly

Who was literature's performing flea . . .? Who wrote 'Live Now, Pay Later . . .'? Keats and Cartland, Balzac and Braine, Coleridge conundrums, Eliot enigmas, Tolstoy teasers . . . all in this brilliant quiz book. You will be on the shelf without it . . .

Voyage through the Antarctic   Richard Adams and Ronald Lockley

Here is the true, authentic Antarctic of today, brought vividly to life by Richard Adams, author of *Watership Down*, and Ronald Lockley, the world-famous naturalist. 'A good adventure story, with a lot of information and a deal of enthusiasm for Antarctica and its animals' – *Nature*

Getting to Know the General   Graham Greene

'In August 1981 my bag was packed for my fifth visit to Panama when the news came to me over the telephone of the death of General Omar Torrijos Herrera, my friend and host . . .' 'Vigorous, deeply felt, at times funny, and for Greene surprisingly frank' – *Sunday Times*

Television Today and Tomorrow: Wall to Wall Dallas?
Christopher Dunkley

Virtually every British home has a television, nearly half now have two sets or more, and we are promised that before the end of the century there will be a vast expansion of television delivered via cable and satellite. How did television come to be so central to our lives? Is British television really the best in the world, as politicians like to assert?

Arabian Sands   Wilfred Thesiger

'In the tradition of Burton, Doughty, Lawrence, Philby and Thomas, it is, very likely, the book about Arabia to end all books about Arabia' – *Daily Telegraph*

When the Wind Blows   Raymond Briggs

'A visual parable against nuclear war: all the more chilling for being in the form of a strip cartoon' – *Sunday Times*. 'The most eloquent anti-Bomb statement you are likely to read' – *Daily Mail*